T0368933

The Handbook of
SOCIAL JUSTICE in
PSYCHOLOGICAL THERAPIES

The Handbook of
SOCIAL JUSTICE in
PSYCHOLOGICAL THERAPIES

Power, Politics, Change

Edited by
LAURA ANNE WINTER & DIVINE CHARURA

Sage

S Sage

1 Oliver's Yard
55 City Road
London EC1Y 1SP

2455 Teller Road
Thousand Oaks, California 91320

Unit No 323-333, Third Floor, F-Block
International Trade Tower Nehru Place
New Delhi – 110 019

8 Marina View Suite 43-053
Asia Square Tower 1
Singapore 018960

Editor: Susannah Trefgarne
Editorial Assistant: Esme Sawyer
Production Editor: Gourav Kumar
Copyeditor: Tom Bedford
Indexer: KnowledgeWorks Global Ltd
Marketing Manager: Ruslana Khatagova
Cover Designer: Naomi Robinson
Typeset by KnowledgeWorks Global Ltd
Printed in the UK

Library of Congress Control Number: 2023932143

British Library Cataloguing in Publication data

A catalogue record for this book is available from the British Library

ISBN 978-1-5296-0484-9
ISBN 978-1-5296-0483-2 (pbk)

At Sage we take sustainability seriously. Most of our products are printed in the UK using responsibly sourced papers and boards. When we print overseas we ensure sustainable papers are used as measured by the Paper Chain Project grading system. We undertake an annual audit to monitor our sustainability.

CONTENTS

Part 3:   Beyond the therapy room

ABOUT THE EDITORS AND CONTRIBUTORS

EDITORS

Laura Anne Winter is a HCPC registered counselling psychologist and BPS chartered psychologist. She works at the University of Manchester as Senior Lecturer in Education and Counselling Psychology and is the Programme Director for the Doctorate in Counselling Psychology and the Associate Director for Equality, Diversity and Inclusion for the School of Environment, Education and Development. Laura's research and writing has focused on social justice, equality and related issues in counselling and psychotherapy, psychology and education. Her clinical practice has been based in NHS, third sector and university counselling service settings.

Divine Charura is a Professor of Counselling Psychology. He is a counselling psychologist and registered as a practitioner psychologist with the Health and Care Professions Council in England. Divine is also an Honorary Fellow of the United Kingdom Council for Psychotherapy (UKCP) and an adult psychotherapist. As a practitioner psychologist, psychotherapist and researcher, Divine's work focuses on psychotraumatology and the impact of trauma across the lifespan. Divine has co-authored and edited numerous books in counselling, psychology and psychotherapy. These include *Love and Therapy: In Relationship* (co-edited with Stephen Paul) and, co-edited with Colin Lago, the following books: *The Person-Centred Counselling and Psychotherapy Handbook: Origins, Developments and Current Applications* (2016), and recently: *Black Identities + White Therapies: Race Respect and Diversity* (2021).

CONTRIBUTORS

Byron Al-Murri is a HCPC registered and BPS chartered counselling psychologist, clinical and research supervisor, and lecturer in qualitative research methods and counselling psychology at undergraduate and doctoral level, at York St John University. Byron's research interests are in difference and diversity in therapy, multicultural competence and social justice, following his thesis on British-Arab client experiences of psychological therapy using interpretative phenomenological analysis. He has worked as a clinician in the third sector, with clients from across the lifespan. He is a pluralistic practitioner, integrating CBT, psychodynamic psychotherapy and humanistic philosophy.

Anne Burghgraef is the Clinical Director of Solace Surviving Exile and Persecution, a specialist therapeutic service for refugees and asylum seekers operating throughout Yorkshire and Humberside. She has been the clinical lead since the founding of Solace in 2006 and has expanded the service to include group and family therapies as well as individual talking, creative and somatic therapies. Anne is a UKCP registered Family & Systemic Psychotherapist and trauma specialist with an interest in the relationship between psychotherapies, worldviews, socio-political structures and human flourishing.

Jasmine Childs-Fegredo is a counselling psychologist registered with the Health and Care Professions Council (HCPC), chartered and accredited by the British Psychological Society (BPS), and a fellow of the Higher Education Academy (FHEA). She is a senior lecturer in counselling psychology at York St John University in the UK and has worked as a clinician in the National Health Service (NHS) in Child & Young People's services. Jasmine's research focuses on contemporary psychological therapies such as yoga-integrated psychotherapy, dialectical behaviour therapy and mental health in schools. She is a humanistic practitioner and educator, with an interest in trauma-informed care.

Mick Cooper is Professor of Counselling Psychology at the University of Roehampton where he is Director of CREST (Cluster for Research in Social and psychological Transformation). Mick is a chartered psychologist and a fellow of the British Association for Counselling and Psychotherapy. Mick is author and editor of a range of texts on existential, humanistic and integrative approaches to therapy. His most recent book is *Psychology at the Heart of Social Change: Towards a Progressive Vision for Society* (Policy Press, 2023). Mick is the father of four children and lives in Brighton on the south coast of England.

Natasha Fiberesima is a neurodivergent trainee counselling psychologist at York St John University. Her thesis focuses on autistic adults' experiences of therapy and well-being, including creative ways of coping.

Lynne Gabriel, OBE, is Professor of Counselling and Mental Health at York St John University, York, UK. She is a British Association for Counselling and Psychotherapy (BACP) accredited and registered counsellor and psychotherapist, an academic activist, and a trained supervisor of practitioners working within the counselling, mental health and helping professions. Lynne is founding Director of the York St John University Communities Centre and founder of its associated Training, Research and Counselling Clinic Consortium (TRaCCs). TRaCCs members are drawn from UK counselling and mental health centres and clinics set in university contexts. Lynne's key research areas include mental health, domestic and relationship abuse, group interventions for bereavement and loss, review and evaluation of standardised mental health measures, and evaluation of the provision of online counselling. Lynne has published books and papers on making sense of ethics in practice and is now editing an *Ethics in Action* series for Routledge, working with Andrew Reeves.

Rachael Goodwin is a HCPC registered counselling psychologist and BPS chartered psychologist. She is white and of working-class heritage from an ex-mining town in Yorkshire, UK. Rachael's varied life experiences and unconventional route into psychology have sparked in her a deep commitment to social justice informed approaches to research and therapy. She has a particular interest in the intersections of social class, gender and wellbeing.

Lorna Hamilton is an Associate Professor of Developmental Psychology at York St John University. Her research focuses on contextual factors that influence educational outcomes for children and young people, including barriers to access for neurodivergent learners at all stages of education.

Brett Heasman is a Senior Lecturer in Psychology at York St John University. His research focuses on neurodivergent communication, participatory research and creating more enabling environments to empower neurodiversity.

Jenny Hui is a graduate student in Counselling and Clinical Psychology at the Ontario Institute for Studies in Education (OISE) at the University of Toronto. Her research focalises the psychosocial wellbeing of racialised and 2SLGBTQ+ individuals, and her scholarship and clinical practice are rooted in anti-oppressive ideologies that reflect her core values of solidarity, compassion and action-oriented change. Most recently, she was published in *Diversity and Social Justice in Counseling, Psychology, and Psychotherapy: A Case Study Approach*, edited by Dr Anusha Kassan and Dr Roy Moodley.

Marja Humphrey is an Assistant Professor in the School Counselling program at Bowie State University in Maryland, United States. Her research interests include Counsellor Preparation, Leadership, Wellness, Spirituality and Online Learning. Identifying social justice concerns and action steps is embedded in how she prepares counsellors-in-training for serving their clients and students. A co-author of *Elements of Culture in Counseling*, a multicultural counselling text, and several published articles, Dr Humphrey has also presented at state, regional and national conferences.

Esther Ingham is a HCPC registered practitioner psychologist (counselling) and a BPS chartered psychologist. She acquired a disability ten years ago and has ever since been fascinated by how she is variously (re)constructed. Esther has taught on the doctoral programme at the University of Manchester in a variety of guises since 2018, and currently also leads the Psychological Service for Merseyside Police, having previously worked in a variety of health and law enforcement services. Her research and clinical work both focus on disability and/or trauma, particularly from a social justice perspective. She aligns strongly with a humanistic and existential integrative approach to her therapeutic work.

Colin Lago, DLitt, retired as Director of the Counselling Service at the University of Sheffield in 2003. Still enthusiastic about the therapeutic task, he maintains a small independent supervision, writing and occasional training practice. He is white British. Trained initially as an engineer, Colin went on to become a full-time youth worker in London and a teacher in Jamaica before becoming a counselling practitioner in the late 1970s. He is a Fellow of the British Association for Counselling and Psychotherapy. Deeply committed to issues of difference and diversity he has published articles, videos and books on the subject.

Courtland C. Lee, PhD, is the author, editor or co-editor of seven books on multicultural counselling and three books on counselling and social justice. In addition, he has published numerous book chapters and articles on counselling across cultures. Dr Lee is the former editor of the *Journal of Multicultural Counseling and Development*. He has also served on the editorial board of the *International Journal for the Advancement of Counselling* and was a Senior Associate Editor of the *Journal of Counseling and Development*. Dr Lee is a Past President of the International Association for Counselling. He is also a Fellow and Past President of the American Counseling Association. He is also a Fellow of the British Association for Counselling and Psychotherapy.

Eden Lunghy was born in England, is Black, Congolese heritage, of working-class origin and has read Human Geography at the University of Reading. Her experience has ranged from local youth politics to youth work and digital marketing as she explores what path she wants to pursue. Outside of academia, Eden has been a Participatory Action Researcher on Take Back the Power based at The Winch where she embarked on a journey into the depths of serious youth violence to gain a deeper understanding and enact positive change. As an individual with lived experience of serious youth violence this project became a saving grace for Eden who continues to use her learnings to be a voice for other young people.

Melernie Meheux was born in Tottenham, North London. She is a chartered senior child psychologist and play therapist. She is an academic tutor at the Institute of Education, UCL and Co-Vice Chair of the British Psychological Society, Division for Child and Educational Psychology. She believes in equitability for all and that play is an invaluable part of a child's life and crucial to their wellbeing. Mel is passionate about supporting children's social and emotional wellbeing and working to reduce school exclusions.

Martin Milton is Professor of Counselling Psychology at Regents University London. He also runs an independent practice in psychotherapy and supervision. Martin's research and interests include eco-therapy and the therapeutic aspects of the natural world. In this regard Martin regularly supervises and examines doctoral theses in the area of the environmental and climate change. He has previously contributed to the Education Committee of the Jane Goodall Institute UK, Bristol Zoo's Advisory Group on the Social Sciences, the editorial board of the journal *Ecopsychology* and the BPS Division of Counselling Psychology Environmental and Climate Crisis Workstream.

Roy Moodley is Associate Professor in Counselling and Clinical Psychology, and the Director for the Centre for Diversity in Counselling and Psychotherapy at the University of Toronto. His research and publications include critical multicultural counselling and psychotherapy; race and culture in psychoanalysis; traditional healing practices; gender and identity.

Nahid Nasrat is a professor, psychologist and diversity and inclusion expert. She has been teaching for over 20 years and providing training, conducting research on diversity issues in clinical psychology, including refugees' and immigrants' mental health as well as psycho-social issues in conflict and post-conflict countries. She currently teaches in the doctoral clinical psychology program at the Chicago School of Professional Psychology in Washington, DC. Professor Nasrat is an International Visiting Professor at Leeds Beckett University, UK.

Silva Neves is a COSRT accredited and UKCP registered psychosexual and relationship psychotherapist, and a trauma psychotherapist. He is a Pink Therapy Clinical Associate. He works extensively with the LGBTQ+ community. Silva is the author of *Compulsive Sexual Behaviours: A Psycho-Sexual Treatment Guide for Clinicians* (2021) and *Sexology: The Basics* (2023). He is a member of the editorial board for the leading international journal *Sex and Relationship Therapy*, and he speaks internationally.

Dan O'Hare was born in Lewisham, South-East London. He is an educational psychologist and tutor at the University of Bristol. At the time of writing he is current Co-Vice Chair of the British Psychological Society Division of Educational and Child Psychology, alongside Mel. Dan's interests are in the communication and dissemination of psychology to wider audiences, with a focus on inclusion and accessibility. Other professional interests include the (mis)application of neuroscience within educational psychology, and the climate crisis.

Olga Oulanova is Assistant Professor, Teaching Stream, in Counselling and Clinical Psychology at the Ontario Institute for Studies in Education, University of Toronto. Her research interests include integration of Indigenous traditional healing practices with Western mental health and the role of peer counselling in suicide bereavement. She works in private practice in Toronto, Canada, as a clinical and rehabilitation psychologist.

Stephanie Petty is Senior Lecturer at York St John University and a chartered clinical psychologist. She provides assessment and therapeutic interventions for neurodivergent clients and carries out complementary research focused on neurodivergence, mental health and wellbeing.

Maryam Riaz is a psychotherapist, supervisor and lecturer with over 17 years' experience of working with trauma, spiritual/religious care and diversity and inclusion. She was the first person of colour to set up counselling/supervision private practice in Bradford city centre, West Yorkshire and has designed culturally adaptive approaches to psychotherapy for her work with minority ethnic, refugee and asylum seeker clients. Maryam's research interests include decolonising client assessments and the role of faith/ spirituality in the therapeutic relationship.

Dwight Turner is the Course Leader in Humanistic Counselling and Psychotherapy within the School of Humanities and Social Sciences at the University of Brighton. Having trained at the Centre for Counselling and Psychotherapy Education, Dr Turner then completed his doctorate through the University of Northampton, where he utilised creative techniques such as active imagination, drawing and sand play to explore the unconscious and internalised phenomenological experience of being the other. Dr Turner is also a psychotherapist and supervisor in private practice, and an activist working towards greater inclusion for disadvantaged groups within the fields of counselling and psychotherapy.

Lita Wallis is a youth worker and participatory action research practitioner. She worked in London for eight years and learned her skills working with housing and migration activist groups, and organisations such as Real Time Ltd (Reading), Voice of Youth (Hackney) and Skills Network (Brixton). She was one of the co-founders of the Take Back the Power project at The Winch (Camden). Since 2020 she has been in mid-Wales working at the Braich Goch, where she visited for the first time with Eden and Take Back the Power in 2019. She is white British.

Sally Zlotowitz was born in England, is White, and is a Clinical Psychologist but now practices as a Community Psychologist. She lives in London and has worked in the charity sector with minoritised young people for about 12 years. She is also an activist on issues around housing, climate justice and poverty and co-founded Psychologists for Social Change. She is Co-Editor of *The Palgrave Handbook of Innovative Community & Clinical Psychologies*. Sally came to co-write this chapter with Eden and Lita as together they offer workshops on community psychology and Participatory Action ResearchPAR.

ACKNOWLEDGEMENTS

Laura Anne Winter

Firstly, I would like to thank colleagues at Sage, Susannah Trefgarne and Sarah Turpie in particular, for helping to make this book happen. To my fantastic co-editor, Divine, it has been a joy to work with and to learn from you. Thank you so much. Also, to all our amazing authors, thank you for making this book what it is.

Thank you to colleagues and students at Manchester who have provided support over the years, and many conversations about psychology, counselling and 'social justice'. Particularly Terry Hanley (who also provided useful comments on Chapter 6).

Finally, thanks to my family: Jack, Rosa, Cerys and Owen. Jack, you have been pivotal both in supporting me to develop my ideas and in practical support. Especially whilst juggling maternity leave and childcare with the final stages of the book! I cannot thank you enough.

Divine Charura

With my thanks to Laura Winter, a wonderful colleague and inspirational editor, for inviting me to help co-edit this book with you and spending many hours working on it. I echo the thanks to colleagues at Sage, Susannah Trefgarne and Sarah Turpie in particular, for your support and guidance.

Thank you to all the wonderful authors and colleagues who have written in this book. It has been a pleasure working alongside you and learning more about social justice from you.

Professor Rachel Wicaksono, Professor Colin Lago and Stephen Paul, I sincerely appreciate you for being wise mentors and colleagues who continually inspire and encourage me.

My parents Alois and Letisia, as well as Helen, Elizabeth and Alois, and the rest of my family, you teach me about life and compassion each day. Thank you for all your love and always being there.

Colleagues, students at York St John University (YSJU) and at Leeds Beckett University, thank you for all the conversations we have had about psychology, life, and about social justice. Professor Mathew Reason, your personal support and support from the institute of social Justice at YSJU is sincerely appreciated.

Thanks to all who have helped and inspired us whose names we may have omitted here: you know who you are.

With thanks for health, strength, faith and love, which make all things possible.

PART 1

SOCIAL JUSTICE THEORY IN PSYCHOLOGICAL THERAPIES

1
AN INTRODUCTION TO SOCIAL JUSTICE IN PSYCHOLOGICAL THERAPIES

Divine Charura and Laura Anne Winter

OVERVIEW

This book focuses on core principles for social justice work in the psychological therapies: from theory, to practice in the therapy room, and beyond. We situate social justice informed work as political, and important for positive change within our professions. In this first chapter, we introduce social justice as a concept: emphasising the diversity in definitions, and the importance of *both* values and action.

WHAT IS SOCIAL JUSTICE?

In this introductory chapter we aim to simply 'set the scene' with regards to defining social justice. Instead of providing a single definition here, we suggest that it is throughout the book that readers get a sense for what social justice *is and can be* within psychological professions. Social justice has been considered a core feature of many branches of the psychological therapies. Nevertheless, the specific term 'social justice' has not always been used, and narrow literature reviews might leave you thinking that the values and ideas were not thought about until quite recently. In reality, the now more popular (in psychological therapies) term 'social justice' is extremely broad in scope and covers a multitude of concepts, many of which were talked about before the language of 'social justice' gained traction. There are a vast array of definitions, and whilst many overlap there are also differences and distinctions which can be drawn. Indeed, we see social justice as 'an umbrella term... for concepts, such as diversity, change, equity, inequality, oppression, marginalization, disruption, and affirmative action' (Peters & Luke, 2021, p. 9). Whilst we would argue it is important to know the limits of social justice to ensure that we are able to apply it and make use of it in our work, in this book the contributors may each understand the term slightly differently. We encourage readers not to view this as a problem, but instead to critically and reflexively approach all things written about 'social justice' (and related concepts) to decide how your understanding of the term fits with the authors'.

Broadly speaking then, what does the term 'social justice' cover? Schenker et al. (2019) note that the concept is constituted by 'social' and 'justice'. They argue that 'social' refers to something that involves collective or group cohesion, and to address the social aspect, action must be on social problems or social cohesion issues. 'Justice' is concerned with equity and the achievement of equitable outcomes. In considering social justice, it has been argued that what must be considered are social constructs such as gender, class, sexuality, social class and economic factors, age, dis/ability and ethnicity (Moodley, 2009). We would also add neurodiversity to this list. In this way justice can be expressed through the notions of fairness and equal opportunity, as well as equitable outcomes. Peters and Luke (2021) outlined ten 'facets' of social justice: cultural, distributive, associational, retributive, restorative, procedural, emancipatory, intergenerational, transformative and transitional.

Bell (2016, p. 3) provides a widely cited definition of social justice, which emphasises the importance of both the process and the outcome:

> The *goal* of social justice is full and equal participation of people from all social identity groups in a society that is mutually shaped to meet their needs. The *process* for attaining the goal of social justice should also be democratic and participatory, respectful of human diversity and group differences, and inclusive and affirming of human agency and capacity for working collaboratively with others to create change.

As outlined in Chapter 6, we see social justice practice as ethical, transformative and political. Research has suggested that action is an important part of understanding social justice (Winter & Hanley, 2015). Various elements of social justice work have been highlighted, including: learning from communities, making yourself uncomfortable, involvement in social action, embracing humility and seeking critical knowledge (Brown & Lengyell, 2022); challenging others, being aware of biases and assumptions, and social justice consultation work (Schulze et al., 2019); and sharing power, facilitating consciousness raising, building on strengths, leaving clients with the tools for social change and 'giving voice' (Goodman et al., 2004).

Context

The Global Socio-Political Context

The need for social justice informed therapeutic and psychological practice could not be clearer than at the time of writing in June 2022. Nationally and internationally there have been numerous significant socio-political events that form the backdrop of this book and of social justice matters in general. These for example include global wars leading to the displacement of millions of people, the climate crisis, political instability and other changes – for example Brexit (the UK leaving the European Union), the overturning of Roe v. Wade in the United States significantly reducing access to legal and safe abortion, and the Covid-19 pandemic. We have also seen various campaigns, movements and associated 'culture wars' around issues such as Black Lives Matter, #MeToo, trans-inclusion and rights, and many more. This is not an exhaustive list but begins to outline the nature of shifts in the socio-political terrain globally. This cannot be separated from the experiences of many who present in the therapy room, or from the call for social justice that therapists need to respond to.

The Psychological Context

Most 'mainstream' theoretical perspectives and research in psychology, psychotherapy and counselling practice have for over a century been drawn from Western, Educated, Industrialised, Rich and Democratic (WEIRD) nations. However, at the time of writing, and over the last couple of decades, there has been a steady rise in psychology, counselling and psychotherapy literature contributions which have illuminated the general lack of equal engagement with other epistemologies (bodies of knowledge). Despite professing to be steeped in understanding human dynamics and the psyche, however, there has remained within the psychological professions a lack of adequate responses to content on social justice, wider global injustices, diversity, culture and ethnicity. The rise of the decolonising the curriculum movement has brought to the fore the urgency of breaking down the status quo of structures that often support power inequalities, discrimination and racism, enabling us to challenge and critically examine the beliefs we hold about other groups and the process of 'othering' (Charura & Lago, 2021).

Through engaging with decolonising approaches and an awareness of the centrality of social justice, and its intricate links to the personal, to society and to our professions, we must respond in and out of the therapy room in ways that demonstrate that we value the views and lived experiences of others. This illuminates the contemporary shift of a social justice informed approach of 'power-with' rather than 'power-over' – the voice of the client and a shift from the position of expert. This has been illuminated through movements like Drop the Disorder (https://adisorder4everyone.com/), which is about challenging psychiatric power and the labelling of psychological distress. This shift is in line with a post-modernist philosophical assumption and stance, which embraces an ethos of 'both/and' rather than 'either/or' (Charura & Lago, 2021; Wachtel, 2014). In line with this there have been many psychotherapy modality and tribal wars. There have, however, been numerous responses to these differences which align well with social justice. These include for example the rise of pluralistic approaches which assert that there are many things that can help people and that the best way to find out what will work is to ask the clients themselves (Cooper & McLeod, 2007). They also include relational perspectives which can be adopted by a diversity of modalities and assert the importance the role relationships play in understanding self and maintaining who we are (Finlay, 2016; Paul & Charura, 2014). Furthermore, another important shift has been the strengthening of trans- and cross-cultural approaches which highlight the importance of understanding transcultural encounters including the lived experience of minoritised groups (Lago, 2011; Moodley, 2009). These approaches are underpinned by a strong commitment to valuing diversity, social justice and the significance of authentic dialogue.

Our Positioning as Editors

Given the centrality of reflexivity to social justice, here we briefly reflect on what we bring to the development of this text. I (Divine) have been interested in social justice from a fairly young age. Some of my early memories are of my parents taking us to South Africa in the late 1980s and experiencing racism and segregation. I remember having conversations about the places I was not allowed to go into, and not being allowed to drink from a tap of water in a park when I was thirsty because of the colour of my skin. Even in the 80s as a young man I was interested in activism for marginalised voices and remember engaging in numerous campaigns for justice and highlighting the importance of antidiscriminatory practice. Fast forward to many years later I started to engage in writing about aspects of my own lived experiences of discrimination and oppression as a black man, alongside the other *isms* relating to for example gender, social class, age, dis/ability, ethnicity and so on that I witnessed and continue to witness in society.

I (Laura) benefit from significant socially structured advantages, being white, middle class, cis and heterosexual, currently non-disabled, and neurotypical. As with everyone this does not mean that I do not have my own experiences of discrimination or oppression, and I have been most aware of that as a young woman and then as a mother in academia. Since a fairly young age I have been actively interested in and engaged with politics and how we structure society. For a long time, however, I would not have known that what I was interested in was 'political'. I knew I was interested in people, and I was interested in how people work together (or don't) in society, and why and how societies include or exclude people. It took me until I was much older to realise that what I was interested in was actually politics. My interest in people had channelled itself towards psychology, but I was forever dissatisfied with the overly individualistic lens through which I was encouraged to look. It took me even longer to realise that I could (and did) have, and voice, an opinion on social and political issues. And probably longer than that still to realise that my interests in psychology, and the social and political, did not need to remain separate.

WHAT FOLLOWS: THE STRUCTURE AND CONTENT OF THE BOOK

The book is divided into three parts. First, we tackle social justice theory, and include chapters from Oulanova, Hui and Moodley on minoritised identities; Lago on intersectionality; Al-Murri and Childs-Fegredo on the individual in context; and finally, Cooper on directionality and the integration of the psychological, the social and the political in our theoretical understandings. Together, these four chapters aim to introduce the reader to various theoretical models and ideas for use when engaging with social justice. This is particularly important given the oft-cited problems with 'mainstream' psychological theory, considered alongside the regular pressures encountered to work with models which are embedded in these traditions. It is our hope that psychological therapists can utilise some of the theoretical ideas presented across these chapters to underpin their social justice informed work.

Part 2 of the book focuses on social justice informed therapeutic practice. We include nine chapters here, beginning with a slightly longer contribution from ourselves, aiming to give a practical introduction to the principles (and practice application) of social justice informed work for professionals in psychological therapies. This provides some introductory content to the chapters which follow, each of which focus on a particular aspect or facet of social justice practice: working with racially minoritised individuals (Nasrat and Riaz); social class (Goodwin); visible and invisible disability (Ingham); neurodiversity (Petty, Hamilton, Heasman and Fiberesima); gender (Gabriel); sexuality (Neves); refugees and asylum seekers (Burghgraef); and the climate and ecological crises (Milton). No chapter should be seen as sitting in isolation, and authors reflect on the importance of intersectionality and reflexivity. Rather than positioning the client as 'the minoritised other', all chapters position their topic in relation to the psychological professions and individuals within that more broadly.

In Part 3, we move beyond the therapy room and look to some of the important ways in which those working in psychological therapies might engage with social justice work: through advocacy (Lee and Humphrey); within clinical supervision (Turner); with communities (Lunghy, Zlotowitz and Wallis); and influencing broader policy and sociopolitical change (O'Hare and Meheux). All these chapters hope to bring to life what macro level social justice work can look like. Finally, we end the book with a postscript bringing together ideas on the practice of social justice.

All chapters aim to be clear and approach the different topics in understandable ways. The authors include counselling, clinical and educational psychologists, counsellors and psychotherapists, participatory action research practitioners and those with lived experience of the topic. No chapters propose a recipe or set out a 'how to' – consistent with the values of social justice outlined. Each chapter ends with questions for critical thinking and reflection, with the hope that ideas prompted can be followed up either individually or in reflexive practice or teaching groups.

A Note on Language

We acknowledge that language evolves quickly and thus in the chosen terminology in each chapter, the aim is to convey and to use language sensitively, and appropriately, in line with social justice principles to avoid repetition of othering and injustice. Inappropriate or outdated language drawn from historical literature will be acknowledged and named, with a particular example being when referring to direct quotes from literature.

REFLECTIVE AND CRITICAL THINKING QUESTIONS

1   When you try to define social justice, how do you feel? What memories, hopes, fears or feelings does this raise in you?
2   How does your social identity (social class, gender, sexuality, ethnicity or other characteristic) influence your feelings about social justice?
3   Can we define everything as being a 'social justice issue' in psychological therapies, or are there some boundaries to the concept, and some issues which do not have a social justice relevance?
4   Do you see any tensions between the definitions of social justice provided above and your understanding of the work of a psychologist or therapist?

RECOMMENDED READING AND RESOURCES

www.psychchange.org/
This is the website of UK-based organisation Psychologists for Social Change. This is a network of psychological practitioners who are interested in applying psychology to social change and action, consistent with the values of social justice.

Cutts, L. A. (2013). Considering a social justice agenda for counselling psychology in the United Kingdom. *Counselling Psychology Review, 28*(2), 8–16.
This article sets out what a social justice agenda might look like in a psychological profession in the UK.

Toporek, R. L., Gerstein, L. H., Fouad, N. A., Roysircar, G., & Israel, T. (Eds.). (2006). *Handbook for social justice in counseling psychology: Leadership, vision, and action.* Sage Publications.
This handbook provides readers with a conceptual road map of social justice and social action to integrate into their practice.

REFERENCES

Bell, L. A. (2016). Theoretical foundations for social justice education. In M. Adams, L. A. Bell, D. J. Goodman, & K. Y. Joshi (Eds.), *Teaching for diversity and social justice* (3rd ed., pp. 3–26). Routledge.

Brown, J., & Lengyell, M. (2022). Psychotherapists' efforts to increase awareness of social privilege. *Counselling & Psychotherapy Research*. https://doi.org/10.1002/capr.12539

Charura, D., & Lago, C. (2021). Towards a decolonised psychotherapy research and practice. In D. Charura & C. Lago (Eds.), *Black identities + white therapies: Race, respect + diversity* (pp. 185–198). PCCS Books.

Cooper, M., & McLeod, J. (2007). A pluralistic framework for counselling and psychotherapy: Implications for research. *Counselling and Psychotherapy Research, 7*(3), 135–143. https://doi.org/10.1080/14733140701566282

Finlay, L. (2016). *Relational integrative psychotherapy: Processes and theory in practice*. Wiley.

Goodman, L. A., Liang, B., Helms, J. E., Latta, R. E., Sparks, E., & Weintraub, S. R. (2004). Training counseling psychologists as social justice agents: Feminist and multicultural principles in action. *The Counseling Psychologist, 32*(6), 793–837. https://doi.org/10.1177/0011000004268802

Lago, C. (2011). *The handbook of transcultural counselling and psychotherapy*. McGraw-Hill/Open University Press.

Moodley, R. (2009). Multi(ple) cultural voices speaking 'Outside the Sentence' of counselling and psychotherapy. *Counselling Psychology Quarterly, 22*(3), 297–307. https://doi.org/10.1080/09515070903302364

Paul, S., & Charura, D. (2014). *An introduction to the therapeutic relationship in counselling and psychotherapy*. SAGE.

Peters, H. C., & Luke, M. (2021). Social justice in counseling: Moving to a multiplistic approach. *Journal of Counselor Leadership & Advocacy, 8*(1), 1–15. https://doi.org/10.1080/2326716X.2020.1854133

Schenker, K., Linnér, S., Smith, W., Gerdin, G., Mordal Moen, K., Philpot, R., Larsson, L., Legge, M., & Westlie, K. (2019). Conceptualising social justice – what constitutes pedagogies for social justice in HPE across different contexts? *Curriculum Studies in Health and Physical Education, 10*(2), 126–140. https://doi.org/10.1080/25742981.2019.1609369

Schulze, J., Winter, L. A., Woods, K., & Tyldesley, K. (2019). An international social justice agenda in school psychology? Exploring educational psychologists' social justice interest and practice in England. *Journal of Educational and Psychological Consultation, 29*(4), 377–400. https://doi.org/10.1080/10474412.2018.1531765

Wachtel, P. L. (2014). An integrative relational point of view. *Psychotherapy, 51*(3), 342–349.

Winter, L. A., & Hanley, T. (2015). 'Unless everyone's covert guerrilla-like social justice practitioners…': A preliminary study exploring social justice in UK counselling psychology. *Counselling Psychology Review, 30*(2), 32–46.

2
ENGAGING WITH MINORITISED AND RACIALISED COMMUNITIES 'INSIDE THE SENTENCE'

Olga Oulanova, Jenny Hui and Roy Moodley

OVERVIEW

This chapter argues that existing psychological theories and therapies have proven problematic for minoritised and racialised communities, with the global pandemic further accentuating this inadequacy. Having established the specific ways psychological therapies have fallen short, we propose broad theoretical frameworks for effectively supporting minoritised clients. The chapter will include a critique of the colonial foundations of psychology, suggest a need to decolonise psychological theories and therapies, and explore what this may entail. We advocate for working from a critical race theory (CRT) and intersectionality lens, while embracing a social justice informed and empowerment approach by exploring relevant theoretical underpinnings and clinical applications. Finally, this chapter discusses how clinicians can use these frameworks to support minoritised and racialised communities in socially just ways.

SETTING THE CONTEXT: THE CURRENT CHALLENGES FACED BY PSYCHOLOGICAL PROFESSIONS

Psychological professions are at a greater crossroads than ever before in their relatively short history. The consequences of the COVID-19 pandemic (i.e., millions of deaths worldwide, especially among older, lower income and racialised individuals) have challenged the epistemological, phenomenological and existential basis of ethical and equitable healthcare. Moreover, climate catastrophes, geo-political events and global economic uncertainties have called into question the very discourse of psychology. The current theories and practices are being seen as limiting and inadequate in meeting the mental health needs of racialised and minoritised communities. Even the foundational principles such as Carl Rogers' 'core therapeutic conditions' – empathy, unconditional positive regard, congruence – appear to need further clinical elaboration and intellectual understanding. For example, concepts such as selective empathy, unconscious racial bias and psychology's hegemonic values are requiring additional research. Clearly, the COVID-19 pandemic and other recent global events have presented psychological professions with an opportunity for creative and revolutionary changes to be made to theory and practice, if the mental health needs of future generations are to be addressed in ways that are equitable, ethical and socially just.

BASIC THEORETICAL PRINCIPLES: MINORITISED AND RACIALISED CLIENTS AND PSYCHOLOGICAL THERAPIES

The multicultural and diversity critique of psychological professions has exposed the underbelly of Western mental health theory and practice as historically racist, sexist and homophobic. Moodley (2011) describes minoritised and racialised clients as falling 'outside the sentence', in which the sentence is defined and conceptualised by a Western, hegemonic and masculine discourse. Minoritised experiences can be encapsulated by Moodley and Lubin's (2008) 'Big 7 intersectional identities', referring to seven different facets of identity: race (inclusive of ethnicity and culture), gender, class, sexual orientation, disability, age and religion. To be 'outside the sentence' is to exist in a subversive and marginal space located outside the conventional, normative epistemologies and theories that inform traditional psychological therapies. For minoritised clients, the experience of being 'outside the sentence' produces the effect of being 'inside' another process: continual engagement with – and resistance in the face of – marginalisation, including racism, colonisation, sexism, ableism, heterosexism, ageism and classism.

Historically, Western psychological therapies have proven inadequate for clients who fall 'outside the sentence'. Minoritised clients are less likely to seek out therapy and often terminate prematurely. Considering that psychological professions operate from an individualistic lens, conceptualise wellbeing in terms of Western worldview and values, prioritise one specific way of knowing and often adopt a medical model, minoritised individuals continue to experience inequality, discrimination and oppression at the hands of professionals. Gone (2009) describes this as a 'monocultural bias', in which 'the procedural norms of the discipline… [are] a source of cultural insensitivity' (p. 751). While it may be uncomfortable for Western-trained clinicians who are members of a dominant group to acknowledge and critically reflect upon 'monocultural biases' and limitations to psychological therapies as well as their own biases and positional-ity, such work is crucial to fostering 'cultural humility' – an ongoing commitment to self-reflection, self-critique and patient-centred relationships founded in collaboration and mutual respect (Tervalon & Murray-Garcia, 1998). In the absence of cultural humil-ity, clinicians risk committing microaggressions, perpetuating stereotypes and thereby undermining the therapeutic alliance.

Mental health disparities among minoritised and racialised patients should be a cause of concern for all therapists. These patients face negative health outcomes at alarmingly disproportionate rates compared to their non-minoritised counterparts, and this is due in large part to unique stressors, including identity-based harassment, discrimination and violence (e.g., Cyrus, 2017). The mental health disparities – and increased dropout rates – of racialised clients can be understood as part of broader systems of oppression and injustice. However, Western psychological theories and therapies have not offered a useful way to address these problematic systems or engage with issues of power and privilege as these play out in clients' lives both outside and within the therapeutic rela-tionship. Sue (2015) argues that psychological professions make problematic assump-tions that 1) psychological theories derived from the dominant group are universally applicable and that 2) techniques and interventions can be removed from cultural and political contexts. These assumptions can harm clients, particularly when unaddressed or unchallenged. Bhugra and Bhui (2006) underscore the damaging consequences when therapists fail to 'empathise' with their minoritised and racialised clients, where empa-thy involves the awareness and honouring of an individual client's relationship to cul-tural and racial differences. These limitations render it even more challenging to address barriers in accessing therapy; work through and navigate differences in the conceptu-alisation of symptoms; concur on treatment plans; and address disagreements, micro-aggressions and strains in the therapeutic bond. The result is therapeutic ruptures that the clinician may not recognise or know how to repair, leading minoritised clients to experience the therapeutic encounter as re-traumatising and unsafe, dropping out of treatment prematurely.

Considering the limitations of Western psychological therapies and therapists, minor-itised clients may prefer to work with clinicians who share their culture, worldview, positionality and lived experiences, as this can facilitate positive therapeutic outcomes (e.g., Constantino et al., 2021). However, as clinicians' demographics do not currently reflect the diversity of the overall populations in the West, a racialised client will likely see a white psychologist who may not share or comprehend important facets of the cli-ent's lived experiences.

An additional significant challenge to psychological professions engaging with minor-itised and racialised populations has been the global COVID-19 pandemic. While men-tal health has declined since the start of the pandemic (e.g., Santomauro et al., 2021), such difficulties are even more pronounced among minoritised and racialised popula-tions (e.g., Diaz et al., 2021). Moreover, the pandemic inflamed racism, discrimination and violence toward racialised individuals. For example, Asian individuals in the West experienced an alarming spike in racist and xenophobic violence, hate crimes and dehu-manising treatment, primarily the result of being scapegoated for the pandemic (e.g., Cheng et al., 2021). Against the backdrop of COVID-19, protests led by Black Lives Mat-ter swelled across the globe, underscoring the injustice of anti-Black racism and police brutality.

This section provided a brief overview of specific traumas and challenges faced by minoritised communities. It is necessary to envision psychological approaches that can actively address sentiments rooted in oppression, colonisation and anti-Black and anti-Asian racism, and promote healing among minoritised and racialised individuals.

CREATING A FRAMEWORK FOR A 'THIRD SPACE IN PSYCHOTHERAPY'

Having established that traditional psychological therapies often prove inadequate for minoritised communities and highlighted the additional challenges faced by these com-munities during the pandemic, we will argue that culturally relevant interventions with minoritised and racialised individuals require decolonising psychological theories and practices. In so doing, we can begin to create a critical space, 'a third space' 'inside' the sentence of psychotherapy within which healing can occur. We will first review the impact of colonialism on psychological theories and therapies and then explore what the process of decolonisation could entail.

Coloniality and Decolonisation

Colonisation and decolonisation as well as coloniality and decoloniality are more than just metaphors and metanomies of challenging 'predominant racial, sexist, homo- and trans-phobic conservative, liberal, and neo-liberal politics' as the continued unfolding of Western modernity is reinforced through crude and vulgar repetitions of coloniality (Maldonado-Torres, 2016, p. 1).

In North America, Ansloos et al. (2021) describe colonialism as 'the complex histori-cal domination of settlers over Indigenous peoples, where through violent means the goal was to erase, remove, and disempower the culture, languages, and socio-political structures of Indigenous peoples' (p. 127). The profound damaging impact of coloni-alism – described by Duran (2006) as a 'soul wound' – is reflected in a loss of iden-tity, spirituality, language and culture that Indigenous communities have experienced, leading to ongoing intergenerational trauma. Reflecting on the impact of colonialism on the field of psychotherapy, Wada and Kassan (2021) explain that colonial values have shaped what is considered '(un)healthy and '(ab)normal' and 'common sense' (p. 357), and that these ideas continue to persist even after countries have gained their independence. Samuel and Ortiz (2021) elaborate further: 'The tools of colonial violence are not always apparent and are often wrapped and concealed within dominant psycho-logical narratives widely accepted as truisms'; including conceptualising mental illness as 'a pathology of the individual self, isolated from relational, social, intergenerational and situational factors' and regarding specific psychological constructs and theories as universally applicable (Samuel & Ortiz, 2021, p. 4). Indeed, Ansloos et al. (2021) remind us that 'colonialism is not only a historical event, but a continuous reality that promotes settler colonized ideals over Indigenous perspectives' (p. 127). Given the dominance of Western ways of knowing that inform psychological therapies and shape how clinicians approach the therapeutic encounter, Wada and Kassan (2021) suggest there needs to be 'a recognition that training has been colonial in nature and may not apply to other clinical contexts' (p. 364). Without such recognition, the clinician risks perpetuating colonial ideas – and thereby the colonial trauma – when working with Indigenous and other minoritised clients (Ansloos et al., 2021).

Decolonising Psychological Therapies

Having established that it is critical for psychological professions to address their colo-nial foundations, what does it actually mean to 'decolonise' therapy and how do we get started? King (2021) argues that:

> Western standards of knowing have become the gold standard by which other cultural knowledges are measured and judged for their validity. Changing our science and psychology to reflect a true global psychology (thus genuine social justice)… would require a major systemic upheaval. (p. 13)

As such, decolonising therapy involves interrogating the fundamental assumptions at the root of clinical theory and practice and challenging the transferability and supposed ubiquity of this approach (Wada & Kassan, 2021). A point reinforced by Ansloos et al. (2021) when they say that 'decolonizing practices in psychotherapy seek to distribute power equally among therapist and client such that structures that have the propensity to oppress can be destabilized' (p. 131). They also note that, 'In counselling practice, this on a basic level looks like taking a more collaborative approach when working with cli-ents, but also allowing clients to guide the therapy in ways that are meaningful to them, and not therapist directed' (p. 131). Samuel and Ortiz (2021) see 'decolonial praxis in psychology as freeing the minds of racialised peoples and creating space for us, our lived experiences, and our epistemologies in psychology' (p. 4). In other words, rather than banish marginalised and racialised populations to the subversive and marginal space located outside the conventional, normative epistemologies and theories that inform traditional psychotherapy, decolonisation involves making room for experiences of minoritised peoples, for other ways of knowing, and for alternative conceptualisations and approaches, 'inside the sentence' of the lived experience of minoritised and racial-ised clients. Regarding other ways of knowing as valid and legitimate and recognising that approaches other than Western ones may be a better fit for working with some minoritised clients offers a more attuned and responsive way of engaging.

Samuel and Ortiz (2021) offer additional practical tools for this endeavour in the form of 'counter-storytelling'. They explain that attending to and making room for counter-narratives can challenge the dominant colonial narratives and 'overwrite' colonial stories with those voiced by racialised peoples – a sentiment echoed by critical race scholars (e.g., Solórzano & Yosso, 2002). King (2021) reminds us that 'Western psychology… has dominated the world with its worldview, all Indigenous knowledges must be seen as equal contributors to how we understand our world' (p. 8). King suggests that a 'major systemic upheaval' is necessary to make space for non-Western ways of knowing 'inside the sentence', or we run the risk of perpetuating those same approaches and limited ways of thinking that we are working to eradicate.

While decolonising psychological professions is an essential first step, we suggest that responsible engagement with minoritised and racialised clients also necessitates embracing a CRT lens, being acutely aware of intersectionality, and working from a social justice and empowerment approach. Indeed, CRT and decolonisation strive in tandem to resist and redefine the oppressive frameworks underpinning Western psychology.

Critical Race Theory and Intersectionality

CRT was developed by activists and scholars of colour in the 1970s in response to unmet demands for social and legal change in the USA. Critical race theorists asserted that substantial change and meaningful racial reform demand a closer examination of how race and power operate in society (Brown & Jackson, 2013). A key CRT idea is that race is a fundamental organising principle in society and that race is socially constructed to maintain the interests of those who constructed it (Taylor, 1998). CRT problematises whiteness as a normative standard and posits that racism is not the exception, but rather a part of daily life. CRT rejects 'colour-blindness' as this stance ignores the racial construction of whiteness and reinforces its privileged and oppressive position. CRT also challenges the belief in meritocracy, recognising the many barriers that exist for minoritised communities and highlighting the inequalities in opportunities to advance.

Another important facet of CRT is 'counter-storytelling' (Solórzano & Yosso, 2002). The act of storytelling can be a powerful tool for creating meaning and disrupting problematic myths and metaphors about minoritised individuals. In particular, CRT emphasises the telling of stories and voices traditionally marginalised by the dominant culture. These counter-narratives resist 'master narratives', which reinforce systems of oppression (Solórzano & Yosso, 2002, p. 27). As such, counter-storytelling can expose, critique and subvert deeply entrenched epistemologies, working to 'inform and transform the dominant narrative' (De Mello, 2021, p. 19). For example, by challenging the belief in meritocracy and the narrative about legal and political systems being 'neutral' and 'colour-blind', CRT addresses minoritised clients' internalised self-blame and shifts these

narratives to underscore the social and political forces that marginalise and inflict violence upon their bodies, identities and experiences. Since therapy entails holding space
for clients' stories, assisting them in making meaning of their stories, and helping them
alter maladaptive stories, CRT offers a tool to engage and contest negative stereotyping
that minoritised individuals face and assist them in re-writing and re-defining harmful,
hegemonic narratives. Through this lens, therapists can acknowledge systemic oppression and racial trauma that minoritised clients face and validate their lived experiences.
It is also a place where these narratives – often different from the dominant narrative –
can find a safe holding space, where alternative narratives can exist and stories of both
trauma and resilience can be told, heard and validated.

Importantly, CRT is rooted in intersectionality (Crenshaw, 1989), which encapsulates
the ways in which a minoritised person's wellbeing can be further complicated by their
'Big 7' multiple identities and experiences of overlapping structural oppressions, including racism, sexism, heterosexism and ableism (see Kassan & Moodley, 2021). Within the
context of therapy, intersectionality encourages therapists to recognise clients' multiple
identities and the resulting complexities that can give rise to uniquely harmful outcomes (De Mello, 2021). In this way, CRT invites the 'full story' – with all its layers and
complexities – to be told.

In the pandemic context, working from a CRT and intersectionality lens encourages
clinicians to refrain from blaming minoritised and racialised clients who fall ill and
from interpreting their physical illness as due to personal wrongdoing. A CRT framework recognises the circumstances that render it difficult or even impossible for some to
self-isolate or work from home and the associated higher risk of exposure to the virus.
This approach helps recognise the underlying conditions stemming from structural inequalities that make these minoritised individuals more vulnerable to severe illness and
present barriers to seeking medical help or taking the time to fully heal and recover. As
Gonzales et al. (2021) explain:

> Racial and ethnic minorities experience a number of disadvantages across their
> lifetimes and across multiple domains of life from education, work, healthcare,
> neighborhoods, and police enforcement. These enduring experiences set a
> context for chronic stress and heighten the risk of disease, disability, and
> complications with the coronavirus. (p. 230)

Working from a CRT framework challenges the commonly held belief during the pandemic that 'we are all in this together'. Instead, there is recognition of the uncomfortable truth that, while as a society, we are all in the same storm of living through a
global public health crisis, we are navigating this storm in dramatically different vessels.
There is tremendous disparity in terms of supports available, financial factors, social
determinants of health and additional stressors such as anti-Asian and anti-Black racism
impacting minoritised individuals. This shift in perspective is essential for responsible
therapeutic engagement with minoritised and racialised communities.

Social Justice and Empowerment

In addition to working from a CRT stance, we suggest that clinicians need to embrace a social justice informed approach when working with minoritised and racialised clients, and work toward empowering these individuals and communities. Social justice is a political and philosophical concept centred around equality along various social dimensions and emphasising equal rights, equal opportunity and equal treatment for all. A society operating from this principle 'promotes individual and community empowerment, attends to societal inequities, distributes economic resources equitably, attends to legal justice, and ensures citizens have access to secure housing, employment, and personal safety' (Sinacore, 2021, p. 315). A social justice approach recognises and works to address systematic discrimination and oppression at structural, institutional and individual levels, while aiming to minimise power imbalances and increase equality (Winter, 2019). Working from a social justice stance, the clinician continually assesses issues of power and representation and monitors processes within organisations to ensure that these are aligned with principles of equity. The clinician closely and critically examines messages in workplaces and the set-up of physical spaces to reflect inclusivity, diversity and equity, engaging in advocacy to address issues (Sinacore, 2021). Considering the inequities that COVID-19 revealed and the particularly adverse impact on minoritised populations, a social justice approach is necessary, even more so during the global health crisis.

Hailes et al. (2021) offer a specific conceptualisation of social justice for the psychotherapy field and identify its three main domains: interactional, distributive, and procedural. According to this, interactional justice is most associated with the interpersonal work of therapy, while distributive and procedural justice are associated with work that targets community-level or structural and societal change. Winter (2019) suggests that these domains may be closely intertwined, as the individual's presenting issues are intimately connected to the broader social and political structures and systems, and proposes that therapy can in turn have an impact on these structures and systems if it challenges unjust structures and fosters new power relations: 'it is an acknowledgment that the work we do occurs in a socio-political context which it cannot be easily disconnected from (and therefore that things like power, discrimination and oppression are important) and that this work can have political implications' (p. 180).

Concrete suggestions for therapists who strive to embrace a social justice approach include engaging in ongoing critical self-reflection on oppression, power and privilege in their own lives and on how their particular social locations have shaped their values and worldview, and how these in turn affect their conceptualisation of a client's presenting issues (Hailes et al., 2021). To mitigate the inevitable power inequalities in the therapeutic relationship, this self-reflection must be coupled with a commitment to collaboration and focus on client and community empowerment and prioritising strengths-based approaches (Hailes et al., 2021). As Sinacore (2021) suggests, when clinical practice is informed by social justice, knowledge and meaning-making are co-created, and there is focus on intersecting identities and acknowledgment of how power and privilege operate (p. 317). The clinician strives for greater reflexivity and awareness of their contribution to inequities 'by examining their personal biases, assumptions, and attitudes' and contemplating whose knowledge and ways of knowing are being prioritised and whose knowledge is being marginalised or excluded (Sinacore, 2021, p. 317). In other words, working from a social justice lens entails critically examining and dismantling the very 'sentence' of psychological therapy, thereby creating a novel healing space 'inside the sentence' where effective and responsible engagement with minoritised and racialised individuals can occur.

CONCLUSION

Considering the historical limitations of psychological professions with minoritised and racialised individuals and the acute need for effective and responsible support for these communities, we suggest that mental health professionals need to critically engage with and dismantle the traditional 'sentence' of therapy to create space for creative and culturally imaginative forms of engagement. What is required is a 'radical healing approach' (Adames et al., 2022) in psychotherapy that resists self-blame by the clients and focuses instead on a critical analysis of systemic superstructures of oppression, addressing the wounds of racism, sexism, homo- and trans-phobic related stress and trauma. This would require clinicians to make space 'inside the sentence' for ways of thinking that may be futuristic, unfamiliar, challenging, yet rich and informative.

REFLECTIVE AND CRITICAL THINKING QUESTIONS

1   A decolonising aesthetic and spirituality shift from the established meanings and effects of traditional psychology. How can a decolonising of counselling psychology and psychotherapy offer a 'third space' that addresses the wounds of oppression, including racism, sexism, homo- and trans-phobic stress and trauma?

2   Overemphasis of Big 7 socio-cultural identities can reinforce negative stereotypes and essentialise identity politics, creating inflexible and harmful understandings of a client's presenting issues. How can psychotherapists avoid boxing clients into a monocultural worldview?

3   A social justice approach challenges existing psychodynamic principles of the unconscious, individuality and self-awareness, and links this to broader communities and systems. How can psychotherapists bridge gaps between the interiority and exteriority of a client's lived experience, so that social justice principles are embodied in clinical practice?

RECOMMENDED READING AND RESOURCES

Arthur, N. (Ed.). (2019). *Counselling in cultural contexts: Identities and social justice.*
   Springer.
This book draws from principles of culture-infused counselling to provide a guide for
working with diverse clients at the personal, relational and community levels; case
studies in each chapter model therapist self-reflexivity while illustrating interventions
for clients across a range of identities.

Duran, E., Firehammer, J., & Gonzalez, J. (2008). Liberation psychology as the path
   toward healing cultural soul wounds. *Journal of Counseling & Development, 86*(3),
   288–295. https://doi.org/10.1002/j.1556-6678.2008.tb00511.x
This article describes a liberation psychology that strives for psychological and spiritual
emancipation of Indigenous individuals and communities afflicted by soul wounding,
oppression and colonialism.

Kassan, A. & Moodley, R. (Eds.) (2021). *Diversity and social justice in counseling, psychology,
   and psychotherapy: A case study approach.* Cognella.
This book takes an intersectional lens to explore social locations, oppression and
privilege in the context of social justice in counselling and psychology. Each chapter
includes a case vignette that illuminates how diversity and social justice theory impact
therapeutic practice, using analytic tools such as anti-racism and critical race theory,
decoloniality and Indigeneity, feminist therapy and more.

Suyemoto, K. L., Hochman, A. L., Donovan, R. A., & Roemer, L. (2021). Becoming and
   fostering allies and accomplices through authentic relationships: Choosing justice
   over comfort. *Research in Human Development, 18*(1–2), 1–28. https://doi.org/10.1080/
   15427609.2020.1825905
This case study explores the process of becoming allies and accomplices across privilege
and identities, with the aim of dismantling oppression at interpersonal and systemic
levels; among other strategies, the article discusses self-reflection, cultural humility,
re-engagement following disconnection and collaborating across differences.

Teachers College, Columbia University. (2021, April 16). *Decolonizing psychology training
   conference* [Video]. YouTube. www.youtube.com/watch?v=d0diS_IMl
   2k&ab_channel=TeachersCollege%2CColumbiaUniversity
This conference recording provides resources for students, scholars and clinicians to
critically reflect on decolonising psychological research, curricula, supervision and
mentorship practices.

REFERENCES

Adames, H. Y., Chavez-Deunas, N. Y., Lewis, J. A., Neville, H. A., French, B. H., Chen, G.
   A., & Mosley, D. V. (2022). Radical healing in psychotherapy: Addressing the wounds
   of racism-related stress and trauma. *Psychotherapy.* http://dx.doi.org/10.1037/
   pst0000435

Ansloos, J., Santos Dunn, N., Ward, K., & McCormick, S. (2021). Indigeneity and coloniality as analytic tools. In A. Kassan & R. Moodley (Eds.), *Diversity and social justice in counseling, psychology, and psychotherapy: A case study approach* (pp. 123–136). Cognella.

Bhugra, D., & Bhui, K. (2006). Psychotherapy across the cultural divide. In R. Moodley & S. Palmer (Eds.), *Race, culture and psychotherapy: Critical perspectives in multicultural practice* (pp. 46–57). Routledge.

Brown, K., & Jackson, D. D. (2013). The history and conceptual elements of critical race theory. In M. Lynn & A. D. Dixson (Eds.), *Handbook of critical race theory in education* (1st ed.) (pp. 29–42). Routledge.

Cheng, H. L., Kim, H. Y., Tsong, Y., & Joel Wong, Y. (2021). COVID-19 anti-Asian racism: A tripartite model of collective psychosocial resilience. *American Psychologist, 76*(4), 627.

Constantino, M. J., Boswell, J. F., Coyne, A. E., Swales, T. P., & Kraus, D. R. (2021). Effect of matching therapists to patients vs assignment as usual on adult psychotherapy outcomes: A randomized clinical trial. *JAMA Psychiatry, 78*(9), 960–969.

Crenshaw, K. (1989). Demarginalizing the intersection of race and sex: A Black feminist critique of antidiscrimination doctrine. *University of Chicago Legal Forum, 1989*, 139–168.

Cyrus, K. (2017). Multiple minorities as multiply marginalized: Applying the minority stress theory to LGBTQ people of color. *Journal of Gay & Lesbian Mental Health, 21*(3), 194–202.

De Mello, T. J. (2021). Integrating antiracism and critical race theory in therapeutic practice. In A. Kassan & R. Moodley (Eds.), *Diversity and social justice in counseling, psychology, and psychotherapy: A case study approach* (pp. 17–30). Cognella.

Diaz, A., Baweja, R., Bonatakis, J. K., & Baweja, R. (2021). Global health disparities in vulnerable populations of psychiatric patients during the COVID-19 pandemic. *World Journal of Psychiatry, 11*(4), 94–108.

Duran, E. (2006). *Healing the soul wound: Counseling with American Indians and other native peoples.* Teachers College Press.

Gone, J. P. (2009). A community-based treatment for Native American historical trauma: Prospects for evidence-based practice. *Journal of Consulting and Clinical Psychology, 77*(4), 751–762.

Gonzales, E., Gordon, S., Whetung, C., Connaught, G., Collazo, J., & Hinton, J. (2021). Acknowledging systemic discrimination in the context of a pandemic: Advancing an anti-racist and anti-ageist movement. *Journal of Gerontological Social Work, 64*(3), 223–237.

Hailes, H. P., Ceccolini, C. J., Gutowski, E., & Liang, B. (2021). Ethical guidelines for social justice in psychology. *Professional Psychology: Research and Practice, 52*(1), 1–11.

Kassan, A., & Moodley, R. (Eds.) (2021). *Diversity and social justice in counseling, psychology, and psychotherapy: A case study approach.* Cognella.

King, J. (2021). Exploring Indigenous ways of knowing. In A. Kassan & R. Moodley (Eds.), *Diversity and social justice in counseling, psychology, and psychotherapy: A case study approach* (pp. 3–16). Cognella.

Maldonado-Torres, N. (2016). *Outline of ten theses on coloniality and decoloniality*. Frantz Fanon Foundation.

Moodley, R. (2011). *Outside the sentence: Readings in critical multicultural counselling and psychotherapy*. Centre for Diversity in Counselling and Psychotherapy, Ontario Institute for Studies in Education (OISE), University of Toronto.

Moodley, R., & Lubin, D. B. (2008). Developing your career to working with multicultural and diversity clients. In S. Palmer & R. Bor (Eds.), *The practitioner's handbook: A guide for counsellors, psychotherapists and counselling psychologists* (pp. 156–175). Sage Publications.

Samuel, C. A., & Ortiz, D. L. (2021). 'Method and meaning': Storytelling as decolonial praxis in the psychology of racialised peoples. *New Ideas in Psychology, 62*, 100868.

Santomauro, D. F., Herrera, A. M. M., Shadid, J., Zheng, P., Ashbaugh, C., Pigott, D. M., … & Ferrari, A. J. (2021). Global prevalence and burden of depressive and anxiety disorders in 204 countries and territories in 2020 due to the COVID-19 pandemic. *The Lancet, 398*(10312), 1700–1712.

Sinacore, A. L. (2021). Critical diversity and social justice: Organizational and systemic considerations. In A. Kassan & R. Moodley (Eds.), *Diversity and social justice in counseling, psychology, and psychotherapy: A case study approach* (pp. 315–327). Cognella.

Solórzano, D. G., & Yosso, T. J. (2002). Critical race methodology: Counter-storytelling as an analytical framework for education research. *Qualitative Inquiry, 8*(1), 23–44.

Sue, D. W. (2015). Therapeutic harm and cultural oppression. *The Counseling Psychologist, 43*(3), 359–369.

Taylor, E. (1998). A primer on critical race theory: Who are the critical race theorists and what are they saying? *The Journal of Blacks in Higher Education, 19*, 122.

Tervalon, M., & Murray-Garcia, J. (1998). Cultural humility versus cultural competence: A critical distinction in defining physician training outcomes in multicultural education. *Journal of Health Care for the Poor and Underserved, 9*(2), 117–125.

Wada, K., & Kassan, A. (2021). The internalization of counseling, psychology, and psychotherapy: Decolonizing diversity and social justice training. In A. Kassan & R. Moodley (Eds.), *Diversity and social justice in counseling, psychology, and psychotherapy: A case study approach* (pp. 355–368). Cognella.

Winter, L. A. (2019). Social justice and remembering 'the personal is political' in counselling and psychotherapy: So, what can therapists do? *Counselling and Psychotherapy Research, 19*(3), 179–181.

3
IDENTITY AND INTERSECTIONALITY

Colin Lago

OVERVIEW

The essentials of life include whatever is necessary to take your place in public
without shame. (Marmot, 2022)

Whilst this book is likely to feature different definitions and descriptions of social
justice, I was deeply touched by Michael Marmot's quote above. To be able to take
your place in public without shame implies a society that aspires towards a compassionate acceptance of each person, that is constituted legally, organisationally and
culturally around values dedicated to decency, equality, ethical perspectives, respect
and care for its citizens. In addition, this would be a society that seeks to have flat-
tened rather than steep differential hierarchies of class and status, of riches and
poverty, of gendered and ethnic equality, of the 'other' who is different (Wilkinson
et al., 2009). This would be a society that has social democracy and social justice at
its heart.

The social vision described above screamed out at me from every page of Harry
Leslie Smith's book *Don't Let My Past Be Your Future* (2017). Purchased in a popular
bookshop on a rainy afternoon at Easter in a seaside resort on the south coast, I
became absorbed in reading this book which reflected upon a lifetime deeply shaped
by growing up in grinding poverty in a northern city in the 1920s. The author's
formative years were subsequently shaped by the impact of the financial depression
and then later by military service during the Second World War. Buoyed up tempo-
rarily by Britain's aspirations towards social democracy after the war, with the advent
of the welfare state, the National Health Service and the investment in education,
the author then strikes a despondent and critical note at current times. 'Democracy
is no longer serving the needs of all its citizens', he asserts (p. 8). Harry's moving
and inspirational story, his commitment and passion for social justice, for reducing
glaring (and increasing) health and financial inequalities, his political activities and

commitment all constitute the elements of an identity profoundly shaped by early personal experience and in continuous growth through his interactions with others and with organisations.

This chapter explores some of the many facets of identity including the exploration of intersectionality, the multi-factorial concept that theoretically embodies the many aspects of identity that symbolise both privilege and 'otherness' (Turner, 2021).

BASIC THEORETICAL PRINCIPLES: IDENTITY

A Brief Introduction

Various definitions of identity have long existed within academic literature spanning the human sciences (sociology, psychology, organisational, political and so on.) Two concise examples follow:

1 'The fact of being who or what a person or thing is'.
2 Identity is the concept of 'who we believe ourselves to be'. It is personal (how you see yourself) and social (how others see you).

Stets and Burke (2003) also allude to the contextual element when they note that identity is enacted within relationships, e.g., parent–child, teacher–student, barrister–client. Beneath these apparently simple ideas inevitably lurks much complexity both within theoretical discourse and social/psychological experiencing. Martin Kettle, a journalist, reflecting upon the nature of identity as played out by one teenage character in a Ken Loach film (*A Fond Kiss*) noted that identity is 'always multiple, always complex, frequently conflicted, and always changing' (Kettle, 2004). This latter description begins to catch the multiple complexities of the lived experience and somewhat anticipates the emergence of intersectionality addressed later in the chapter.

Determinants of Identity from the Past

The television programme *Who Do You Think You Are?* has become immensely popular in recent years. Focusing each episode upon a particular (well-known) personality, the programme presents a process of discovery of the subjects' familial and historic antecedents. Perhaps mirroring trends in society where personal interest in your origins and activities of ancestors has become a popular pursuit, this programme not only stimulates reflections upon historical identity but also evidences the enormous reservoir of records available for such research. A further dimension of this reservoir of information has been the extraordinary developments within the field of genetics and DNA. Historic and geographic origins can now be traced over centuries, frequently revealing previously completely unknown aspects of one's genealogical origins. Where one comes from is a key aspect of identity, which over recent decades is an enquiry from others that has unfortunately stimulated 'the effects of racism and perceived discrimination on people of colour' (Dass-Brailsford, 2021).

Erikson and Identity Development

The theoretical conceptions of identity by Erikson first appeared in the 1950s and were geared towards understanding the nature of identity and its development over a lifetime. Given Erikson's background, it comes as no surprise that he devoted his professional life to unravelling the nature of identity. Fleeing from her estranged husband, his pregnant mother relocated to Germany where she eventually married again. Erik was told that her new husband was his real father, only revealing the truth later in his life. He reports remaining bitter about this deception throughout his life.

He was raised in the Jewish religion but suffered bullying and bigotry because of his physical characteristics (tall, blond and blue eyed), from both Jewish and Gentile (not Jewish) children for either being Jewish or too Nordic. Reflecting on these experiences later in life he describes his complex 'identity confusion' and believed himself to be on the borderline between neurosis and adolescent psychosis. Perhaps it is no wonder that Erikson later believed that identity formation was the major task of adolescence. He proposed that identity is the awareness of the consistency of self over time combined with the recognition of this consistency by others (Erikson, 1980). We can see from this perspective that the process of identity development is both an individual and social phenomenon (Adams & Marshall, 1996). For those seeking asylum, fleeing from civil, political and military unrest in their countries of origin, there can be major interruptions to identity development for young people (Charura, 2022), and recent research has revealed the considerable challenges to identity that are experienced by those of refugee and asylum-seeking status (Taylor et al., 2020).

Erikson proposed that there were nine stages of psychosocial development within his theory of personality which were each framed within a spectrum of 'virtues' or 'potencies' (strengths). Thus, for example, the initial virtue 'hope', which considers the first 18 months or so of life, is characterised by the elements of trust and mistrust, and the second stage, 'will', is reflected in the tension between autonomy and shame. Similar to Jung's assertions that maturity can be defined as the capacity to hold a creative tension between opposites, Erikson's theory posits that it is only when both ends of each life-stage challenge are understood and accepted can the optimal value or virtue of that stage emerge. His nine stages, which he approximates, though rarely mentions, to age, have the following developmental tasks. (Stages one and two are briefly mentioned in the above paragraph.)

- Stage 1. (Ages 0–18 months). Hope: trust vs. mistrust.
- Stage 2. (Ages 18 months–3). Will: autonomy vs. shame.
- Stage 3. (Ages 3–6). Purpose: initiative vs. guilt.
- Stage 4. (Ages 7–11). Competence: industry vs. inferiority.
- Stage 5. (Ages 12–18). Fidelity: identity vs. confusion.
- Stage 6. (Ages 19–29). Love: intimacy vs. isolation.
- Stage 7. (Ages 30–64). Care: generativity vs. stagnation.
- Stage 8. (Age 65+). Wisdom: integrity vs. despair.

Joan Erikson, his wife with whom he developed some of these ideas, contributed a ninth stage to the above conceptual framework which she wrote at the age of 93 (Erikson & Erikson, 1997)! Projecting this final stage into much older age, Joan argued that, to a greater or lesser degree, each of the developmental challenges previously described all have to be confronted again as the older person has to cope with deteriorating physical, mental and possibly relational circumstances.

There is no doubt these propositions created a significant theoretical base upon which later hypotheses concerning identity development have been built (see, for example: Archer & Waterman, 1983; Marcia, 1966, 1980). Subsequent attention has also been given to gender differences in adolescent identity development (Sandhu & Tung, 2006) and career development.

Identity: The Shifting Sands of Meaning

Erikson's ideas were critically developed on the basis that identity development was a psycho-social process. That is, identity emerged from the potent interaction of the individual with others. Whilst this essential core foundation process still, somewhat, holds sway, there have been shifts in the perception, connotations and meanings of identity in more recent decades. Discussions within various oppressed groups during the last two decades have led to the development and adoption of many new terms for identity description. One source suggests that contemporary identity privileges the 'psycho' over the 'social' (Schachter & Galliher, 2018).

Whilst it is important within this chapter to introduce these recent and relevant developments, I did not want to overlook the article by Syed and Fish (2018) who argue that Erikson's work is 'seldom associated with work on culture, race and ethnicity', (p. 274) They assert that Erikson not only incorporated these elements, but that they 'figured prominently into his theorizing'. They advance the view that his work recognises the impact of historical trauma which damages the identity development of those in marginalised groups; and it is from within these groups that the awareness and creation of new and continually developing descriptions and terminology have been emerging.

Danielson and Engle (1995) articulate the complex paradoxes emerging from traditional identity politics. They note the tension between the diversity of discourses engaged in by differing oppressed groups (e.g., women, sexual minorities, black groups) which assumed 'similarity of experience within those groups and ignored the significance of multiple allegiances, communities, and experiences in the construction of those identities' (p. xiii). They later suggest that the beginning point of this spectrum within identity politics was founded upon the early civil rights and women's movements, where the dominant argument was based upon equality with white, able-bodied men. As such, these early aspirations aimed towards achieving a society through which neither sex, disability or skin colour determined one's position in society. Later, this 'paradigm of liberal pluralism' was contested and rejected on the basis that its colour-blind and sex-blind thinking camouflaged real differences between the groups. This later position facilitated, for many, a (re)claiming of their identities. Concisely described, this book constitutes a collection of voices from within the field of American legal scholarship that aspired towards 'methodologies for thinking affirmatively about cultural identity without freezing differences among social groups'. I will return to this text later when considering intersectionality.

Cultural Identity Development Models

From the late 1970s onwards a raft of cultural identity development models were developed within the USA. Based upon considerable research, these models described a series of (attitudinal and emotional) stages that people would proceed through in moving from positions of self and group deprecation through to full appreciation of themselves as cultural/ethnic beings within the context of contrast and comparison to other ethnic groupings, with selective appreciation of the dominant group in society (Sue & Sue, 2013). Within this canon of work, a considerable range of such models were developed, and include for example: disability, biracial, LGBT, Hispanic, African American, white consciousness, adolescent, etc. Though somewhat critiqued as 'stage' models of development rather than 'process' conceptualisations, the research base of descriptions offered for each stage offers considerable nuanced information to readers wishing to explore their own attitudinal base towards others. The value of these models to professional therapeutic practice was established by the research of Carter (1995) who reported that the psychotherapist's levels of identity development compared to the client were directly related to the efficacy of therapy.

Reconceptualising 'Stigmatised' Identities

> If you don't control your narrative, someone else will. (Henry, 2022)

The big eight 'stigmatised' identities in society are deemed to be ethnicity, race, gender identity, sexual orientation, ability, spirituality/religion, nationality and socio-economic status (see the video 'Social identities and the Big 8' on YouTube). Within each of these categories, the advances in research, data collection and conceptual categorisation has exploded in recent times. Further, there has continued to be vigorous reflective and projective debates within 'minority' groups as to the issues they face and the philosophical/ social/ political outcomes they wish to see when applied to them as a group. Within this sociological arena concerned with 'difference and diversity' and certainly reflecting the expansion, indeed explosion of conceptualisations in recent decades, there has been an ever-increasing number of publication platforms (social media, YouTube, alternative sources) through which ideas have been communicated about concepts and terminology that more accurately reflects people's experiencing of their identities and the issues they face.

In many cases, formal academic pieces have not kept up with these changes. For example, originating in the 1960s, 'gender identity' was used to describe a person's own sense of identifying as either male or female. Facebook has, in recent years, published lengthy lists of gender identity terminology, thus moving away from society's previous usage of (what now seems extraordinarily) simplified binary descriptions of male/female/intersex. This list now offers more than 50 custom gender options, for example: genderqueer, gender questioning, gender nonconforming, agender, bigender, cisgender and so on. The term has not only substantially expanded in concept to include those who identify in many other ways but also such expansion, by implication, may encourage those to create self-definitions that are not already included.

Similarly, the core statistics related to neurodiversity (just one aspect of the ability category noted above) reveal that:

- 1 in 20 have ADHD.
- 1 in 10 have dyslexia.
- 1 in 60 have autism.
- One-fifth of the human population are neurodiverse.

The above figures reveal the extraordinary extent of diversity in human neuro-cognitive capacity (Chan, 2022), and indicates both the number and complexity of those occupying categories of stigmatised identity. Certainly, it has long been recognised that the movement from 'other-attribution' to 'self-attribution' signals a critical and profound moment of personal and group identity change that has emancipatory consequences for individuals and groups.

Finally, it is important to acknowledge the work of Altman (2020) who discusses 'nonlinear dynamic systems of identity formation'. That is, the categories of stigmatised identities detailed above are overly simplistic descriptions that do not accord with the complexity of peoples' lives, how they see themselves and how they manage their social contexts. Each facet of identity interacts uniquely with other facets and changes over time.

BASIC THEORETICAL PRINCIPLES: INTERSECTIONALITY

Intersectionality is a sociological concept for unravelling the complexities of systems of power... as they actually exist in our daily lives. (Romero, 2018, p. 36)

A Brief History

The concept of intersectionality shifts us from a previous position of singular or binary category thinking and conceptualisation regarding oppressed groups and persons within them. Angela Davis, the black liberation and feminist activist and Professor Emerita at the University of California, recalls being asked the following question in the 1970s: 'are you black or are you a woman?' She goes on to comment that 'there was such backwardness in the early days of feminism' (Davis, 2021). This singularity of issue was also reflected in the issues that separated white and black feminist thought in the USA during these times (Kendall, 2020).

Despite the above, Ted Brown, a UK domiciled black gay rights activist, remembers hearing stories from his mother, who had been a civil rights campaigner in the USA, noting the similarities between the three movements of the Black Panthers, the women's movement and the gay rights movement. This story 'galvanised the Gay Liberation Front (GLF) in the UK (in 1970), to be intersectional before there was a word for it!' he retorts (Abraham, 2021, p. 31). Later in the same article Peter Tatchell reports how the GLF supported the black community, trade unions under Tory attack, anti-Vietnam war protests and the Troops Out (of Ireland) movement. Within these examples, social activists from one societally discriminated-against group were recognising similar and parallel phenomena occurring within other discriminated groups and consequently seeking to lend their voices of support. Almost three decades later, Sanders (2006) wrote a critical chapter exploring the intersections between psychotherapy and politics, quoting George Albee who argued that 'psychologists must join forces with persons who reject racism, sexism, colonialism and exploitation and must find ways to redistribute social power and to increase social justice' (1996).

Crenshaw, an American legal scholar, is frequently cited as the initial architect of the concept of intersectionality (1991). Notwithstanding this popular interpretation of intersectionality's history, Hill Collins and Bilge (2020) complain about academics' selective amnesia and devote a densely detailed chapter to exploring its many historical antecedents in social activism. They do, however, acknowledge the importance of Crenshaw's naming of the concept, which has acted as a springboard for many, surprisingly different, applications. They suggest that six core ideas underpin intersectionality: social inequality, intersecting power relations, social context, relationality, social justice and complexity (p. 31).

Defining 'Intersectionality'

Writing from within the legal framework, Crenshaw contested that, for example, a black woman, whilst straddling two oppressed identities, nevertheless could only be judged against a single aspect of law, be that either race discrimination or sex discrimination. The legal system failed to recognise, in this example, the simultaneous joint impact of both sexism and racism. Intersectionality seeks to recognise the complex and multiple facets of social identity that impact people's experiencing of the world. The central thrust of this conceptualisation is in its application to and pursuit of social equity and justice.

Hill Collins and Bilge (2020), whilst recognising how this concept has now been applied in a wide variety of different settings for different purposes, suggest the following definition which they believe would likely be acceptable to a variety of researchers and theorists:

> Intersectionality investigates how intersecting power relations influence social
> relations across diverse societies as well as individual experiences in everyday

life. As an analytic tool, intersectionality views categories of race, class, gender, sexuality, nation, ability, ethnicity, and age – among others – as interrelated and mutually shaping one another. Intersectionality is a way of understanding and explaining complexity in the world, in people and in human experiences. (p. 2)

It is thus directly related to matters of power, privilege, social inequalities and discrimination as they manifest within society between and across groups and between people.

Intersectionality has been inappropriately and incorrectly likened to the movements celebrating multiculturalism and diversity that became popular in the 1970s and 1980s. Whilst the many educational, workplace and social work development initiatives based upon multicultural perspectives have been promulgated over recent decades, they have not been based, as intersectionality is, upon addressing the realities of the social inequalities embedded within society.

Applying Intersectionality

The concept of intersectionality has been embraced by a plethora of researchers, scholars, policy makers and social activists. Intersectionally informed research has challenged previously held, generalised, assumptions by policy makers, who do not anticipate the everyday negative implications in practice upon those from other intersectional identities (Romero, 2018).

As an encompassing methodology, Hill Collins and Bilge (2020) note a range of social context arenas where intersectional approaches have been applied including reproductive justice, anti-violence initiatives, workers' rights and school and college transformation. Detailed accounts are given in their text of the use of intersectionality as an analytic tool into three quite distinct and different arenas: international football and its governance, worldwide economic inequalities, and the Brazilian black women's movement. Each of these quite disparate subject arenas foregrounded four critical themes: social inequalities, intersecting power relations, the complexity of social context and just how important relationality is in informing all aspects of intersectionality. They cite Cho et al. who argue that 'the important focus of intersectionality is on what it does rather than what it is' (2013, p. 795).

CASE STUDY: THE INTERSECTIONAL CHALLENGE WITHIN PSYCHOTHERAPEUTIC DYNAMICS

Some years ago, I was informed of a case of an international student who had already completed several years of graduate study in his own country. Following a harrowing arrest and subsequent torture, he had fled his country of origin and gained political asylum in the UK. Sadly, he had already lost several members of his family who had been killed by the same forces that arrested and tortured him.

He recommenced his studies in a British college, having to start in year one again. In the final year of his new course, he failed a 'viva' in which he was interviewed by senior academic figures in his department. Alarmingly for him, this situation immediately sparked the traumatic memory of his previous torture. Frozen and dissociating, and therefore completely unable to answer the questions posed, he was deemed to have failed. He was referred to the welfare officer and the college counsellor, both of whom were British, white, middle class, middle aged and degree educated.

In reflecting upon this situation, and stimulated by the texts of both Belkin and White (2020) and Turner (2021) it is relatively straightforward (with either of the above helping colleagues) to become acutely aware of the multiple differences between them and the traumatised student when considered within the 'privilege–otherness' spectrum:

- He was a traumatised immigrant having sought asylum, and being ousted through tragic circumstance from his own country (major losses of family, belonging, culture, nationality, relationships, language, home, etc.).
- He had been subjected to violence by his own state and countrymen, a major cause of loss of trust in the world.
- Not only was he shamed and humiliated by the original torture but was now 'failing' again at his chosen subject and life aspiration.
- Driven by desperation of circumstance and desperately wanting and needing to qualify, he experienced a re-traumatisation, not only through the viva experience, but also through having to face the subsequent helping and appeal processes.

Within the context of these helping relationships, this client's agony, trauma, powerlessness and statelessness contrasts desperately and graphically with the power and privileged position of both helpers.

'Nothing more drives a spirit into creative acts of survival than the stifling experience of coercion and control that subvert complexity of being'. So writes White in her account of her therapeutic work with a fellow Jamaican immigrant, now both living in the USA (Belkin & White, 2020, p. 148). From an intersectional perspective, whilst both shared national and cultural origins and similar status within their adopted country, they also occupied differing gender, class and heritage origins. In Jamaica, the patient had come from a poor, black, working-class family whilst the therapist, being middle class and lighter skinned, had grown up in a very different and privileged social milieu. Whilst profoundly recognising the patient's accounts of a tough upbringing in an impoverished area, White realised she had been spared such a hard reality. She reports catching herself experiencing fear and then shifting into an act of 'othering' when he discussed gang violence, only to be followed, fortunately, by another sensibility of shame. Later in the chapter she notes that what the two of them could not name was her 'unwitting participation in social structures that perpetuated his unfortunate plight' (p. 158). 'We avoided talk of racial difference', she reports, perhaps both fearing the 'destructive power that symbolizing this truth might potentiate'. Both participants in this therapeutic relationship were simultaneously both joined and separated by their shared, though very different, backgrounds in Jamaica as well as their experiences of 'immigrantism' and racism within the USA. Reggae music, and particularly Bob Marley's lyrics (which constituted a meaningful shared background to their joint national origins), acted as a powerful symbolic, metaphorical resource in their relationship. It facilitated the exploration of anxiety and hope. In concluding her chapter, White cites the poetry of Bromberg (2011) with the quote 'the most valuable gift that any human being will ever receive is the gift of intersubjectivity' (p.14).

The nature of the discourse around otherness is profoundly complicated. Turner (2021) challenges therapists to recognise how they might be, consciously or unconsciously, oppressive to their clients and warns against the tendency to reduce the complex identity of the other into a part which can be used and projected upon. Hatred, shame, privilege, superiority and narcissism are some of the multiple aspects of intersectional relating succinctly explored and explicated by Turner in his (very rare) book within the British canon on intersectionality and psychotherapy. The complexities of intersectionality certainly disrupt any possibilities of accurately predicting 'ethnic matching' of client and therapist. An intersectional approach reminds us that therapeutic work is not just about responding to the individuality of the client, but rather is a profound relational dynamic of considerable complexity and demanding in many different ways of both therapist and client.

CONCLUSION

This chapter has explored and reflected upon the changing socially constructed nature of the term 'identity' and noted some of the many associated concepts that have been linked to it. Intersectionality has provided an overarching concept that recognises and respects the multiple dimensions of identity within a framework which recognises the relativity of power differentials within a person's life circumstances. The relative speed of development of emerging linguistic descriptors and the movement from binary to nonbinary identities is of extraordinary value to many who previously have been unable to fully express meaningful parts of their identity. From another perspective, the usage of appropriate and sensitive language has become a challenge, indeed, even a 'minefield' to enter, as evidenced in the recent publishing situation where a book, initially a prize-winner, went on to attract virulent criticism on social media leading to publishers now employing 'sensitivity advisers' to ensure that contemporary accuracy in descriptive language is used (Hinsliff, 2022). The pathways towards social justice are complex, challenging and contested as this brief trajectory through the concepts of identity and intersectionality has demonstrated.

REFLECTIVE AND CRITICAL THINKING QUESTIONS

1 How would you describe your identity? Would your answer differ if you had been asked by a friend, or a colleague or a client? How?

2 How might you describe the most significant (5–10) aspects of your intersectional identity? Imagine or recall a client who was significantly, intersectionally, different to you on each of the criteria you selected. Look at each category and either interrogate each of the differences between you and the fictitious client (a) in terms of privilege and otherness or (b) in terms of the knowledge, awareness and skills you would require to interact with them sensitively and skilfully. (This is a development of an original exercise devised by Janis Galway in *Counselling Skills for Immigrant Workers: A Training Guide*. Toronto, Ontario Council of Agencies Serving Immigrants.)

RECOMMENDED READING AND RESOURCES

Belkin, M., & White, C. (Eds.). (2020). *Intersectionality and relational psychoanalysis: New perspectives on race, gender and sexuality*. Routledge.
This text looks at the ways privilege and marginalisation are reproduced in therapy.

Lowe, F. (2014). *Thinking space: Promoting thinking about race, culture and diversity in psychotherapy and beyond*. Karnac.
This book celebrates curiosity in learning about difference and intersectionality.

REFERENCES

Abraham, A. (2021, June 25). We broke through a barrier to change the world. *The Guardian colour supplement.*

Adams, G., R. & Marshall, S., K. (1996) A developmental social psychology of identity: Understanding the person-in-context. *Journal of Adolescence, 19(5)*, 429–442.

Albee, G. W. (1996) Revolutions and counterrevolutions in prevention. *American Psychologist, 51*(11), 1130–1133. https://doi.org/10.1037/0003-066X.51.11.1130.

Altman, N. (2020) Intersectionality: From politics to identity. In M. Belkin & C. White (Eds.), *Intersectionality and relational psychoanalysis: New perspectives on race, gender and sexuality* (pp. 218–226). Routledge.

Archer, S. L., & Waterman, A. S. (1983). Identity in early adolescence: A developmental perspective. *The Journal of Early Adolescence*, 3(3), 203–214. https://doi.org/10.1177/0272431683033003

Belkin, M., & White, C. (Eds.). (2020). *Intersectionality and relational psychoanalysis: New perspectives on race, gender and sexuality*. Routledge.

Bromberg, P., M. (2011). *The shadow of the tsunami and the growth of the relational mind*. Routledge.

Carter, R. (1995) *The influence of race and racial identity in psychotherapy: Towards a racially inclusive model*. Wiley & Sons.

Chan, C. (2022, April 30). Could I have adult ADHD? *The Guardian colour supplement*.

Charura, L. (2022, June 24). Experiences of unaccompanied refugee/asylum seekers living in the UK, as well as social workers who support them during the asylum seeking process, post-resettlement and through integration. Presentation at 'We all share the same sky' conference, Institute for Social Justice, York St. John University.

Cho, S., Crenshaw, K., & McCall, L. (2013). Towards a field of intersectionality studies: Theory, applications and praxis. *Signs, 38*(4), 785–810.

Crenshaw, J. W. (1991). Mapping the margins: Intersectionality, identity politics and violence against women of color. *Stanford Law Review, 46*, 1241–1299.

Danielson, D., & Engle, K. (Eds.). (1995). *After identity: A reader in law and culture*. Routledge.

Dass-Brailsford, P. (2021). 'Where are you from?' The effects of racism and perceived discrimination on people of colour. In D. Charura & C. Lago (Eds.), *Black identities and white therapies: Race, respect and diversity* (pp.77–87). PCCS Books.

Davis, A. (2021). *An autobiography*. Hamish Hamilton/Penguin.

Erikson E. H. (1980) *Identity and the life cycle*. W.W. Norton.

Erikson, E., H. & Erikson, J., M. (1997) *The life cycle completed*. W.W. Norton.

Henry, L. (2022). *Lenny Henry's Caribbean Britain* [TV series episode]. BBC2.

Hill Collins, P., & Bilge, S. (2020). *Intersectionality*. Polity.

Hinsliff, G. (2022, June 18). Damaged Goods [Magazine article]. *The Guardian colour supplement*.

Kendall, M. (2020). *Hood feminism: Notes from the women white feminists forgot*. Bloomsbury.

Kettle, M. (2004, October 19). Identity. *The Guardian*, 24.

Marcia, J. E. (1966). Development and validation of ego-identity status. *Journal of Personality and Social Psychology, 3*(5), 551–558. https://doi.org/10.1037/h0023281

Marcia, J. E. (1980). Identity in adolescence. In J. Adelson (Ed.), *Handbook of adolescent psychology* (pp. 109–137). Wiley and Sons.

Marmot, M. (2022, April 9). What's about to happen to health equity is terrifying [Newspaper article]. *The Guardian*.

Romero, M. (2018). *Introducing intersectionality*. Polity Press.

Sanders, P. (2006) Politics and therapy: Mapping areas for consideration. In G. Proctor, M. Cooper, P. Sanders & B. Malcolm (Eds.), *Politicizing the person-centred approach* (pp. 5–16). PCCS Books.

Sandhu, D., & Tung, S. (2006). Differences in adolescent identity formation. *Pakistan Journal of Psychology Research, 21*(1–2), 29–40.

Schachter, E. P., & Galliher, R. V. (2018). Fifty years since 'identity: Youth and crisis': A renewed look at Erikson's writings on identity. Identity: *An International Journal of Theory and Research, 18*(4), 247–250. https://doi.org/10.1080/15283488.2018.1529267

Smith, H. L. (2017). *Don't let my past be your future*. Constable.

Stets, J. E., & Burke, P. J. (2003). A sociological approach to self and identity. In M.R. Leary & J.P. Tangney (Eds.), *The handbook of self and identity* (pp. 128–152). Guilford.

Sue, D. W., & Sue, D. (2013). *Counseling the culturally different: Theory and practice* (6th ed.). John Wiley.

Syed, M., & Fish, J. (2018). Revisiting Erik Erikson's legacy on culture, race and ethnicity. *Identity: An International Journal of Theory and Research*, *18*(4), 274–283. https://doi. org/10.1080/15283488.2018.1523729

Taylor, S., Charura, D., Williams, G., Shaw, M., Allan, J., Cohen, E., Meth, F., & O'Dwyer, L. (2020). Loss, grief, and growth: An interpretative phenomenological analysis of experiences of trauma in asylum seekers and refugees. *Traumatology*. http://dx.doi. org/10.1037/trm0000250

Turner, D. (2021). *Intersections of privilege and otherness in counselling and psychotherapy: Mockingbird*. Routledge.

Wilkinson, R., & Pickett, K.(2009) *The spirit level: Why more equal societies almost always do better*. London: Penguin.

4
THE INDIVIDUAL IN CONTEXT

Byron Al-Murri and Jasmine Childs-Fegredo

OVERVIEW

As therapists, we remain vigilant to the possibility that experiences of *social injustice* may be a part of the lived experience of what clients bring to therapy. To make sense of this, we view the client not as a mere 'individual', but as an *individual in context* embedded in social and contextual systems which can impact psychological and emotional wellbeing. Having this awareness facilitates an embracing of the complexity likely to be contributing to psychological and emotional distress and could assist in capturing meanings attributable to the client's lived experience. This chapter will aim to present the main theories which underpin the individual in context, encompassing the places and systems which hold meaning for us as socially embedded beings. The first part of the chapter considers Bronfenbrenner's ecological systems theory (1979), with each of the systems being noted in turn, in addition to referencing more contemporary thought of 'context' and the limitations of the theory. The second part of the chapter discusses the concept of 'socially just' psychological therapy. It emphasises the value of reflexivity and phenomenology, and how psychologists can support clients by navigating their ecological systems. This entails going 'beyond therapy', into advocacy outreach, and highlights the need for the psychological professions to embed social justice as part of their integrative practice. Finally, the chapter argues for the importance of seeing trauma through the lens of social injustice and understanding how social systems oppress and stigmatise various identities.

BASIC THEORETICAL PRINCIPLES

Bronfenbrenner proposed his seminal ecological systems theory of child development in 1979. This has undergone multiple revisions to be updated to the Bioecological model (Bronfenbrenner & Ceci, 1994), the Process, Person, Context, Time model

(Bronfenbrenner, 1995), and included an additional system related to the changes and (in)consistencies of time called the Chronosystem (Bronfenbrenner, 1994). Starting firstly from the individual or Nano-level and moving outwards, we have the Micro-, Meso-, Exo-, Macro- and Chronosystems. All these various socio-cultural-political influences affect the individual and, when aligned with intersectionality theory, interact with the person's various identities to create unique 'kaleidoscopic' experiences of oppression and privilege.

Bronfenbrenner (1995) refers to 'proximal processes', which are multifaceted, repeated and enduring bidirectional interactions between an individual (person) and their environment. The proximal processes involve people (relationally significant others), symbols (societal constructs, e.g., childhood, culture, customs, and language) and objects (toys, activities, books, stories), which act as drivers for realising genetic potential, to promote effective psychological functioning for a child (Bronfenbrenner & Ceci, 1994). This psychological functioning relies upon sufficiently meeting bio-psychological developmental outcomes in the following domains for the individual: perception and response, directing and controlling behaviours, managing stress and stressors, knowledge and skill acquisition, forming and sustaining relationships, and changing and preserving an appropriate environment for the individual. However, while genetic expression and 'heritability' are emphasised by Bronfenbrenner and Ceci (1994), these can only be partially realised and actualised, necessitating the consistent reciprocal interactions of the environmental-relational proximal processes which mediate the biological. This has been seen in mental health research, in trying to distinguish the effects of parental genetics and parental environment, and quality and consistency of child–parent relationships (McAdams et al., 2014). For Bronfenbrenner and Ceci (1994), it is this intersection of an individual's biology and their environment (peoples, symbols and objects) that results in child development. Over the lifespan, an individual's schemata will diminish or augment the impact of such external processes on behaviours and subsequent personal development (Bronfenbrenner, 1995).

Bronfenbrenner (1995) refers to four aspects of proximal processes: form, power, content and direction. Each is dependent upon the contextual system's elements, particularly the Microsystem, which, in turn, facilitates consistency and safety within the individual's environments and ultimately realise one's genetic potential. Conversely, if an individual's proximal processes are harmful or deficient, this inversion disrupts and damages one's psychological functioning (Merçon-Vargas et al., 2020). Indeed, multiple scholars have emphasised the consequences of adversity upon development and pathogenesis (Ceccarelli et al., 2022; Thomason & Marusak, 2017). This highlights the need for practitioners to utilise such a model in therapeutic practice to formulate a client's past and present systems. This guides the subsequent actions and the compassionate 'response-abilities' (Levinas, 2002) to systemic oppression and promoting social justice.

Ecological Systems Theory

Firstly, the individual level (Nanosystem) refers to a person's genetic predisposition, from which the various environments (systems) activate or inhibit gene expression

(Bronfenbrenner & Ceci, 1994). Aside from the biological aspects, the Nanosystem also encompasses an individual's cognitive, behavioural and intrapsychic mechanisms, including motivations, desires and drives. This interplay between the brain, body, mind and psyche show that far from being wholly environmentally influenced, the first system level is individually biopsychological. Social justice for our clients within this system may be in facilitating additional physical and mental healthcare access.

Secondly, the Microsystem comprises of primary interpersonal relational others, such as family and friends. This system is important to an individual's early development, with influences and socialisations from caregivers and relatives, and later, friends. This acts as the first instance of identity formation, in being like others: generating the relational model to be used throughout the lifespan, based upon early interactions.

Friendships and relationships are vital resources for clients, which may also be considered within the systems model; both in the past and present. The Microsystem is bidirectional, meaning that the individual (person) influences, and is influenced directly by, the relational others in this system. In relation to therapy, we may need to consider working within this immediate system, to fully incorporate others into a client's assessment, formulation and treatment planning. 'Socially just' practice within this system may be to consider group, couples or family therapy, to consolidate and strengthen this integral relational-cultural system with clients. It may also be appropriate to consider others' additional needs, necessitating Mesosystemic interaction between formal and informal supportive services and entities with the family or relational Microsystem.

The next level is the Mesosystem. This refers to the permeable space that allows the interactions between the Microsystem of households and family, and the more indirect organisational and institutional structures located in the Exosystem. This essentially demarcates the individual and immediate group levels from community and locality influences within the Exosystem. Within this are physical entities such as businesses, councils or local government, or religious, educational and social bodies. Moreover, it is the organisational culture and *modus operandi* of how these entities function and interact with the individual (albeit indirectly), families and groups within communities. On this level, the fundamental rules for living and participating within such a community are housed, with specific, formal or informal rules, laws, practices and philosophies. Social justice within this system may be connecting or signposting clients to structures and organisations, which require clients – rather than us as therapists – to interact with such third-sector charities, financial and debt advice, employment and voluntary opportunities and local council support and initiatives.

For Bronfenbrenner (1994), the Macrosystem refers to the overarching socio-cultural elements of the Micro-, Meso- and Exosystems. Examples of this include: specific wider belief and knowledge systems, material resources, societal customs, laws, histories, ideologies and socio-political-economic structures. The Macrosystem also encompasses regulatory bodies, such as the HCPC and the BPS, who standardise and offer a 'blueprint' for the profession and therapeutic practice. In relation to social justice, the political and economic climate, judicial system, welfare, immigration and national interests are important constituents of the Macrosystem to consider for practitioners. Promoting social justice and challenging systemic inequality within this level is perhaps the most difficult for both clients and therapists, given the magnitude and pervasiveness of the societal problems: sexism, racism, classism, ageism, ableism, nationalism, sexual and gender discrimination. Tackling such issues requires individual introspection, as well as unique pro-action and intersectional conceptualisation for each of the 'isms' (Brown, 2019): how they damage, oppress, stigmatise individuals and malignantly permeate through all system levels. Within our own psychotherapeutic Macrosystem, our attitudes, guidelines and regulatory entities are ascribing to proactive anti-discriminatory practice and social justice.

Bronfenbrenner (1994) argued that 'a chronosystem encompasses change or consistency over time not only in the characteristics of the person but also of the environment in which that person lives' (p. 40). It is within this system that changing geo-political and socio-economic phenomena occur over the lifespan, which impact both positively and negatively upon the corresponding system levels, through to the individual level. Such contemporary phenomena may include: the COVID-19 pandemic, the cost-of-living crisis, war, political instabilities, and wider pressures of globalisation and climate change.

In the UK, we are already seeing the impact of such phenomena at the Nano-level, with brain damage and grey matter loss following COVID-19 (Douaud et al., 2022), which extends to the Microsystem with families and immediate others. Moreover, staying within the British context, UK Government policy and lockdown measures have influenced individuals from the Macrosystem. This has exacerbated pre-existing health inequalities and worsened mental health, through influencing and impacting corresponding internal levels, through to the Nanosystem, as experienced by the individual.

Other global events such as the 'War on Terror', political instability, civil war and the conflict between Russia and Ukraine have also created unique migratory pressures. As such, previous system levels of refugees and asylum seekers interact with those of their host country and population. Research suggests that navigation of the asylum process and policy, coupled with socio-economic and interpersonal issues, negatively impact refugee psychological wellbeing (Li et al., 2016). Therefore, rather than conventional therapeutic intervention, we as practitioners must address harmful policy, challenge stigmatising attitudes, and facilitate helpful client interaction with these new systems, which is discussed later in the chapter.

Critiques and Additions to the Ecological Systems Theory

Naslund et al. (2020) discuss how social media can offer a lifeline to those experiencing mental ill health. Clients can find information on diagnosis and therapeutic and pharmacological intervention, and use informal peer networks to both offer and receive support and to express themselves, their stories and mental health journeys. This may represent another dimension to the systems theory, that of the technological through internet, digital and social media, and telecommunications.

Identities (Nano-level) and relationships are maintained or damaged through social media interactions, which cascades to the Macro- and Chronosystems, intersecting all levels. All systems can be influenced, impacted and maintained through technology. Technology facilitates access to new information, which is integrated into the Nano-individual level, through 'real-time' reflection and awareness of Chronosystemic events via news, social media, and the internet. This supports the existence of the digital (online) and physical (real) dimensions to multiple Microsystems (Navarro & Tudge, 2022) and of a phenomenological variant of an individual's ecological systems (Spencer et al., 1997).

In sum, given the current and future direction of teletherapy and online practice this creative and accessible use of technologies offers a strong rationale for an additional digital system – not fully realised or considered in Bronfenbrenner's original or subsequent theories. Practically, this offers a new platform to both conceptualise and manage digital influences for an individual, and to facilitate and actualise social justice through teletherapy. Such a system has been incorporated into Figure 4.1, and amalgamated with culture, to create the cultural-technological system. This is due to the symbiotic nature of cultural transmission and emission, through digital telecommunication.

A criticism of the Bronfenbrenner is the lack of definition regarding the location of cultural influences (Vélez-Agosto et al., 2017). Bronfenbrenner amended the model in 1994 to accommodate social interactional components of the Microsystem, to include symbols and objects, yet culture was not fully integrated within the systems model. Culture appears to have been placed within the Macrosystem, therefore prioritising top-down national views of culture, at the expense of more bottom-up phenomenological accultured or encultured processes within the Microsystem. This effectively separated the individual from their own and differing cultures.

Contemporary thought places a more symbiotic relationship between cultures, individuals, and groups, such as Berry's (1997) acculturation pathways and societal pathways (2009). Berry (1997) notes four specific pathways for acculturation (acclimating or non-acclimation of a majority or dominant culture). These are assimilation, separation, integration and marginalisation. Assimilation is the complete incorporation, to the detriment, and the cessation of, the original culture. Separation is the denunciation of the new culture and conservation of one's original culture. Integration is the dialectical balance and reconciliation between both the new and original cultures. Finally, marginalisation is the concurrent rejection of both new and original cultures, which may lead to an incoherency of identity.

Berry's acculturative pathways and enculturation (an individual's return to ethnic cultural background) are substantiated by Yoon et al. (2013), who highlight that marginalisation had the worst outcome, followed by separation, with assimilation and integration being more associated with better mental health. This validates the need for culture to

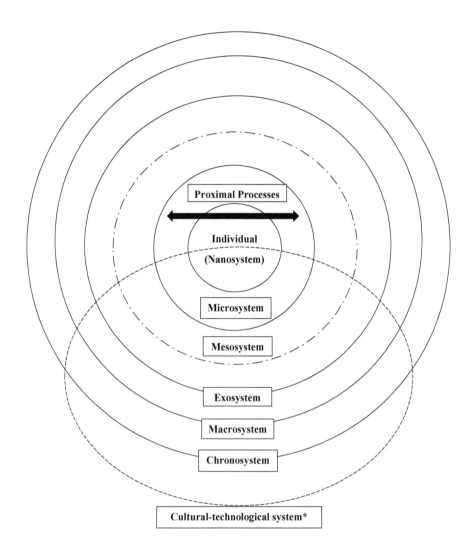

Figure 4.1 Ecological Systems model (adapted from Bronfenbrenner, 1994)

be its own system, rather than be moved to the Microsystem (Vélez-Agosto et al., 2017) or to be viewed from the Macrosystem (Bronfenbrenner, 1994), given its transcendence throughout all systems.

Acculturation and enculturation are not singular individual and group processes, but rather facilitated, or impeded by, social and political structures, which are located within the Macrosystem and Chronosystems. Berry (2009) considered these to correspond with the individual's acculturative pathways, in relating to society's treatment and attitudes towards minority ethnic peoples: multiculturalism (integration), melting pot (assimilation), segregation (separation) and exclusion (marginalisation). While these attitudes are internalised and can become self-stigmatising to the person, society also can directly or indirectly discriminate and oppress, or privilege others. In understanding such conceptualisations with our clients, we can start to begin to challenge systemic inequality and tackle current, historical, and emerging phenomena within the Chronosystem and its artifacts within the Macrosystem.

Finally, Christensen (2016) argues for the inclusion of both resilience and entrepreneurship in Bronfenbrenner's model, to allow for a more holistic conceptualisation of an individual's developmental history and current life trajectory, schemata and skills within their environments. These two elements allow for an individual to engage with their various systems more proactively and functionally, to promote reflection upon their personal development, identity as individuals and their external systems and relationships.

RELEVANCE TO SOCIAL JUSTICE IN THE PSYCHOLOGICAL THERAPIES

Having looked at ecological systems theories, we now turn to what this means in practice in the therapy room and other therapeutic contexts.

At the time of writing, real-life examples of social injustice at the Chronosystem level are prominent across the globe. For example, increasing numbers of migrants are making perilous journeys to flee war-torn countries, such as Ukraine and Afghanistan. Asylum seekers are subject to overloaded spaces and systems in host countries, which struggle to welcome individuals in need of safety, let alone reach the position of acculturation. These difficulties run in parallel with the Black Lives Matter and #MeToo movements, discussions about societal antisemitism, gender-specific discrimination, homelessness and domestic abuse. This list is by no means exhaustive and a mere representation of the wider social landscape. Perhaps therapists today are in positions to assist, where those who seek help from mental health services are likely to have been subject to social injustices. The question becomes, how do therapists make use of theories of the individual in context in their work with clients who present with distress explicitly rooted in social injustice?

We consider a few aspects in relation to this question. Firstly, the process of engaging in reflexivity to enhance the therapist's understanding of their own experiences of social injustice in relation to their clients. Second, to consider the individual in context in relation to Bronfenbrenner's theory in the process of assessing and formulating the client and building a therapeutic relationship. Thirdly, the types of action the therapist can take in relation to aspects of social justice, where therapists who are embedded in the systems of society have a wealth of knowledge which potentially can be of assistance to the client. Finally, we consider the role of social justice within the framework of psychological therapy, with a proposed approach to incorporating the principles of social justice into traditional notions of therapeutic practice.

Reflexivity

The interrelated psychological therapy professions require trainees and therapists to have a certain level of understanding of their own life-worlds and experiences. Some disciplines do this explicitly as part of training programmes which require trainees to experience a certain number of hours of personal therapy. The overarching principle aligns with the notion that therapists can achieve a sense of integrity, connection and authenticity with their clients which may be less accessible without deeper insight into their own experiences. To achieve this, Gelso (2018) posited that in-depth understanding of the therapeutic relationship and notions of transference and countertransference pave the way for rich and authentic therapeutic work. Here it is argued that reflexivity and self-awareness on the part of the therapist is the first step to becoming competent in the area of delivering therapy with an underpinning or focus on social justice. Practitioners are encouraged to be aware of the self and how their own relationship to the various stigmatised identities could contribute to the therapeutic dynamic.

Reflecting on past experiences and coming to therapy with a reflexive stance would appear crucial, with many texts available to both trainees and professionals to decipher this concept. Using personal therapy as trained therapists can develop a continued sense of connection with deeper feelings and experiences which can assist in therapeutic work with clients (Rizq & Target, 2008). In terms of working with disentangling from personal experience of social injustice to avoid enactment, therapists could consider their historical and ongoing relationships to the various stigmatised identities. The stigmatised identities have been listed in the introduction to this book, with editors suggesting that neurodiversity would be a welcome addition. It could also be argued that trauma plays a role here, impacting the individual at the Macrosystem and Exosystem levels, through a lack of social and wellbeing support, which cascades into the Mesosystemic space between Microsystemic relational others down to the Nano-level.

The aim of reflexivity is to become as aware as possible of potential prejudices, judgements and biases, so that therapists can meet clients from a position of clarity and non-judgemental awareness. This in turn can lead to more robust formulations where there is more clarity about the impact of past experience of social justice or injustice, and how that could be impacting the therapeutic dynamic. This stance would achieve a skilled approach to seeing the boundary between therapy and other roles the therapist may want or need to take up on behalf of a client when it comes to working with the principles of social justice.

Assessment, Formulation and Action

The National Institute for Health and Care Excellence recommends practitioners to fully incorporate other people into a client's assessment, formulation and treatment planning. Therapists using various approaches to therapy will likely have different approaches to assessment and formulation. This variety in practice is essential to meet the diverse needs of individuals presenting to therapy. Bronfenbrenner's model provides a helpful framework to assist in formulating clients from the perspective of the individual in context. We further suggest that Clarkson's 5 Aspects model of the therapeutic relationship (2003) could provide a framework for practitioners in terms of how social justice can be viewed and realised in each of the five aspects, in alignment with Bronfenbrenner's systems.

Firstly, the *working alliance* would be attended to whereby the therapist and client undertake contracting in the early phase of the relationship, taking time to consider what it may be like for a client to (re)engage in professional services and how therapy may differ from formal assessment or medicalised or occupational therapeutic intervention. This represents the interaction of small system entities of the Exosystem (therapy) interacting within the Mesosystem that permeates to the individual client-level between the client (individual). Moreover, this process simultaneously occurs for the therapist on a Nano-level in both parties occupying the Microsystemic space.

Secondly, the *transference and countertransference dynamic* would be considered to attend to internalised societal stigma and shame as well as socio-cultural values playing out for both parties. This may be conceptualised in being expressed within the Mesosystemic level (if the transferential processes are more societal or cultural). Additionally, such early life patterns of relating may be an attempt to draw the therapist from the Exosystem into the client's phantastic Microsystem. Additionally, the therapist's countertransference may mirror this process, placing the client into the practitioner's phantastic Microsystem from the boundaried and professional Exosystem.

The third stage is *reparative*, where the therapist would recognise any trauma in the client's history with the aim of breaking this cycle within the various systems. As this is reparative, this interaction may also occur at the client's Nanosystem, in creating new neural pathways, dampening of the fight or flight response and the internalisation of quasi-Microsystemic consistency and therapeutic modelling.

The fourth stage is an emphasis on the *person-to-person interaction*, which would take a humanistic phenomenological approach with sensitive curiosity to prompt a compassionate 'response-ability' (Amari, 2021) from which to work with and challenge such adversity. This may represent a healthy and helpful Exosystemic alignment or re-adjustment, as well as reconnecting to the wider Macrosystem, in cultivating authentic and positive change for clients by links and signposts to supportive services and structures (NHS services, government departments, third sector organisations such as Citizens Advice). The aim is to recognise the limitations of the systems surrounding the individual in context, and that action on the part of the client may be extremely challenging, whilst therapists are in a position to offer support in the form of action on behalf of the client. This also proactively starts to reconnect the individual and their families (Microsystem), with Exosystemic and Macrosystemic supportive entities.

Finally, the *transpersonal element*, which would incorporate the spiritual and the experiential. This is underpinned by being alongside clients, through advocacy, outreach, shared navigation and successful arbitration of the 'systems' and 'structures'. This intangible aspect of the relational model may be conceptualised as the realised form of socially just therapy, in working to not only relieve symptoms but to empower and support clients in the liberation of the challenges posed by systemic inequality.

Approaching therapy from the stance of engaging with principles and action of social justice could give rise to further questions. For one, where does therapy end, and acting on the principles of social justice begin? Secondly, can therapy in fact be *therapy* if the therapist is engaged in active participation in the client's life? In some therapeutic modalities such as person-centred therapy or psychodynamic psychotherapy, therapy arguably ceases to be therapy when therapists take on action-orientated roles outside the therapy room and 'within systems'. In doing so, therapists likely become a resource for help and advice, as well as therapy. However, in contexts where systems can diminish client accessibility to helping services, it could be seen as another injustice to deny clients the right to '*know what the therapist knows*', if this knowledge or action can address the issues which marginalised, displaced and disenfranchised clients bring to the therapy room. This could be especially pertinent in services for the homeless, asylum seekers and refugees, who may be struggling to cope with daily living and engaging in societal systems.

It is suggested that actions which take place outside the therapy room should be undertaken in a way that underscores the importance of maintaining at the fore *therapy as therapy* and taking a boundaried approach to any actions that might need to be taken in the name of social justice. If a helping relationship needs to take a purely social justice and active focus, the therapist could consider if there are other professionals available who would be more suited to help at this stage. If not, then contracting with the client and stating what the relationship comprises would be a key factor in ensuring the boundaries of therapist-activist are not blurred.

Theories of psychological integration are well documented, and studies reveal that a large proportion of psychological therapists practice using an integrative approach (Norcross & Alexander, 2019). The same concept could apply to integrating aspects of social justice into therapy. In this approach, 'therapy' would be seen as the core approach, and elements of working with the ecological systems theory and principles of social justice would be assimilated into this way of working. The definition of social justice in the context of therapy would include being orientated to social justice; undertaking advocacy when required; and seeing therapists as 'change agents' whose role it is to 'promote change at the level of institutions, community or society' (DeBlaere et al., 2019).

CONCLUSION

Bronfenbrenner has made a substantial theoretical contribution to the field of developmental psychology, which can be transposed into current psychotherapeutic practice.

This is through updates to the chronology of the system, offering a dual formulation of the past and present systems for clients, as well as identifying inequalities and oppression through using an intersectional lens. Moreover, acculturation and enculturation processes and digital technologies, that were not present in the original theory, have now been incorporated into the *Cultural-Technological* system. The second part of this chapter considered how practitioners foster and facilitate social justice within and external to their therapeutic work, viewing trauma as systemic oppression and inequalities through the stigmatisation of one's multiple identities.

REFLECTIVE AND CRITICAL THINKING QUESTIONS

1 Which cultural and technological systems and changes have impacted or altered your therapeutic practice?
2 Consider your developmental and current influences within your own ecological systems and evaluate the impact of recent socio-political-economic events on your life.
3 Create a client formulation using Bronfenbrenner's system theory.

RECOMMENDED READING AND RESOURCES

Brown, J. D. (2019). *Anti-oppressive counseling and psychotherapy: Action for personal and social change.* Routledge.
The practical application of social justice in therapy.

DeBlaere, C., Singh, A. A., Wilcox, M. M., Cokley, K., Delgado-Romero, E. A., Scalise, D. A., & Shawahin, L. N. (2019). Social justice in counseling psychology: Then, now, and looking forward. *The Counseling Psychologist, 47*, 938–962.
The trajectory of the principles of social justice in counselling psychology.

Rizq, R., & Target, M. (2008). 'Not a little Mickey Mouse thing': How experienced counselling psychologists describe the significance of personal therapy in clinical practice and training: Some results from an interpretative phenomenological analysis. *Counselling Psychology Quarterly, 21*(1), 29–48.
The role of personal therapy in being reflexive.

REFERENCES

Amari, N. (2021). Social justice in counseling psychology practice: Actualizing the ethics of compassion. *Journal of Humanistic Psychology.* https://doi.org/10.1177/00221678211039968

Berry, J. (1997). Immigration, acculturation, and adaptation. *Applied Psychology, 46*(1), 5–34. https://doi.org/10.1111/j.1464-0597.1997.tb01087.x

Berry, J. (2009). A critique of critical acculturation. *International Journal of Intercultural Relations, 33*(5), 361–371. https://doi.org/10.1016/j.ijintrel.2009.06.003

Bronfenbrenner, U. (1979). *The ecology of human development: Experiments by nature and design.* Harvard University Press.

Bronfenbrenner, U. (1994). Ecological models of human development. *Readings on the Development of Children, 2*(1), 37–43.

Bronfenbrenner, U. (1995). Developmental ecology through space and time: A future perspective. In P. Moen, G. H. Elder Jr., & K. Lüscher (Eds.), *Examining lives in context: Perspectives on the ecology of human development* (pp. 619–647). American Psychological Association.

Bronfenbrenner, U., & Ceci, S. J. (1994). Nature-nurture reconceptualized in developmental perspective: A bioecological model. *Psychological Review, 101*(4), 568–586. https://doi.org/10.1037/0033-295X.101.4.568

Brown, J. D. (2019). *Anti-oppressive counseling and psychotherapy: Action for personal and social change.* Routledge.

Ceccarelli, C., Prina, E., Muneghina, O., Jordans, M., Barker, E., Miller, K., Singh, R., Acarturk, C., Sorsdhal, K., Cuijpers, P., Lund, C., Barbui, C., & Purgato, M. (2022). Adverse childhood experiences and global mental health: Avenues to reduce the burden of child and adolescent mental disorders. *Epidemiology and Psychiatric Sciences, 31*, e75. https://doi.org/10.1017/S2045796022000580

Christensen, J. (2016). A critical reflection of Bronfenbrenner's development ecology model. *Problems of Education in the 21st Century, 69*(1), 22–28. https://doi.org/10.13140/RG.2.1.2959.7681

Clarkson, P. (2003). *The therapeutic relationship.* John Wiley & Sons.

DeBlaere, C., Singh, A. A., Wilcox, M. M., Cokley, K., Delgado-Romero, E. A., Scalise, D. A., & Shawahin, L. N. (2019). Social justice in counseling psychology: Then, now, and looking forward. *The Counseling Psychologist, 47*, 938–962.

Douaud, G., Lee, S., Alfaro-Almagro, F., Arthofer, C., Wang, C., McCarthy, P., ... & Smith, S. M. (2022). SARS-COV-2 is associated with changes in brain structure in UK Biobank. *Nature, 604*(7907), 697–707. https://doi.org/10.1038/s41586-022-04569-5

Gelso, C. (2018). *The therapeutic relationship in psychotherapy practice: An integrative perspective.* Routledge.

Levinas E. (2002). Useless suffering. In R. Bernasconi & D. Wood (Eds.), *The provocation of Levinas: Rethinking the other* (pp. 168–179). Routledge. (Original work published 1982). https://doi.org/10.4324/9780203402047

Li, S. S., Liddell, B. J., & Nickerson, A. (2016). The relationship between post-migration stress and psychological disorders in refugees and asylum seekers. *Current Psychiatry Reports, 18*(9). https://doi.org/10.1007/s11920-016-0723-0

McAdams, T. A., Neiderhiser, J. M., Rijsdijk, F. V., Narusyte, J., Lichtenstein, P., & Eley, T. C. (2014). Accounting for genetic and environmental confounds in associations between parent and child characteristics: A systematic review of children-of-twins studies. *Psychological Bulletin, 140*(4), 1138–1173. https://doi.org/10.1037/a0036416

Merçon-Vargas, E. A., Lima, R. F., Rosa, E. M., & Tudge, J. (2020). Processing proximal processes: What Bronfenbrenner meant, what he didn't mean, and what he should have meant. *Journal of Family Theory & Review*, *12*(3), 321–334. https://doi.org/10.1111/jftr.12373

Naslund, J. A., Bondre, A., Torous, J., & Aschbrenner, K. A. (2020). Social media and mental health: Benefits, risks, and opportunities for research and practice. *Journal of Technology in Behavioral Science*, *5*(3), 245–257. https://doi.org/10.1007/s41347-020-00134-x

Navarro, J. L., & Tudge, J. R. (2022). Technologizing Bronfenbrenner: Neo-ecological theory. *Current Psychology*. https://doi.org/10.1007/s12144-022-02738-3

Norcross, J. C., & Alexander, E. F. (2019). A primer on psychotherapy integration. In J. C. Norcross & M. R. Goldfried (Eds.), *Handbook of psychotherapy integration* (3rd ed., pp. 3–27). Oxford University Press.

Rizq, R., & Target, M. (2008). 'Not a little Mickey Mouse thing': How experienced counselling psychologists describe the significance of personal therapy in clinical practice and training: Some results from an interpretative phenomenological analysis. *Counselling Psychology Quarterly*, *21*(1), 29–48.

Spencer, M. B., Dupree, D., & Hartmann, T. (1997). A phenomenological variant of ecological systems theory (PVEST): A self-organization perspective in context. *Development and Psychopathology*, *9*(4), 817–833. https://doi.org/10.1017/S0954579497001454

Thomason, M. E., & Marusak, H. A. (2017). Toward understanding the impact of trauma on the early developing human brain. *Neuroscience*, *342*, 55–67. https://doi.org/10.1016/j.neuroscience.2016.02.022

Vélez-Agosto, N. M., Soto-Crespo, J. G., Vizcarrondo-Oppenheimer, M., Vega-Molina, S., & García Coll, C. (2017). Bronfenbrenner's bioecological theory revision: Moving culture from the macro into the micro. *Perspectives on Psychological Science*, *12*(5), 900–910. https://doi.org/10.1177/1745691617704397

Yoon, E., Chang, C., Kim, S., Clawson, A., Cleary, S., Hansen, M., ... & Gomes, A. M. (2013). A meta-analysis of acculturation/enculturation and mental health. *Journal of Counseling Psychology*, *60*(1), 15–30. https://doi.org/10.1037/a0030652

5
INTEGRATING THE PSYCHOLOGICAL AND THE SOCIO-POLITICAL: A DIRECTIONAL FRAMEWORK

Mick Cooper

OVERVIEW

To develop a social justice agenda in the psychological therapies, we need models of well-being and distress that take socio-political factors into account. The *directional framework* presented in this chapter is one attempt to integrate psychological and socio-political understandings. The basis for this framework is that human beings are agentic and purposeful, striving to realise their needs and wants. People experience distress when they fail to realise their most important needs and wants, and this can be for socio-political or psychological reasons. Hence, both socio-political or psychological channels can be means for ameliorating distress. There are striking parallels between positive change processes at the psychological level and the socio-political level: developing an understanding of such processes can help to advance psychological, social and global wellbeing and justice.

BASIC THEORETICAL PRINCIPLES

How do we conceptualise human beings? It is clear from the empirical evidence that socio-political factors – such as homophobia, poverty and political oppression – are key sources of psychological misery. But how do we develop psychological understandings – rich, complex and compelling – that have such factors at their very heart?

The Apoliticism of Classic Therapy Models

Today, the dominant models in the psychological therapies are almost exclusively apolitical. This is not to say that they deny the influence of socio-political factors, but the influence of such forces is conceptualised outside of the predominant theories of distress. Take, for instance, Rogers' (1959) classic theory of development. Rogers' approach is an avowedly 'humanistic' model, with an explicit orientation to such liberal concerns as individual freedom, self-worth and growth. Yet, here, the origins of distress are located in the 'conditional positive regard' that parents, carers or other significant individuals hold for an infant, and not in wider socio-political structures. Certainly, in Rogers' classic theory, sexism, homophobia or other forms of prejudice may affect an individual through the expectations placed upon their experiencing (for instance, 'Women should be meek and not feel anger'). But structural, 'real world' factors – such as poverty, racial discrimination or the threat of gender-based violence – do not have an explicit place in Rogers' developmental model. Only in more recent years, in the person-centred field, has work been done on racialised and gendered conditions of worth (e.g., Chantler, 2005; Proctor, 2008). Another example is cognitive-behavioural therapy (CBT). Here, distress is classically conceptualised in terms of 'distorted' thinking, such as making false over-generalisations (for instance, 'If one person at a party does not like me, then everyone hates me') (Beck et al., 1979). Again, this does not deny the role that socio-political factors may have on wellbeing or distress, but there is no specific place for them in the classic models. Even contemporary forms of CBT, such as acceptance and commitment therapy, tend to locate distress around such intrapersonal processes as 'psychological flexibility', rather than conceptualising how socio-political factors can have a profound impact on wellbeing.

Throughout the history of the psychological therapies, however, there have also been attempts to develop models with a socio-political and social justice core (for an excellent review, see Totton, 2000). Adler, for instance, developed an approach oriented around a human need for community and social connectedness, with an appreciation of the 'inferiority complexes' that can emerge when people are not treated as equal human beings. In the latter part of the twentieth century, feminist clinicians developed 'relational-cultural' models of therapy (e.g., Jordan et al., 1991), which recognised the crucial role that gender and cultural factors can have on an individual's development. Most recently, there is the Power Threat Meaning Framework, published by the British Psychological Society's Division of Clinical Psychology (Johnstone et al., 2018). This is a strengths-based alternative to the medical model that locates psychological difficulties in the social adversities, threats and abuses people face, rather than in people's internal 'deficiencies'.

This chapter presents a framework for integrating the psychological with the socio-political that is aligned with such developments but has several distinctive features (Cooper, 2019, 2021, 2023). First, grounded in a 'pluralistic' approach to therapy (Cooper & McLeod, 2011), it strives to be inclusive to *all* models of psychological therapy, including humanistic, psychodynamic, cognitive-behavioural, and existential. Second, in contrast to some of the earlier models of psychological and socio-political integration, it draws extensively from contemporary psychological theory and evidence. Third, going beyond 'surface-level' links between socio-political factors and wellbeing, it aims to tie socio-political thinking to an understanding of people at the deepest existential levels. Fourth, as well as understanding people within their socio-political context, it strives to develop parallels between psychological and socio-political levels of functioning, developing broader, systemic principles of what is 'good'.

The aim of this framework is not to construct a new model, but to create a language and set of concepts through which we can bring together many different pre-existing understandings. In essence, it is striving to 'get underneath' such understandings and to articulate their fundamental principles, so that we can develop more comprehensive, meaningful and effective models of social and psychological analysis and change.

Directionality: An Integrating Theoretical Construct

The starting point for this framework is an understanding of human existence as *directional*: that is, agentic, intentional and purpose-oriented. This is an understanding of human beings derived from existential and humanistic thinking, but shared – in different terminologies and conceptualisations – across the psychological therapies. To see human existence as directional is to challenge the assumption that human beings are passive, sponge-like 'things'; blank screens; or machine-like automatons. Rather, it holds that we are all, always, intentionally reaching out towards our worlds: striving along particular lines of *direction*. These directions can range from long-term, explicitly-set objectives (such as completing a book) to implicit, bodily-desires, motivations and instincts (such as desiring food). But to describe human beings as directional is to say that there are always needs and wants behind what we do.

While directionality is manifest as an individual's needs and wants, these directions do not reside 'within' the person, but between the person and their world. Every desire needs something desired; and these 'directional objects' are as integral to the direction as the 'inner' impulse itself. This *in-the-world*-ness of directionality is essential to emphasise because it sets the basis for understanding distress and wellbeing in socio-political, as well as psychological, terms. Directionality is also in-the-world in the sense that the directions we adopt are often – and, perhaps, always – infused with the meanings, values and directions of those around us. Hence, the directional framework is consistent with both realist understandings of human being and also more socially constructionist ones.

A 'Hierarchy' of Directions

A basic assumption amongst many psychological and psychotherapist theorists (e.g., Powers, 1973) is that directions can be conceptualised as existing in a hierarchical structure. Here, there are a small number of *highest-order* directions (for instance, for relatedness), beneath which are *lower-order* 'sub-directions' (for instance, 'to spend time with my partner', 'to play with my children'). These, then, have further sub-sub-directions (for instance, 'To book a restaurant'); cascading down to the lowest-order needs and wants (for instance, 'to move my fingers to type out the restaurant booking form'). Within such structures, lower-order directions can be considered the *means* by which individuals try to realise their higher-order directions. Conversely, higher-order directions form the *reference value* for lower-order directions. Hence, as we go up the hierarchy, we ask 'why?' something is done. By contrast, when we go down the vertical hierarchy, we ask 'how?' something is done.

Different psychotherapeutic models have posited different needs and wants as being of the ultimate highest order. For instance, the person-centred approach argues that it is actualisation, logotherapists argue that it is meaning (Frankl, 1986). In the psychological field, numerous different models of highest-order directions have also been posited, such as self-determination theory's relatedness, autonomy and competence (Ryan & Deci, 2000). There are few today, however, that would claim that there is one, ultimate, highest-order direction for all. It is recognised, for instance, that highest-order directions are likely to vary across cultures (with Global South cultures, for instance, tending to place greater emphasis on community over individuality, as compared with Global North cultures); and considerable variation may also exist at the individual level. Furthermore, as Berlin (2003) argues, the hallmark of a democratic society is that each person, or each community, has the right to determine its own highest-order directions for itself.

Wellbeing as the Realisation of Highest-Order Directions

From this standpoint, and drawing on the empirical evidence (see Cooper, 2019), we can say that wellbeing is the extent to which an individual can realise those needs and wants that are of the highest order to them. A good life, then, might be one in which we have our physical needs met; feel safe, free and of worth; and experience happiness, relatedness, growth and a sense of meaning. 'Realising' our needs and wants, however, does not just mean achieving them; it also means being oriented towards something (rather than having a sense of purposelessness), progressing towards our realisation of them, feeling confident we can achieve them and then being able to celebrate their achievement.

RELEVANCE TO SOCIAL JUSTICE IN THE PSYCHOLOGICAL PROFESSIONS

The principles outlined here – that human beings are directional, and that wellbeing is the realisation of our highest-order directions – has the potential to serve as the basis for an integrated psychological and socio-political understanding of psychological distress; and the means by which such distress may be ameliorated.

The Origins of Psychological Distress

If wellbeing is the realisation of our highest-order directions, then psychological distress is the failure to realise such needs and wants. Why might this come about? Three basic sources of psychological distress can be proposed: the first socio-political (a lack of external resources) and the second and third more intrapersonal (intrapersonal conflicts and ineffective means towards ends). These sources, however, are fundamentally interlinked: in particular, the more limited the external resources, the more likely individuals may be to experience intrapersonal conflicts, and/or to adopt ineffective means towards their ends.

Lack of External Resources

The most obvious reason for failing to realise our directions – and one that social justice advocates will be acutely aware of – is a lack of external resources. Poverty, insecure housing, back-breaking working conditions: all are examples of socio-economic conditions that limit people's abilities to realise such directions as safety, pleasure or growth (Cooper, 2021). These external limitations may not just be material. Domestic violence, for instance, can be understood as a situation in which a person's interpersonal context violates – rather than sustains – their need for safety; homophobia can be considered a context in which lesbian and gay people must struggle for security, autonomy and self-worth.

Of course, as Marcuse (1966) states, the fundamental fact of scarcity means that the struggle for existence will inevitably take place 'in a world too poor for the satisfaction of human needs without constant restraint, renunciation, delay' (p. 42). Put more prosaically, we cannot always get what we want. But restrictions such as insecure housing or homophobia are what Marcuse (1966) terms 'surplus repression', in that they do not need to be there. Rather, in this instance, there is the possibility of creating a more 'resource-rich' world: one in which all people can have decent homes, or live without the threat of violence.

Intrapersonal Conflicts

Yet limited external resources cannot explain all psychological distress. Why is it, for instance, that two people with seemingly equal levels of resources can experience such different levels of distress? Similarly, why is it that some people with access to every possible resource can still be so miserable, while others that have 'nothing' can experience such satisfaction and fulfilment? As psychological therapists, we know the reality of these 'paradoxes' every day in our therapy rooms: a wholly socially determinist account of mental distress, from a psychological therapy perspective, is just not accurate, compelling or complete.

A concept that can add here to an understanding of the aetiology of distress, pervasive across the psychological therapies (albeit, often, implicitly), is that of *intrapersonal conflicts*. This conflict is seen as taking different forms. In the Freudian school, this conflict is between 'id' and 'superego'; for person-centred, between self-concept and actual experiencing; for CBT, between short-term heuristics and longer-term rational thought. A conflict that, as psychological therapists, we frequently witness is between a person's desire to be close to others (a direction towards relatedness), and a fear that they will be damaged or hurt if they do so (a direction towards safety). In such examples, opposing needs and wants are present at the same time, but conflicts can also be between 'parts' or 'voices' that take over at different times. For example, a client may become consumed with a desire for revenge ('No-one should be able to treat me like that'), and only later shift into the opposing position ('I'm terrified people hate me for being angry'). When a person becomes 'taken over' by a particular direction, to the exclusion of all other needs and wants, we can describe that direction as going *rogue* (Cooper, 2019).

As at the interface between person and society, we can never realise all of our needs and wants all of the time: some degree of 'restraint', 'renunciation' and 'delay' is inevitable. Indeed, existential therapists have emphasised the need to accept such conflicts as part of living, rather than striving to attain a conflict-free and entirely harmonious life. But, again, the problem is where there is 'surplus conflict': more discord between a person's needs and wants than there needs to be. A client, for instance, might be pulled between wanting to present a confident front to the world, and desperately yearning for love, care and affection from others. In a relatively 'functional' configuration, the person may be able to recognise both needs, and move fluently between them. Less functionally – and as an example of surplus conflict – the person's 'confident' side may despise and berate their vulnerability: 'I hate you inside of me and I hate what you reveal to other people. I just want to destroy you'.

Here the role of a therapist – of any orientation – is to help the person move towards less conflictual, and more cooperative, solutions. We help clients, within their given circumstances, to bring such conflicts to the fore, and then look at ways in which more of their highest-order needs and wants can be met more of the time. This might be through, for instance, 'two-chair work', in which the person's confident side can listen to their vulnerable side and find mutually compatible solutions. Alternatively, a therapist might use such strategies as interpretation, to help the client understand what they are unconsciously striving for, such that they can find more constructive ways of progressing towards it.

Such cooperative solutions can also be termed *synergetic*. Here, in abstract terms, $1 + 1 > 2$. That is, two sets of needs and wants can come together and make something 'more than' than either direction alone. They support each other, pull in similar directions. The opposite to this – another term for unproductive conflicts – is *dysergies*, where $1 + 1 < 2$. Here, where you get one need or want met, you undermine the achievement of others. 'Synergies' and 'dysergies' are useful concepts when we begin to consider the maximisation of wellbeing across different *levels of organisation* (see below), because they indicate how we can get more (or less) benefit within the same set of resources.

Ineffective Means

Across the psychotherapeutic fields, there is also an understanding that sometimes people fail to realise their higher-order needs and wants because the lower-order means that they adopt to try and get there are just not very effective. Take the example of a person who is trying to get rid of panic attacks. As they start to feel anxiety, the person grits their teeth and tries to compel themselves not to feel anxiety. Such a response is totally understandable – I know it myself very well when I used to get panic attacks – but the problem is that it generally has the opposite effect: we become more afraid that we will panic, and so our symptoms (like feeling nauseous) worsen, leading to an ever-tightening vicious spiral. In fact, as behavioural therapy teaches us, when people are starting to panic, they are generally better off saying to themselves things like, 'If I have a panic attack, then that's OK, I will survive', which can then defuse the cycle. But this is not something we are born knowing, and it is not something that is absent because of our socio-economic context.

In some instances, ineffective strategies may have arisen because we have learnt ways of doing things in the past that are no longer 'fit for purpose' in the present. This is, de facto, the basis for many counselling and psychotherapy practices: helping clients trace back dysfunctional thoughts, feelings and actions to their childhoods; and finding ways of being that are more 'fitted to' their current circumstances.

Ameliorating Distress

So how can we help people who are distressed? The three factors described above point to an understanding that fluently integrates psychological and socio-political strategies. If people are experiencing distress because their external circumstances do not allow them to realise their needs and wants, then there is a need to change those external circumstances – through, for instance, advocacy – so that the person can have more of what they need and want more of the time. But if people are experiencing distress because their directions are configured in dysergetic ways, then therapeutic strategies may be needed to help the person find more cooperative and synergetic modes of intrapersonal cooperation. And, if the problem is that the person is striving through ineffective means, then psychoeducation or other forms of self-reflection may be most helpful in supporting change. Different ameliorating strategies, then, suit different types of problems, but there is no conceptual break between them. Rather, they are all means of helping people realise what they need and want more of the time: sometimes with a focus on the external correlates of this direction, sometimes with more of a focus on the internal correlates.

Mapping across Psychological and Socio-Political Levels of Organisation

Directionality and Wellbeing at Higher Levels of Organisation

There is a second way in which this framework allows us to integrate the psychological and socio-political: by creating a model of intrapsychic processes – of multiple, interacting directions or 'agencies' – that can be closely aligned to ways of understanding processes on the interpersonal plane.

Koestler's (1967) concept of a *holarchy* is useful here. Koestler envisioned different *levels of organisation* (such as the self, the community or the nation), with the 'organising unit' at each level sitting within an open-ended hierarchical structure (see, for instance, Figure 5.1). Here, higher-level organising units are made up of lower-level units. So, for instance, the individual is made up of intrapersonal directions, the family is made up of individuals, and the community is made up of families. But because the higher-level units are formed through the relationships between the lower-level units, they are never simply reducible to them. This means, then, that at each level of organisation, the units can be considered functioning whole – self-regulating and semi-autonomous – with none more 'real' or significant than the others.

Such a model opens up the possibility that we can articulate concepts and processes that are common across different levels of organisation: that is, we can understand such phenomena 'systemically', in terms of abstract, structural principles. And, indeed, the core principles discussed so far in this chapter can all be seen as transposable to levels of organisation beyond the individual. Directionality, for instance, can be considered a quality of organisational units across multiple levels: whether an organisation's

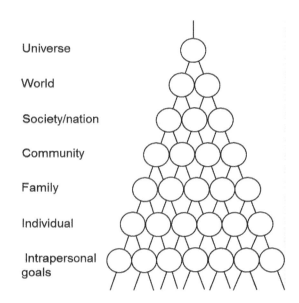

Figure 5.1   An illustrative holarchy

'mission', or the needs and interests of different social classes. And, as at the individual level, the 'wellbeing' of each unit of organisation can be conceptualised in terms of the maximal realisation of its needs and wants. A family or community, for instance, succeeds to the extent that it achieves its goals for safety, prosperity or creativity. The success of any one organising unit, however, only serves the common good to the extent that it contributes to the maximal realisation of directions at higher levels of organisation. This, then, brings us back to the issue of synergetic and dysergetic modes of relating; and whether the realisation of one unit of organisation's directions is supportive, or undermining, of the realisation of another's. Racism, for instance, can be understood as one form of inter-community dysergy. Here, one group may actualise its desires (for instance, for self-worth) but at the expense of many other communities' needs and wants (for instance, for self-worth, safety and freedom). Capitalism, of course, is another form of dysergy, this time between classes. Indeed, capitalism can be understood as a rogue goal at the inter-class level, in which one group's social interests take over to the exclusion of all others. And, of course, war – the social ill that causes an abundance of misery, terror and loss – can be considered the most macro form of dysergetic relating.

Common Principles of Positive Change across Levels of Organisation

So how can we create more synergetic, and less dysergetic, modes of relating? What is striking here is that, while different theorists, practitioners and activists have focused on answering this question at very different levels of organisation (with psychological therapists, for instance, focusing on the intrapersonal; mediators on the interpersonal; and ecological activists on the global), the synergistic strategies that are described are actually very similar (Cooper, 2023). And, indeed, these also closely align with principles emerging from *game theory*: 'the study of strategic interdependence – that is, situations where my actions affect both my welfare and your welfare and vice versa' (Spaniel, 2015, p. 1).

Drawing this theory, research and practice together, I have suggested eight cross-level principles for developing synergies (Cooper, 2023). First, here, is *seeing the bigger picture*, whether this is mentalisation at the individual level or recognising the needs and wants of other countries in international negotiations. We cannot act synergistically if we cannot 'move up a level' and see the greater whole. Second is *taking responsibility*: at any level of organisation, entities need to proactively initiate the development of synergistic processes. It is not enough to wait for something to happen, or for someone else to forge them. Third there is a *willingness to trust*: at the individual level, for instance, to listen to the different internal 'voices'; at the dyadic level (for instance, in couple's counselling), to move beyond blame and contempt. Closely related to this is *being nice*: starting from a position of friendliness, openness and warmth; catalysing a virtuous cycle of cooperation and good will, whether towards internal or external others. Fifth, and again closely related, is *prizing difference and diversity*: valuing the other whether marginalised internal voices; marginalised communities; or, at an ecological level, marginalised non-human organisms. Sixth is *being assertive*: having the capacity to calmly, non-aggressively and non-manipulatively state our own needs and wants, and to hold them as of equal value to others. Being nice means starting from a position of good will, but it does not mean being gullible or naïve. Synergies require an openness to all, and if some agencies are acting to shut down or minoritise others (whether as oppressive inner voices, classes or nations), then they need to be resisted. Seventh, and critically, synergies require *effective communication* between different entities, to understand the other's needs and wants, and to creatively generate synergetic ways forward. In two-chair work for instance, as above, a person's voices talk to each other; couples therapy invites both parties into a communicative space; international negotiation requires countries to articulate their needs, listen to the needs of others and find mutually compatible solutions. Finally, at whatever level of organisation, synergies require *fairness*: equal access to resources, power and the capacity to realise one's highest-order directions. As *The Spirit Level* shows, everyone is worse off when things are unequal, because the disadvantaged feel mistreated; and the advantaged feel threat, stress and vulnerability (Wilkinson & Pickett, 2010). Democracy, though complex and hard won, is a general systemic principle for what maximises benefit overall. When voices are excluded from power, they, as well as others, almost always lose out.

CONCLUSION

In this chapter, I have mapped out a conceptual framework that can bring psychological and socio-political understandings into an integrated whole. This is in two main ways. First, it provides a means of understanding distress, and its amelioration, that can move fluently between psychological and socio-political accounts. This supports psychological therapists in bringing together intrapsychic work with more advocacy and social justice practices. Inviting clients to reflect on the childhood roots of their difficulties, for instance, or advocating for them to tackle discrimination in their workplace, are no longer conceptually distinctive practices. Rather, they are part of an integrated psychosocial therapeutic whole, focused on helping clients realise more of their directions, more of the time. Second, this framework provides a means of exploring, across different levels of organisation, common processes and principles of change. Developing such a systemic view is helpful because it means that psychological therapists can learn from, and contribute to, other understandings of positive, synergetic developments. For instance, how might principles of democracy, developed in the socio-political arena, be applied to an understanding of clients' inner worlds? What might this mean for therapeutic practices? And conversely, how might such intrapsychic phenomena as insight or self-care be applied at the inter-community or international levels?

The directional framework described in this chapter also shows how principles of social justice are 'best', overall. Not just for ethical reasons, but because fairness and a prizing of difference and diversity are key principles in maximising benefit for a system as a whole. Closely related to this, the framework shows how cooperative, synergetic functioning is a fundamental component of wellbeing. Whether at the intrapsychic, interpersonal, inter-community or international level, we all do better when we work together, rather than against each other. Finding pathways towards more synergetic solutions, at whatever level of organisation, is an essential concern for today – and one that psychological therapists, like other progressive forces, have much to contribute.

REFLECTIVE AND CRITICAL THINKING QUESTIONS

1   What is your own, personal model of human being? To what extent, and in what ways, do socio-political factors feature in it?
2   What parallels do you believe exist, if any, between processes at the intrapersonal level (that we work with in therapy), and processes at the interpersonal? Do you agree that there are common processes of positive change?
3   Where are synergies in your own life: both within you, and between you and others? And where are dysergies?
4   What might a 'socially just' inner world look like? Would you say that that is how your being is configured, or those of your clients?

RECOMMENDED READING AND RESOURCES

Cooper, M. (2019). *Integrating counselling and psychotherapy: Directionality, synergy, and social change*. Sage.
An extensive account of directionality and how it can serve as an integrating basis for therapeutic practice. The implications of this for a progressive politics is further developed in Cooper, M. (2023). *Psychology at the heart of social change: Developing a progressive vision for society*. Bristol University.

Powers, W. T. (1973). *Behaviour: The control of perception*. Aldine.
Classic, albeit highly technical, account of a hierarchy of needs and wants.

Psychotherapy and counselling's contribution to global peace, justice, and wellbeing: What difference can we make? [Online Conference] (2022, March 26, Online Events and University of Roehampton). Access recordings at: www.courses-onlinevents. co.uk/courses/UKRAINE-FUNDRAISER-Emergency-Summit-Contributing-to-Global-Peace-and-Justice
A treasure trove of talks on the relationship between social and psychological change, including my own: 'Common principles of positive change: Bridging the intrapersonal and socio-political divide'.

REFERENCES

Beck, A. T., Rush, A. J., Shaw, B. F., & Emery, G. (1979). *Cognitive therapy of depression.* Guilford.

Berlin, I. (2003). The pursuit of the ideal. In H. Hardy (Ed.), *The crooked timber of humanity: Chapters in the history of ideas* (pp. 1–19). Random House.

Chantler, K. (2005). From disconnection to connection: 'Race', gender and the politics of therapy. *British Journal of Guidance & Counselling, 33*(2), 239–256. https://doi.org/10.1080/03069880500132813

Cooper, M. (2019). *Integrating counselling and psychotherapy: Directionality, synergy, and social change.* Sage.

Cooper, M. (2021). Directionality: Unifying psychological and social understandings of wellbeing and distress through an existential ontology. *The Journal of Humanistic Counseling, 60,* 6–25. https://doi.org/10.1002/johc.12148

Cooper, M. (2023). *Psychology at the heart of social change: Developing a progressive vision for society.* Policy.

Cooper, M., & McLeod, J. (2011). *Pluralistic counselling and psychotherapy.* Sage.

Frankl, V. E. (1986). *The doctor and the soul: From psychotherapy to logotherapy* (R. Winston & C. Winston, Trans.; 3rd ed.). Vintage Books.

Johnstone, L., Boyle, M., Cromby, J., Dillon, J., Harper, D., Kinderman, P., Longden, E., Pilgrim, D., & Read, J. (2018). *The power threat meaning framework.* British Psychological Society.

Jordan, J. V., Kaplan, A. G., Miller, J. B., Stiver, I. P., & Surrey, J. L. (Eds.). (1991). *Women's growth in connection: Writings from the Stone Centre.* The Guilford Press.

Koestler, A. (1967). *The ghost in the machine.* Pan.

Marcuse, H. (1966). *Eros and civilization.* Sphere.

Powers, W. T. (1973). *Behaviour: The control of perception.* Aldine.

Proctor, G. (2008). Gender dynamics in person-centered therapy: Does gender matter? *Person-Centered & Experiential Psychotherapies, 7,* 82–94. https://doi.org/10.1080/14779757.2008.9688455

Rogers, C. R. (1959). A theory of therapy, personality and interpersonal relationships as developed in the client-centered framework. In S. Koch (Ed.), *Psychology: A study of science* (Vol. 3, pp. 184–256). McGraw-Hill.

Ryan, R. M., & Deci, E. L. (2000). Self-determination theory and the facilitation of intrinsic motivation, social development and well-being. *American Psychologist, 55*(1), 68–78. https://doi.org/10.1037/0003-066X.55.1.68

Spaniel, W. (2015). *Game theory 101: The complete textbook.* William Spaniel.

Totton, N. (2000). *Psychotherapy and politics.* Sage.

Wilkinson, R., & Pickett, K. (2010). *The spirit level: Why equality is better for everyone.* Penguin.

PART 2

SOCIAL JUSTICE INFORMED THERAPEUTIC PRACTICE

6
CORE PRINCIPLES FOR SOCIAL JUSTICE INFORMED THERAPEUTIC WORK

Laura Anne Winter and Divine Charura

OVERVIEW

Social justice informed practice is about how we translate the ideas, values and theoretical perspectives introduced earlier in this book into therapeutic work across psychological therapies. In this chapter we introduce social justice informed therapeutic work and provide some core principles alongside their application to practice. This is not about providing a recipe or template for social justice informed practice but offers something that psychological practitioners can integrate into their own practice. It is important to note from the outset of this section of the book that social justice informed practice is not reducible to 'work with minoritised clients', nor is it only relevant if you as a therapist identify as being from a minoritised group or identity. Instead, this is relevant to *all* psychological practitioners and clients, thus improving the discipline for everyone.

CONTEXT

As we discussed in Chapter 1, 'social justice' has a long history in the fields of psychology, psychotherapy and counselling, though it may not always have been referred to by that label. Critical and community psychologists and others have written about the problems with the traditional applied understandings of psychological distress and associated practice (e.g., Smail, 2001, 2015). Furthermore, authors from within counselling and psychotherapy have written about difficulties reconciling mainstream therapeutic approaches with values such as social justice and equality (e.g., Proctor, 2017).

What we aim to do in this chapter therefore is not startlingly new (like much academic writing!). We do not claim to be the first authors to try to set out what social justice might look like in practice (indeed we are indebted to many authors before us, including but not limited to those referenced in our chapters and this book). Instead, we synthesise some of what has come before us, combine this with some of our own experiences and ideas, and create practice-oriented principles applicable to social justice therapeutic work. We aim for these to be as clear as we can, to avoid the trap of keeping 'social justice' at the level of a well-meaning but obtuse buzzword in psychological therapy (Winter, 2019).

SOCIAL JUSTICE IN THE THERAPY ROOM

Social justice is not just an issue for those of us who experience minoritisation and marginalisation. Apart from important ethical and professional reasons to engage with social justice in the psychological professions (Winter, 2023), research also tells us that a more equal and just society benefits not only those who are oppressed or discriminated against, but the whole of society including those occupying positions of power or holding greater privilege (Wilkinson & Pickett, 2009, 2019).

In therapeutic work the impact of injustice and inequality is also plain to see. Many researchers have documented clients' experiences of microaggressions and discrimination in counselling and psychotherapy spaces. For example, Shelton and Delgado-Romero's (2013) study highlighted lesbian, gay, bisexual and queer (LGBQ) psychotherapy clients' experiences of sexual orientation microaggressions. This included experience with therapists: assuming all problems are caused by their sexual orientation; avoiding and minimising their sexual orientation; making stereotypical assumptions based on their sexual orientation; or warning about the dangers of identifying as LGBQ. Along a similar vein, Constantine (2007) found that African American clients experience numerous racial microaggressions when working with white therapists, including therapist colour-blindness (denying or ignoring the impact of skin colour on individuals' experiences); denial of personal or individual racism; minimisation of racial or cultural issues; and being accused as a client of being over-sensitive to issues of race and culture. Clients identifying as religious have also described various religious microaggressions such as therapists avoiding discussion of religion; making stereotypical comments about clients based on religion; suggesting or providing interventions which were unhelpful or at odds with religious beliefs; or incorporating their own rather than their clients' religious beliefs into therapy (Trusty et al., 2021). These three studies are only the tip of the iceberg, but what they do illustrate is that psychological practice can be harmful and can reinforce injustices we see outside of the therapy room. Within this chapter we hope to illustrate some of the principles and ways of applying these that can actively challenge such harm and instead work towards increasing social justice.

Our Positioning

Given the centrality of reflexivity and self-awareness to the process and practice of social justice informed work (discussed below), we wanted to include at the beginning of this chapter a note about our own positioning and relationship with the *practice* of social justice, following on from our reflexive contribution in Chapter 1. Firstly, I (Laura) am reminded of the quote from Layla Saad when I think about the process of engaging with this rewarding but challenging part of our work:

> ...I want to remind you that we are not looking for the happy ending, the teachable moment, or the pretty bow at the end of all the learning. We are also not looking for dramatic admissions of guilt or becoming so frozen with shame that you cannot move forward. The aim of this work is not self-loathing. The aim of this work is truth – seeing it, owning it, and figuring out what to do with it. This is lifelong work. Avoid the shortcuts, and be wary of the easy answers. (Saad, 2020, p. 74)

I entered this area of work initially through my research, and I did so from a position of what I would reflect on now as being 'naïve good intention'. As noted in the introduction, I benefit from significant socially structured advantages. Like others, this does not mean that I do not have my own experiences of discrimination or oppression. If I look at my connection to social justice *practice*, I have experienced a steep learning curve building from my initial 'naïve good intention', and I regularly ask myself whether others look at me and think 'what a hypocrite'. I am aware that my volunteering, clinical practice and activism has probably had a relatively minimal impact. More importantly I am acutely aware of the many times in which I have got things wrong, and I continue to get things wrong. But as Saad notes above, this is lifelong learning, and I endeavour to learn and to continue to do better. For me, one important thing to note at the outset of this chapter is that social justice work can sometimes feel incredibly daunting. We can feel scared, afraid of getting things wrong, saying or doing the wrong thing or not knowing where to begin. For me, the act of trying is an important part of the process. Reflecting on when things do go wrong is important. Being paralysed by fear of not knowing the right words, offending or getting things wrong will not change anything. Nevertheless, trying to improve things can make a difference, however minimal each of us believes our contributions to be.

Given my life experiences as a black person I (Divine) have been interested in social justice from a fairly young age. As a young man training in psychotherapy, and later as a psychologist and supervisor, I witnessed, heard and read narratives of students from diverse ethnic communities engaged in training in different institutions, who spoke about experiences of racism, discrimination and other '...*isms*'. They also spoke of limitations of the theoretical orientations which were mostly Eurocentric, and written from a patriarchal perspective, and then had to be applied to all communities. Similarly, I have been engaged in activities of activism, including numerous campaigns to promote social justice for marginalised groups, i.e., refugees and asylum seekers' lived experiences of discrimination. These social justice activities are important. However, it is also important that I highlight and engage with intersectionality. Namely I state here my own to start with and note that I also recognise and benefit from significant socially structured advantages, as a man, as an academic (a professor within a university in the UK), middle class and heterosexual, able-bodied and 'neurotypical'. I believe engaging with our own intersectionality illuminates the complexities and tensions or dynamics of oppression/being othered/dislocation and connection/belonging/privilege. Given my own lived experiences I am interested in how society is structured, and how as individuals and as psychological professions we challenge all forms of discrimination and achieve equal opportunities.

CORE PRINCIPLES

In this part of the chapter, we aim to set out what we have come to view as the three core principles of social justice informed therapeutic work, which provide important scaffolding for any enactment of social justice informed therapeutic practice. These are (1) relational, socially just ethical practice, (2) transformative practice and (3) politically informed practice. Here we introduce each of these principles before looking at them in practice below:

1. Relational, socially just ethical practice

First and foremost, social justice practice in psychological therapy should be underpinned by ethical practice (common to all good psychological work), and specifically by a relational, social justice informed ethical practice. Gabriel and Casemore (2009) present multiple examples of relational ethics in practice in counselling and psychotherapy. Finlay (2019) describes 'relational ethics' as seeing ethics and ethical practice in terms of relationships, rather than solely ethical codes or guidelines (directives). She states that 'relational ethics drive us towards collaborative, responsive, respectful, compassionate and authentic relationships as opposed to exploitative, instrumental or habitual ones' (p. 4). Collaboration, responsiveness, respect, compassion and authenticity are all core aspects to social justice. Social justice informed practice surely must then be grounded in this relational understanding of ethical practice.

Beyond this, it is important to note that the histories, identities and socio-political contexts of both therapist and client, and the relational space between these for both parties, all inform ethical decision making in practice, and ethical codes, though useful guidance, are not enough on their own. Thus, we suggest that relational ethics should also be grounded in an understanding of social justice as described throughout this text. Simply put: *the relational is grounded in, and inseparable from, social justice.* Finlay (2019) notes that underneath relational ethics are our values: social justice values shape and inform our relational ethical decision making. As with all good ethical practice, this should be considered, reflexive and explicitly articulated.

2. Transformative practice

Building on this relational ethical stance, social justice informed practice is also grounded in transformative practice principles. Prilleltensky (2008) notes that 'transformational validity derives from the potential of our actions to promote personal, relational, and collective wellness by reducing power inequalities and increasing political action' (p. 130). Our social justice informed practice should therefore be underpinned by an understanding of our work as having the potential to change the unjust status quo, to promote not only individual but social, political and collective wellness. Social justice has regularly been defined as both a process as well as a goal (Cutts, 2013), and our understanding of transformative practice is consistent with that. Transformative practice can be contrasted with ameliorative practice (Nelson & Prilleltensky, 2010) because it aims to go *beyond* solely reducing distress.

3. Politically informed practice

Critics of social justice suggest that it is an unnecessary and unethical intrusion of political attitudes and beliefs into psychological practice (see for example https://criticaltherapy-antidote.org). We would argue that yes, social justice is political (Schmid, 2012; Totton, 2006), and politically informed practice is an important core principle underpinning our social justice therapeutic work. However, social justice practice in the psychological professions is *not* about forcing one's beliefs on electoral politics onto those that we work with.

The well-known and often-cited feminist activist phrase 'the personal is political' cannot go without a mention. This phrase exemplifies the broad reach and understanding of politics, and the intertwined nature of things that can be sometimes erroneously classified as *either* personal *or* political. Instead, as Hanisch (1970, 2006) writes, 'the personal is political' demonstrates that personal problems *are* political ones, and for psychological practitioners this means acknowledging that the work we do occurs in a social environment structured by both electoral politics and everyday political structuring of power and relationships. It also means acknowledging that the work we do can have (and often does have) political implications (Winter, 2019). These are perhaps not implications for electoral politics, or things that for example happen at Westminster in the UK. But it might be about implications for the everyday political relationships in our communities for example.

There are a whole range of ways in which we can think about therapy as being political (in relation to everyday politics) and Political (in relation to electoral politics). For example, it might be that your client (or you as the therapist) are particularly impacted by an issue which is not in itself about who you vote for but is structured by political systems: such as the climate and ecological crises. Or it could be about the impact that explicit Political decision making has on you or your client: for example, the influence of asylum and refugee policy on how you live. Or it could be about everyday circumstances which are political, such as a client who comes to you experiencing depression, and as part of your assessment you find that they are very socially isolated, living in damp and cold social housing provision.

We should therefore not create an artificial divide between politics and therapy. Politics cannot be completely off our radar in our therapeutic work, and we cannot remain neutral if therapy is political. Remembering that the broader social and political climate affects all of us and will structure and interact with the things you are talking about in therapy (not only those negatively impacted by it – all of us). This does not mean that therapists should reduce all problems to *solely* those that can be looked at politically, and it does not mean that therapists should tell their clients who to vote for, but it does mean we need to reject the idea of keeping politics out of the therapy room, because therapeutic work is always to some degree political. We need to be open to engaging with that, rather than adopting a position which says that is not our business.

PRINCIPLES IN PRACTICE

Now we move on to outline how the core principles described above might manifest in our social justice informed therapeutic work. This is not about manualising or providing a blueprint for our therapeutic conversations, instead it is a way of considering the principles above in an applied sense. In presenting these for psychological therapists, we hope to encourage practitioners to stay true to the creative and relational processes which underpin any good therapeutic encounter.

Collaboration

Much has been written in recent years about the importance of collaboration, and topics like shared decision-making have gained some ground in the therapeutic literature, after developing a strong base in medical and other areas (Gibson et al., 2020). Winter (2019) writes about the idea of 'collaboration as a matter of principle', which connects with the principle of a relational ethics discussed above. What is suggested here is that the primary reason for collaborating with your clients, on all (or as close to all as practical) elements of therapeutic decision making, should be because we are treating our clients as moral equals, and relate to them as such (Fitzgibbon & Winter, 2021). Others have written about the importance of shared decision making as an 'ethical imperative' (Cooper et al., 2006). For us, this ethical imperative is rooted in an important part of social justice: egalitarianism, and relational equality (Proctor, 2019; Winter, 2018). If we truly want to communicate to our clients that we view them as equals then collaboration around the goals of therapy we can address together, and how we might work, seems to be an important application of the principles of social justice informed practice.

What might this look like? Cooper et al. (2006, pp. 47–51) outline nine principles for metatherapeutic conversation, which is the process of talking with clients about therapy: what they want and how they want to approach the therapy itself. These can be easily considered as supporting social justice informed practice:

- Address metatherapeutic issues from the start of therapy.
- Actively invite clients to share their views.
- See metatherapeutic communication as an ongoing process rather than as a one-off event.
- Uncertainty is a good predictor of when metatherapeutic communication may be helpful.
- Be part of the dialogue.
- Describe what the options might be.
- Use measures.
- Tailor levels of metatherapeutic communication to the particular client.
- Adopt a whole service approach.

We also must recognise, however, from a social justice perspective, that collaboration and metatherapeutic communication will undoubtedly be influenced by the broader context of the therapeutic relationship: by power, identities and histories. It is therefore vital that when we talk about collaboration, we remember our social justice principles and consider the way in which these might manifest. We go on to consider this further in the following sections.

Broaching and Epistemic Justice

Authors have written about the importance of a social justice approach which relays cultural competence, humility, an awareness of intersectionality, reflexivity and anti-oppressive practice (Lee, 2019; Lee et al., 2022; Oulanova et al., 2022). Engaging with minoritised and racialised clients through *broaching* is recommended by such authors. In this we understand broaching as an intentional task and approach for understanding of the lived experience and systemic oppression in the client's life-in-context (Lee et al., 2022). A therapist who does not avoid 'broaching' refers to and raises difficult client experiences of oppression, discrimination, disempowerment experiences in therapy and society (Lee et al., 2022). Thus, they *deliberately engage in explicit discussions in therapy as well as supervision on this*, demonstrating their understanding, openness and willingness to learn with the client. We would argue that this is not just about racialised or minoritised clients, but all clients we work with. But how can injustice occur in the therapeutic context, when therapists are so deeply committed to antidiscriminatory practice? Lee et al. (2022) argued that this can occur through what they termed epistemic and social justice:

> Epistemic and social injustice occurs when therapists implicitly and explicitly impose personal, professional, and institutional power onto clients, and dismiss client experience which is embedded in cultural identity and social location. (Lee et al., 2022, p. 322)

It is important for the concept of social justice not to be arbitrarily related to the practices of counselling and psychotherapy. We concur with Lee et al. (2022) whose previous quote speaks to the considerations that therapists should make in their work. They argue that epistemic injustice has two types or forms – namely testimonial and hermeneutic injustice. What they term *testimonial injustice* is when clients' experience of marginalisation is decentred or discredited. The second form of epistemic injustice relates to not providing clients with opportunities to share their experiences in therapy of marginalisation, and where there is little shared understanding in the cross-cultural therapeutic process. This form of injustice they termed *hermeneutic injustice* (Lee et al., 2022).

Therapists therefore need to have an awareness of visible versus invisible diversity and how inadvertently injustice can be caused, particularly when dealing with invisible diversity. Visible diversity relates to for example age, sex, some disabilities, ethnicity etc., whilst invisible aspects of diversity relate to some disabilities, religion, sexual orientation, socio-economic background, marital/relationship status and so on (though even the visible/invisible divide can become blurred and should not be viewed as a strict binary). When an individual is in the majority the paradox is that they are in some ways invisible. However, at the same time it is also possible to feel visible because of one's differences when in the majority. The opposite is also true, that those in the minority can feel visible and hence do not have the privilege of at times hiding their visibility, and the pain that comes with this can include being oppressed or discriminated against because of one's visibility. *All of* your own facets of identity - privileged or otherwise, will influence your interactions as a therapist or as a client, for example your whiteness, class, religion, ethnicity, gender, etc. So how can practitioners ensure that they do not inadvertently cause testimonial or hermeneutic injustice? Therapists should remain open, curious and seek to understand what emerges in the therapeutic process, from the client's frame of reference. Furthermore, therapists should ensure that they demonstrate their openness and curiosity by asking questions like 'what have been your experiences of marginalisation and being othered'? or 'I don't know much about X, but I would love to hear more…'. Lastly, engaging in supervision which specifically explores one's own responses to a client's/one's own experiences in society and how they are mirrored or avoided in the therapy room is important.

Relationality

We spoke above about the importance of relationality in terms of our ethics, but relationality is broader than this, and is an important way in which social justice principles might manifest in action. The therapeutic relationship is viewed as important by all theories of and approaches to psychological practice but is conceptualised differently in different approaches. Some approaches for example view the therapeutic relationship as the vehicle for change (e.g., person-centred therapy (PCT), Rogers, 1951). Others view it as most certainly necessary, but not sufficient, and instead we need therapeutic techniques and skills in the context of a strong relationship, such as in cognitive-behavioural therapy (CBT; Leahy, 2008). Understandings of what a good therapeutic relationship looks like vary too, with CBT for example emphasising collaboration and psychoeducation, PCT emphasising congruence, unconditional positive regard and empathy, and psychodynamic approaches generally emphasising the importance of the relationship as a way of seeing how a client's experiences may impact their current situation and relationships. In social justice informed therapy, we do not have a single model of relationality, as indeed it cuts across all therapeutic approaches potentially. Instead, we can see how social justice may inform and influence the way in which the therapeutic relationship unfolds.

Two important ways in which we can make concrete our understanding of relationality in social justice informed therapy is by considering (1) rupture and repair in therapeutic relationships and (2) therapeutic endings.

1. Dealing with ruptures

As the therapeutic encounter is a meeting in time between two people who lead different lives, and it is undoubtable that for many practitioners when the therapeutic relationship gets challenged in some way in a session or over a series of sessions, a rupture can emerge in the work (Paul & Charura, 2014). When working in social justice informed therapy, we can expect dynamics to emerge in which we are drawn in as a sounding board, on socio-political matters, 'isims/othering' or injustice that have/are impacting the client in society. Thus, ruptures in the therapeutic relationship may be catalysed by the therapist's inability to engage in social justice informed therapy which enables the safe exploration of negative feelings or experiences of social injustice or consistent failure to appropriately broach or respond to what the client (groups, couple or family bring) as therapy progresses (Paul & Charura, 2014). If ruptures emerge, to repair them, we again suggest collaborative working in a non-defensive way. The therapist should be open to feedback and express cultural humility to acknowledge shortcomings on the experiences of social injustice that they overlooked which may have contributed to the rupture.

2. Working through therapeutic endings

Although both clients and therapists know that their therapeutic relationship will end at some point, preparing for endings is an essential therapeutic process which requires the therapist and client to collaborate (Paul & Charura, 2014). It is important however that in social justice informed therapy, the therapist takes responsibility in systematically drawing attention to, and addressing, the client's reality of experiences of injustice, as well as their defences, feelings, unconscious processes and anxieties or perceived loss about the ending of therapy. These feelings of perceived loss having felt supported and understood, they may mirror or parallel other feelings, for example of disempowerment, loss exclusion and injustice in society. Thus, the ending phase of social justice informed therapy is an opportunity to re-visit and refocus on what has been achieved or changed and collaboratively reflect on the social reality that the client will continue to face posttherapy. Where appropriate, therapists can act and use their power to challenge injustice, for example writing a letter to the housing authority in relation to the impact on their wellbeing of a client living in damp conditions.

Reflexivity, Curiosity and Openness

To engage in social justice informed therapeutic work, we need to be reflexive as psychological professionals. Reflexive practice involves the process of reflecting on and in action, with the intention to engage in experiential learning and development (Schön, 1982). Most branches of the psychological professions include some reference to the importance of being a reflexive practitioner (Donati, 2016; Rose, 2023). Practices such as personal therapy, supervision and journaling are all used to support this reflexive process. Therefore, it is no wonder that we are suggesting that a core applied principle underpinning social justice informed therapeutic work is reflexivity. Nevertheless, here reflexivity must take a particular shape and adopt a particular stance: as with collaboration discussed above, we need to go beyond how this is sometimes talked about in the literature. Specifically, we suggest that reflexivity must become *political* and *intersectional*. What this means in clinical practice and in supervision is that we must turn our reflexive gaze to our political selves, and our intersectional identities in relation to oppression, discrimination and socially structured advantage.

This will take different forms depending on who you are, and what your various identities and positionings look like. Importantly, however, it is not just a process of learning about the other, and those who experience socially structured advantage or privilege do not simply need to reflect on 'what are things like for X group'. Instead, they should turn their gaze to how their own positionings and power influence their life and the lives of others. This is not about experiencing shame or guilt, it is about understanding how we are social and political beings, embedded in broader complex structures. For example, for me (Laura), my social justice reflexivity should consider how I benefit from my whiteness, and how it influences my interactions with my environment and those around me, just as I reflect upon my experiences of sexism and what it means to be a woman in society. Intersectionally, this also means considering my experiences as a white woman with children who is currently able-bodied and heterosexual for example.

This social justice informed reflexive process is far from easy and can involve some painful unearthing of an awareness of the ways in which *we play a role* in the systems around us. Rather than leading us to despair, inaction, guilt or defensiveness, to engage fully with this social justice informed reflexivity, we require attitudes of openness and curiosity, non-defensiveness and a willingness to learn (which involves not always getting things right). Importantly, this is not about claiming all responsibility, and there is a balance to be struck between recognising our individual roles and recognising the social and political contexts which structure our relations.

CONCLUSION

We conclude this chapter with some points of reflection on social justice principles in psychological practice. We reiterate the benefits of remaining curious, of not assuming the power or disempowerment that those accessing our service may have experienced.

We also highlight the importance of engaging in dialogue, and challenging systemic discrimination and oppression at structural, institutional, societal and individual levels, while aiming to minimise power imbalances. Whilst we do not believe that social justice engagement can be done by going through a tick list, we note here themes of exploration and suggest that as practitioners it is important to:

1   Reflect on whether your practice (including supervision) is underpinned by relational socially just ethics, transformative practice, and politically informed practice.
2   Explore these matters in supervision: collaboration, broaching and any difficulties you may have with relationality, as well as your own positionality in society and with those who are marginalised.
3   Pay attention to the potential relationships between therapy and the process of othering.
4   Engage critically with literature and research to engage with a decolonised, culturally sensitive, social justice informed approach.
5   Consider cultural factors and cultural humility when engaging in social justice work.

Thus, we conclude by championing a social justice definition and approach that recognises and works to address systemic discrimination and oppression at structural, institutional, societal and individual levels, while aiming to minimise power imbalances, and endeavouring to have power with rather than power over and increasing equality (Winter, 2019; Schenker et al., 2019).

REFLECTIVE AND CRITICAL THINKING QUESTIONS

1   How do your own social identity and histories influence your engagement with social justice practice? What might be some of the personal barriers you might encounter in this work?
2   How comfortable are you with the idea of therapy as political?
3   What difficulties can you see with social justice informed therapeutic practice? How might these be overcome in our work?
4   How might your practice differ from someone who is socially and politically very different to you, as opposed to when you work with someone with whom you share more social and political identities or beliefs?

RECOMMENDED READING AND RESOURCES

Milton, M. (2018). *The personal is political: Stories of difference and psychotherapy*. Palgrave.

This text provides beautifully written illustrations of some of the social justice principles we have described above in case examples of therapeutic work.

Lee, C. C. (2019). *Multicultural issues in counselling: New approaches to diversity*. American Counselling Association.
This text provides material for therapists to engage with to inform their own development towards opposing all forms of discrimination, oppression and marginalisation of clients, thus becoming agents of social justice.

Audet, C., & Paré, D. (2017). *Social Justice and Counseling: Discourse in Practice*. Routledge.
This text offers a critical interrogation of the concept of social justice and offers in each chapter reflection questions to experientially engage with.

REFERENCES

Constantine, M. G. (2007). Racial microaggressions against African American clients in cross-racial counseling relationships. *Journal of Counseling Psychology, 54*(1), 1–16. https://doi.org/10.1037/0022-0167.54.1.1

Cooper, M., Dryden, W., Martin, K., & Papayianni, F. (2006). Metatherapeutic communication and shared decision-making. In M. Cooper & W. Dryden (Eds.), *The handbook of pluralistic counselling and psychotherapy* (pp. 42–54). Sage.

Cutts, L. A. (2013). Considering a social justice agenda for counselling psychology in the United Kingdom. *Counselling Psychology Review, 28*(2), 8–16.

Donati, M. (2016). Becoming a reflective practitioner. In B. Douglas, R. Woolfe, S. Strawbridge, E. Kasket, & V. Galbraith (Eds.), *The handbook of counselling psychology* (4th ed.). (pp. 55–73). Sage.

Finlay, L. (2019). *Practical ethics in counselling and psychotherapy: A relational approach*. Sage.

Fitzgibbon, A., & Winter, L. A. (2021). Practical applications of a social justice agenda in counselling and psychotherapy: The relational equality in education framework (REEF). *British Journal of Guidance and Counselling*. https://doi.org/10.1080/03069885. 2021.1981230

Gabriel, L., & Casemore, R. (Eds.). (2009). *Relational ethics in practice: Narratives from counselling and psychotherapy*. Routledge.

Gibson, A., Cooper, M., Rae, J., & Hayes, J. (2020). Clients' experiences of shared decision making in integrative psychotherapy for depression. *Journal of Evaluation in Clinical Practice, 26*(2), 559–568. https://doi.org/10.1111/jep.13320

Hanisch, C. (1970). The personal is political. In S. Firestone & A. Koedt (Eds.), *Notes from the second year* (pp. 76–78). Published by Editors.

Hanisch, C. (2006). *The personal is political: The women's liberation movement classic with a new explanatory introduction*. www.carolhanisch.org/CHwritings/PIP.html

Leahy, R. (2008). The therapeutic relationship in cognitive-behavioral therapy. *Behavioural and Cognitive Psychotherapy, 36*(6), 769–777. https://doi.org/10.1017/S1352465808004852

Lee, C. C. (2019). Multicultural competency: A conceptual framework for counseling across cultures. In C. C. Lee (Ed.), *Multicultural issues in counseling: New approaches to diversity* (5th ed.) (pp. 3–13). American Counseling Association.

Lee, E., Greenblatt, A., Hu, R., Johnstone, M., & Kourgiantakis, T. (2022). Developing a model of broaching and bridging in cross-cultural psychotherapy: Toward fostering epistemic and social justice. *American Journal of Orthopsychiatry.* http://dx.doi.org/10.1037/ort0000611

Nelson, G., & Prilleltensky, I. (2010). *Community psychology: In pursuit of liberation and wellbeing* (2nd ed.). Palgrave.

Oulanova, O., Hui, J., & Moodley, R. (2022). Engaging with minoritised and racialised communities 'inside the sentence'. In L. A. Winter & D. Charura (Eds.), *Handbook of social justice theory and practice in the psychological therapies: Power, politics and change.* Sage.

Paul, S., & Charura, D. (2014). *An introduction to the therapeutic relationship in counselling and psychotherapy.* Sage.

Prilleltensky, I. (2008). The role of power in wellness, oppression, and liberation: The promise of psychopolitical validity. *Journal of Community Psychology, 36*(2), 116–136. https://doi.org/10.1002/jcop.20225

Proctor, G. (2017). *The dynamics of power in counselling and psychotherapy: Ethics, politics and practice* (2nd ed.). PCCS Books.

Proctor, G. (2019). Acknowledging inequalities and meeting the unknown other: Facilitating encounter. *Person-Centered & Experiential Psychotherapies, 18*(3), 243–254. https://doi.org/10.1080/14779757.2019.1650811

Rogers, C. R. (1951). *Client-centered therapy.* Constable & Robinson.

Rose, C. (2023). Personal and professional development. In T. Hanley & L. A. Winter (Eds.), *The SAGE handbook of counselling and psychotherapy* (5th ed.). Sage.

Saad, L. F. (2020). *Me and white supremacy.* Quercus.

Schenker, K., Linnér, S., Smith, W., Gerdin, G., Mordal Moen, K., Philpot, R., Larsson, L., Legge, M., & Westlie, K., (2019). Conceptualising social justice – what constitutes pedagogies for social justice in HPE across different contexts?, *Curriculum Studies in Health and Physical Education, 10*(2), 126–140, https://doi.org/10.1080/25742981.2019.1609369

Schmid, P. F. (2012). Psychotherapy is political or it is not psychotherapy: The person-centred approach as an essentially political venture. *Person-Centered & Experiential Psychotherapies, 11*(2), 95–108. https://doi.org/10.1080/14779757.2012.682441

Schön, D. A. (1982). *The reflective practitioner: How professionals think in action.* Basic Books.

Shelton, K., & Delgado-Romero, E. A. (2013). Sexual orientation microaggressions: The experience of lesbian, gay, bisexual, and queer clients in psychotherapy. *Psychology of Sexual Orientation and Gender Diversity, 1*(S), 59–70. https://doi.org/10.1037/2329-0382.1.S.59

Smail, D. (2001). De-psychologizing community psychology. *Journal of Community and Applied Psychology, 11*(2), 159–165. https://doi.org/10.1002/casp.621

Smail, D. (2015). *The origins of unhappiness: A new understanding of personal distress.* Routledge.

Totton, N. (Ed.). (2006). *The politics of psychotherapy: New perspectives*. Open University Press.

Trusty, W. T., Swift, J. K., Black, S. W., Dimmick, A. A., & Penix, E. A. (2021). Religious microaggressions in psychotherapy: A mixed methods examination of client perspectives. *Psychotherapy*. https://doi.org/10.1037/pst0000408

Wilkinson, R., & Pickett, K. (2009). *The spirit level: Why equality is better for everyone*. Penguin.

Wilkinson, R., & Pickett, K. (2019). *The inner level: How more equal societies reduce stress, restore sanity and improve everyone's wellbeing*. Penguin.

Winter, L. A. (2018). Relational equality in education: What, why and how? *Oxford Review of Education, 44*(3), 338–352. https://doi.org/10.1080/03054985.2017.1391761

Winter, L. A. (2019). Social justice and remembering 'the personal is political' in counselling and psychotherapy: So, what can therapists do? *Counselling and Psychotherapy Research, 9*(3), 179–181.

Winter, L. A. (2023). The social and political context. In T. Hanley & L. A. Winter (Eds.), *The SAGE handbook of counselling and psychotherapy* (5th ed.). (pp. 8–14). Sage.

7
SOCIAL JUSTICE INFORMED THERAPY AND RACIALLY MINORITISED INDIVIDUALS

Nahid Nasrat and Maryam Riaz

OVERVIEW

This chapter explores socially just psychological practices with racially minoritised individuals. We introduce the reader to the theory of liberation psychology as anti-oppressive and socially just psychological practices. We discuss the foundation and key concepts of liberation psychology as they pertain to the liberation of psychological oppression and servitude of racial minorities. In the context of therapy, the minoritised individuals are the clients as well as the therapists. We conclude with a few case vignettes applying liberation psychology tools and practice.

CONTEXT

The field of psychological therapies and counselling has historically been influenced by Western culture, philosophy and theories. The birth of 'talk psychotherapy' is credited to Freud, the father of psychoanalysis. Since their inception, psychological therapies have mainly focused on diagnosing and treating mental health challenges without much consideration of the social, political and ecological systemic context. The field's ethnocentric emphasis has long failed to include clients' experiences with racism, systemic oppression and other 'isms'. There is an extensive body of literature that points out to the adverse impacts of racism on the psychological wellbeing of individuals (Carter et al., 2017). The emergence of social justice to be incorporated in the psychological therapies in the counselling profession and training has been very slow. Working toward human rights and social justice includes a broader awareness and emphasis on the intersecting factors that impact clients' lives and complex lived experience. To truly attend to and capture the rights of clients and empower them, one needs to go beyond intrapsychic processes. The emergence of COVID-19 has provided an opportunity for the helping professionals to become more aware of inequality, inequity and social injustices that have long affected the social wellbeing of marginalised communities.

Throughout the history of Western colonisation, racial minorities have been offered at different points various narratives which have undermined their humanity, dignity and wellbeing. Consequently, the field of psychological therapies was missing a deeper understanding of the lived experiences of racial minorities, and the helping professionals historically have not contextualised the suffering of racial minorities. They have in the West directly or indirectly played a role to perpetuate the belief in human superiority and hierarchies through scientific racism, defined as 'the use of scientific concepts and data to create and justify ideas of an enduring, biologically based hierarchy' (Winston, 2020, p. 2). Without addressing systemic and structural issues that contribute to the oppression of racial minorities, the helping professionals will continue to be unsuccessful to stop the cycle of oppression and injustices that are the major source of psychological suffering in their clients. Traditional and classical psychological theories and concepts did not include a discussion of social injustices in their conceptualisation of racially minoritised clients' psychological pain.

Community psychologists, in contrast, have been advocating for the teaching and application of *liberation psychology* that looks at societal and ecological oppression, historical trauma, colonisation and racial healing. To conduct socially just psychological therapies and counselling with racial minorities, psychologists are slowly developing an appreciation of the cultural and socio-political context of their racial minorities. There is much advocacy work needed to address the racial trauma and facilitate healing (French et al., 2020).

History of Race (In)Equality

The narrative for race equality in the UK and USA is complex; the trends in legislation provide a societal context of how people of racially marginalised communities experience oppression psychologically and societally.

The Black Lives Matter Movement in the USA, established in 2013, took international momentum in 2020 following the brutal and fatal treatment of George Floyd in Minneapolis, Minnesota by the police, and with the post-Covid levelling up agenda in the UK. We have seen globally increased awareness of histories, systems and structures that oppress or perpetuate oppression and racism, challenging practitioners to take a holistic view of the conversation about race and social justice between therapist and client. Racism can be subtle, woven into the tapestry of institutions and establishments; systemic oppression and injustice is embedded in policies, systems and networks as well as in hearts and minds. Liberation psychology responds to racial inequality: it questions, does not reinforce patterns of power, and seeks to liberate people from societal and psychological oppression. Liberation psychology considers the structural and personal power and privilege differentials that manifest in society and how these are deeply embedded and expressed within the identity, attitudes and behavioural responses of both therapist and client (Charura & Lago, 2021).

Liberation psychology promotes a model for social justice that truly liberates a person to live and be accepted in their authentic self. We hope it offers practitioners a decolonial approach to racial healing. It empowers clients and fosters a healing relationship, and is a move towards a collective responsibility, to recognise we all have a worldview and position that can support equality with equity for social justice.

CORE PRINCIPLES

Ignacio Martín-Baró (1942–1989) is considered the first person to introduce the concept of liberation psychology. He was a Jesuit priest born in Spain, but worked all his life in Central America, particularly El Salvador. Martín-Baró advocated for the field of psychology to recognise the psychological and community wounds caused by socio-political violence, including wars, poverty, racism and a long history of Western colonisation. He was vocal about the fact that liberation psychology was not only a tool to resist oppression but also to provide a framework for purposeful and meaningful living of racial minorities and marginalised people whose lives had been impacted by the long-lasting effects of Western colonisation (Martín-Baró, 1994).

Liberation psychology was also influenced by the work of Paulo Freire, a Brazilian lawyer, who experienced hunger and poverty and soon realised that the most important task to end oppression and systemic injustices is to promote education. He promoted a grassroots approach of achieving this goal. He advocated for oppressed individuals to develop a *critical consciousness* which he called '*conscientization*' of the oppressed (Freire, 2000). He later wrote the book *The Pedagogy of the Oppressed* which was the foundation for liberation psychology. Freire argued that 'critical consciousness' of the systemic oppression is the process of developing a deep consciousness and ability to recognise and analyse systems of inequality and the commitment to take actions against them.

According to Freire, the oppressed individuals carry within an internalised oppressor. This is an aspect of the self that needs liberation. He further postulated that the marginalised and oppressed people experience a sense of powerlessness, disconnections, internalisation of the oppressor's consciousness, unawareness of being manipulated and exploited by those who are privileged. At the same time, individuals with privilege benefit from having power, yet are unaware of their privilege. They believe that the status quo is the 'normal way' for everyone. They may use their power to preserve their position in society at the cost of the powerless without recognising and acknowledging their behaviour (Freire, 2000).

Martín-Baró (1994) challenged the field of psychology by arguing that psychologists must promote a more balanced, socially just and mentally healthy context for marginalised individuals. This can be accomplished only if they critically analyse the dominant messages in light of the experiences of those living as racial, social and economic minority contexts. Liberation psychology recognises that the Western colonisation had long-lasting effects on the lives of many generations through the continuation of exploitation, discrimination, racism and systemic oppression, hindering many racial groups from becoming actualised and having equal and equitable access to resources. Martín-Baró (1994) further criticised the field of traditional psychology as being neutral as a science, making universal assertions about human conditions, and not considering the social context of racial and economic minority populations. He even went further by stating that without considering the sociopolitical context, psychologists may risk perpetuating the cycle of oppression when offering psychological therapies. Some refer to liberation psychology as postcolonial psychology (Duran et al., 2008).

Concepts of Liberation Psychology

Since its inception, liberation psychology has emphasised an anti-oppressive stance and was designed to respond to marginalisation and oppression of minoritised people. It is based on two main ideas, namely ontology and epistemology. Ontology involves the question of how people interpret their reality. Epistemology is concerned with how people gain knowledge. Martín-Baró criticised Western psychology by pointing out that it only served the interests of those in power dominating the oppressive system, hence supporting it. He challenged the field by stating that psychology needed to liberate itself from its 'own chains' through changing its focus from its scientific position to addressing the long-lasting challenges of marginalised populations (Martín-Baró, 1994). Furthermore, psychology must develop a new epistemology recognising the truth within oppressed and marginalised peoples to properly shed light onto their anguish, pain and struggles. He advocated for a new *'praxis'*, a new application, to help marginalised people transform. The foundation of liberation psychology is based on the notion that all knowledge has a socio-political agenda. In other words, social reality results from peoples interacting with each other. As such, liberation psychology proposes that the idea of social reality is fluid and subject to change.

According to liberation psychologists, the helping professionals have an ethical responsibility to help marginalised and racial minorities develop critical conscientiousness about *how their social reality was created and imposed on them*. Liberation psychology is concerned with the promotion of psychological theories and practices that reflect a clear set of moral principles that promote the liberation of individuals, groups and collectives. As a value-based psychology, liberation psychology is concerned not only with what is but also with what should be. Ultimately, psychology can contribute toward social change, transformation and collective healing.

From a liberation psychology perspective, there are at least three types of well-being, namely personal, relational and collective. Personal wellness is achieved when individuals perceive themselves as having self-determination, have engaged in internal liberation from intrapsychic oppressive forces, and have created meaning through spirituality and collective Indigenous wisdom and knowledge. Relational wellbeing is achieved through respecting diversity, showing caring and compassion for each other, and liberating oneself from internal oppression. Lastly, collective wellbeing, defined as social justice, is achieved through support for social structures, support for the environment and liberation from societal oppressive forces. All three types of wellness are interconnected and have direct relationship with each other. There are barriers at each level through which an individual can experience oppression. If any of the three wellbeing levels are not in balance, individuals, communities and societies will continue to suffer from social injustice and psychological pain (Ginwright, 2010).

Socially Just Informed Liberatory Psychological Tools with Racially Minoritised Clients

It can be concluded that liberation psychology is a healing method that focuses on the lived experiences of racially and economically oppressed and marginalised individuals, groups and communities. The main goal of liberation psychology is to promote social justice action through the integration of emancipatory approaches and culturally grounded healing methodologies into mainstream psychotherapy.

Unlike mainstream psychological therapies, liberation psychology as a theoretical concept promotes racial healing and criticises the helping professionals for teaching the racially minoritised clients to cope with oppression, racism and discrimination. As such, healing comes from within. Racial trauma is real and must be addressed differently from the traditional interventions. There are several tools and concepts that are offered to bring racial and social justice to the clients and provide healing rather than a sense of coping with racism. Coping with racism would normalise the act of racism and may even further negatively affect the psychological wellbeing of racial minorities. Liberation psychology offers specific tools that may help racially and economically oppressed people heal from the effects of colonisation. These tools are discussed below (Comas-Díaz & Torres Rivera, 2020).

Internal Liberation

Firstly, internal liberation from the oppressive narratives must take place. According to Martín-Baró, to liberate someone, psychologists themselves need to be liberated at a personal level. Racially minoritised clients must become aware of their internalised racism, oppression and victimisation and recognise their own cultural and Indigenous health practices. Through enabling the oppressed racially minoritised clients to self-reflect and achieve self-transformation, a true shift will emerge from within promoting psychological cultural liberation. This will ultimately liberate the society as a whole (Watkins & Shulman, 2008).

Psychosocial Accompaniment

Secondly, the helping professionals cannot continue holding power in the therapy process by serving as subject matter experts. Instead, they need to provide a sense of accompaniment to their racially minoritised clients. Specifically, psychosocial accompaniment is an ethically and socially responsive intervention which is grounded on mutuality and interdependence. It is not hierarchical, nor is it unidirectional which decontextualises suffering (Martín-Baró, 1994).

As a tool, psychosocial accompaniment counters the cultural invasion (Freire, 2000). Western helping professionals are not to export psychiatric diagnoses and psychological treatment interventions to non-Western communities and assume a universal notion of the position to demonstrate cultural supremacy. To engage in psychosocial accompaniment, the helping professionals and researchers must move toward accompaniment and not serve as so-called experts. Psychosocial accompaniment is grounded on the notion of social decolonisation. The helping professionals must know that people in their community know what they want and need. Hence, mental health professionals need to accompany oppressed communities to reach their goals of liberation. Those professionals who are providing psychosocial accompaniment know how to ground their practice based on an understanding that psychological and community wellbeing are interconnected and refuse to follow an individualistic paradigm of psychological suffering.

Radical Healing

The third tool of liberation psychology is radical healing. French et al. (2020) describe radical healing as the process of racial minorities and Indigenous individuals healing from historical racial trauma. For radical healing to occur, one must understand the history of oppression and trauma and address the individual and collective harm that resulted from centuries of colonisation and subjugation of people of colour. It entails allowing the individual to resist oppression while being able to gain access to their freedom. This approach is meant to be a holistic one and does not have to occur to the exclusion of other psychological interventions. Traditional interventions for racial minorities focused on helping people manage racial trauma that they have encountered. However, radical healing moves away from teaching clients various coping strategies with racism and other 'isms'. Instead of coping with racial trauma, radical healing helps them heal from their experiences. It does this by using its concept of radical healing and its five grounded liberatory components – namely critical consciousness; strength and resistance; cultural authenticity and self-knowledge; radical hope; and emotional and social support – as well as connecting with communities.

The concept of radical healing forces us to consider how psychological rehabilitation must go past standard concepts of psychotherapy, which focuses on helping individuals cope with racism, and destroying structures that contribute to race-based trauma. As a result, radical healing acknowledges oppression's grief while encouraging hope for justice and liberation. The foundation of radical healing is collectivism, and it evolves through different criteria that are important for change.

For radical healing to occur, the helping professionals must understand the history and the many socio-political issues pertaining to the oppression of racial and ethnic minorities. Healing from racial trauma involves much more than the typical psychotherapy to help individuals cope with racism and traumas they may have endured. It is critical to go beyond the basics of learning to cope with racial trauma because it does not help the social justice that needs to occur. The liberatory psychological framework identifies concepts that include collectivism, critical consciousness, hope, resilience, resistance and authenticity.

Radical Hope

Racial trauma is conceptualised as a long-lasting trauma emerging from inequalities and racism. Hence racial trauma should not be pathologised and treated as a psychopathology. Radical healing needs a shift away from a deficit-based standpoint and adopts a sense of agency to encounter and transform oppressive conditions. Ginwright (2010) pointed out that social wellness is achieved through social, community and individual tools. Creating a sense of action and solidarity, engaging in resistance and transforming systems of oppression are processes that help to achieve wellness on multiple levels that are congruent with the call for social action among the helping professionals. This process is called radical hope. No challenge should be viewed as a problem by itself, but rather in the context of social inequality, inequity and injustice. An ecological and systemic approach must be taken to address the psychological oppression of racial minorities.

CASE STUDY: IMAAN

Banter can often be used to mask a person's racist and prejudiced views. It is considered to stem from unconscious bias and can lead to micro-aggressions against racially marginalised clients which can trigger racial trauma and cause psychological distress. In the following case study, we invite you to consider the impact of 'banter', how it has contributed to Imaan's psychological distress and made her question her racial and ethnic identity. Can you recognise systemic oppression? Reflect on the best ways to support a client like Imaan; considering Imaan's social and personal history, fleeing war and her need to be accepted and seeking a 'safe space' and the family's cultural views, for example of education being a 'safe-space', can Imaan really share her experience of racial injustice with her parents and shatter their narrative of hope? How would you address the psychological distress?

Imaan is a young female studying engineering and the only student of colour in her group. Imaan is the first generation from her family to attend university, and there is family history of racial trauma. Her parents migrated to the UK fleeing war. Her family's cultural philosophy of education is based on the notion that education is empowering, and the university environment and structure is a safe space that promotes equality and social justice, which is why they encouraged Imaan to attend. Imaan worked hard to settle into the university environment, however over time, banter from her peers made her become conscious of her 'otherness' (her difference in race and cultural heritage). She regularly experienced microaggressions about her country of origin, her racial identity and culture. Nonetheless, she continued to socialise with her peers as she wanted to belong and feel accepted. Sadly, over time 'banter' from colleagues became racially motivated, Imaan's attendance dropped and she stopped socialising, she began to feel marginalised and isolated from the group. Imaan was conscious of not wanting to fall behind in her studies and raised her concerns with her professor, who told her, 'banter is normal amongst peers, and it takes time for students to settle in'. Imaan left the meeting feeling demoralised.

Imaan is close to failing her first year, she is referred for therapy because she is experiencing severe anxiety and depression, and is scared she may be hearing voices because the 'banter' and racial comments are ruminating day and night. Imaan is also experiencing insomnia.

What might your social justice informed perspective look like working with Imaan? From a liberation perspective it might include radical hope – providing support for Imaan to feel her racial and cultural identity is not oppressive, so that she develops a narrative of hope which challenges oppression and provides her with a sense of 'belonging' and acceptance of her authentic self. It might also include radical healing – exploring ways for Imaan to feel safe and confident in spaces that oppress and marginalise her, to help her psyche heal from racial trauma; for example, developing a network of supportive peers to accompany Imaan's journey to liberation.

CASE STUDY: NOAH

In this case study, we invite you to consider the role of power, privilege and unconscious bias. Unconscious bias, with the use of personal and institutional power, can lead to systemic oppression which can trigger experiences of prejudice, marginalisation and racism. We see the manager's unconscious bias towards colleagues has affected his decisions concerning work allocation, selection and recruitment for a leadership role. Stereotypes of 'angry person of colour' are used by his team as an explanation rather than understanding the systemic oppression and racial trauma that have contributed to Noah's frustration and anger. Consider, what is the root cause of the anger/frustration? Is this triggering a threat response from racial trauma? For example, if Noah experiences daily discrimination and is perceived as a threat as a Black male, are societal injustices and discrimination being triggered in the place of work?

Noah is a chartered accountant and the team leader in the accountancy company. He has a good work ethic, is always the first to arrive and last to leave. He is aspiring to become a senior director in the business and is working 'above and beyond' to demonstrate his potential. He often receives microaggressions from his colleagues regarding his race and ethnicity: 'there are not many people from your community in this profession, or at this senior role', and 'you dress really smart for someone from your community', or 'your accent doesn't sound like a Black person, where are you from?'

Recently, Noah has noticed his manager is increasing his workload in comparison to white colleagues, however he does not complain and perseveres with the hope that doing the extra work will demonstrate his potential to be a senior director in the business.

Sadly, Noah tested positive for Covid-19 and was forced to take time off to self-isolate. He has mild Covid symptoms, but he does not want to disappoint his colleagues, so he continues to work from home and returns to work two weeks later. On his first day back, Noah is reading through the minutes of the last board meeting. He is surprised no one sent him an online meeting link for the meeting since his colleagues and manager were speaking to him daily regarding clients when he was self-isolating. Noah discovered that a white colleague, fairly new to the team, has been given the senior director role. Noah is devastated and starts to feel depressed and very angry. His colleagues do not understand why Noah is upset. They want him to attend anger management classes to address his frustration and 'baseless anger'.

What might your social justice informed perspective look like working with Noah? Radical hope: Noah's experience of social discrimination and racism and the impact it is having on him needs to be acknowledged and validated to allow him to move forward free from any narrative of oppression. From a liberation perspective it might include radical healing: recognising the effect of unconscious bias and the role of power and privilege his manager has played, and offering anti-oppressive solutions to help Noah manage systemic problems. For example, identifying an advocate and/or support network for Noah, raising awareness of unconscious bias to peers, understanding white fragility and privilege to ensure conversations remain authentic and are understood from a position of social justice and equality, not reinforcing stereotypes of 'angry person of colour'.

CONCLUSION

It is crucial that helping professionals engage in advocacy, naming the systemic socio-political issues that keep racial minorities oppressed and dehumanised. To define mental health without considering the socio-political context is to ignore the source and causes of racially minoritised people's suffering. It is hoped that the readers realise that it is time to move away from a hierarchical modality of providing psychological therapies where the therapists serve as 'experts' to place bandages on the psychological wounds of their clients whose pain is caused by inequality, social injustice, inequity and social and economic exclusion. Instead, the helping professionals need to become conscious of the deep connection between social wellbeing which includes physical, mental, cultural and economic wellbeing. A socially just helping professional is one who is actively participating in the political process, advocates on behalf of and with their clients, and works toward prevention of further inequality, injustice and oppression which are the basis of psychological pain in the general population, but particularly among racial minorities.

Liberation psychology offers tools to facilitate healing from racial trauma through critical consciousness raising, forming radical hope and envisioning possibilities, strength and resistance, as well as cultural authenticity and self-knowledge, and collectivism (Adames et al., 2022). Liberation psychology advocates that it is not enough just to use intervention strategies to address the psychological impact of marginalisation and discrimination. The helping professionals must also actively advocate for their clients, directing them to resources that empower them. They must also push for changes that decrease the conditions leading to their client's oppression at whatever level is possible. For example, an obvious utility of therapists' role in the collectivism step of the radical healing framework may be that we become familiar with different formally composed ethnic communities that we can direct our racialised clients towards who feel some lack in their sense of belonging to their group. The helping professionals' main role in helping the racial and marginalised populations is to '*accompany*' them on their journey of liberation from all historical and political oppressive forces that caused them to feel dehumanised.

REFLECTIVE AND CRITICAL THINKING QUESTIONS

1 Liberation psychology practice moves beyond descriptions of the nature of oppression to vigorous and innovative ways of working. Using liberation psychology theory, identify three specific methods you will adopt in your personal life and professional role to challenge the impact of inequalities and promote social justice in your practice.

2 When you incorporate tenets of social justice for racially marginalised clients, how will you monitor your practice to ensure consistency in your approach? For example: attending regular CPD related to race and social justice; document, reflect and monitor progress in supervision; reflection on cultural and racial identities in therapeutic conversations; including and exploring racial identity in client assessments and treatment plans?

3 Recognise your blind spots: can you identify aspects of privilege and power in your identity and consider how this may help or hinder you in your social justice approach?

4 Authentic support is one way to instil radical hope for radical healing; however, without critical reflection you may fall into a 'saviour/rescuer' role which can further silence/oppress a client's voice. Consider the meaning of authentic support. What critical considerations do you need to include for authentic allyship?

RECOMMENDED READING AND RESOURCES

The Implicit Bias test by Harvard University: https://implicit.harvard.edu/implicit/aboutus.html
This tool helps you understand your unconscious bias and recognise your blind spots.

Charura, D., & Lago, C. (2021). *Black identities + white therapies: Race, respect + diversity.* PCCS Books.
One of the first books of its kind for counselling and psychotherapeutic practice, bringing together a comprehensive collection of over 20 papers, written by authors who have lived experience of being marginalised and have experienced racism.

Lee, E., Greenblatt, A., Hu, R., Johnstone, M., & Kourgiantakis, T. (2022). Developing a model of broaching and bridging in cross-cultural psychotherapy: Toward fostering epistemic and social justice. *American Journal of Orthopsychiatry.* http://dx.doi.org/10.1037/ort0000611
A much-needed paper on defining social injustice, use of personal, professional and institutional power with clients, and developing a model of 'Broaching and Bridging' when working with cross-cultural psychotherapy.

www.racialequitytools.org/
This fully accessible website offers a range of resources that reflect language justice principles to support practitioners to develop their social justice practice.

https://learningtoforgive.com/about/
Forgiveness can be a vital tool in healing from social injustice. This website provides a useful framework and '9 steps' to use with clients to support the forgiveness methodology.

REFERENCES

Adames, H. Y., Chavez-Dueñas, N. Y., Lewis, J. A., Neville, H. A., French, B. H., Chen, G. A., & Mosley, D. V. (2022). Radical healing in psychotherapy: Addressing the wounds of racism-related stress and trauma. *Psychotherapy.* https://doi.org/10.1037/pst0000435

Carter, R. T., Johnson, V., Roberson, K., Mazzula, S. M., Kirkinis, K., & Sant-Barket, S. (2017). Race-based traumatic stress, racial identity status, and psychological functioning: An exploratory investigation. *Professional Psychology: Research and Practice, 48,* 20–37. https://doi.org/10.1037/pro0000116

Charura, D., & Lago, C. (Eds.) (2021). *Black identities + white therapies: Race, respect, + diversity.* PCCS Books.

Comas-Díaz, L., & Torres Rivera, E. (Eds.). (2020). *Liberation psychology: Theory, method, practice, and social justice.* American Psychological Association. https://doi.org/10.1037/0000198-000

Duran, E., Firehammer, J., & Gonzalez, J. (2008). Liberation psychology as the path toward healing cultural soul wounds. *Journal of Counseling & Development, 86*(3), 288–295. https://doi.org/10.1002/j.1556-6678.2008.tb00511.x

Freire, P. (2000). *Pedagogy of the oppressed* (30th anniversary ed.). Continuum.

French, B. H., Lewis, J. A., Mosley, D. V., Adames, H. Y., Chavez-Dueñas, N. Y., Chen, G. A., & Neville, H. A. (2020). Toward a psychological framework of radical healing in communities of color. *The Counseling Psychologist, 48*(1), 14–46. https://doi.org/10.1177/0011000019843506

Ginwright, S. A. (2010). *Black youth rising: Activism and radical healing in urban America.* Teachers College Press.

Martín-Baró, I. (1994). *Writings for a liberation psychology* (A. Aron & S. Corne, Eds.). Harvard University Press.

Watkins, M., & Shulman, H. (2008). *Toward psychologies of liberation.* Palgrave Macmillan.

Winston, A. S. (2020). Scientific racism and North American psychology. In O. Braddick (Ed.), *The Oxford research encyclopedia of psychology.* Oxford University Press.

8
SOCIAL JUSTICE INFORMED THERAPY AND SOCIAL CLASS

Rachael Goodwin

OVERVIEW

Despite the well-known impacts of social class on mental health and wellbeing, social class remains a neglected topic in counselling, psychotherapy and psychology. This chapter aims to contextualise social class in a social justice framework and offer some core principles to consider when working with social class in therapy. I begin by highlighting several definitions of social class and classism, before outlining a broad context for considering the importance of social class and classism in therapy. Three core principles for therapy are then offered, which include: 1) Ending class blindness in therapy: Becoming aware of classism and classist microaggressions and potential impacts on clients; 2) Therapy and therapists as perpetuators of classism: Becoming aware of social power in the therapeutic relationship; 3) Moving towards anti-classist therapy: What can we do as practitioners? The chapter ends with a case study and some questions for self-reflection and critical thinking, as well as recommended further reading and resources.

CONTEXT

What Is Social Class and Classism?

Social class is a complex construct, which is historically, politically and culturally influenced. Various histories of social class exist which are too far-reaching for a summary in this chapter (see Savage, 2015 for a comprehensive overview). Broadly speaking, however, class has historically been defined using objective measures (e.g., income, occupation, status) or subjective measures (e.g., self-definition, identity, culture). Increasingly, class is conceptualised as multi-dimensional, which includes both objective and subjective measures (Savage, 2015). Many sociologists draw upon Bourdieu's (1986) concept of forms 'capital' or 'power and privilege' to understand how class-based inequalities are shaped and maintained in society. Bourdieu outlines four types of capital, including economic (income and assets), cultural (education and leisure pursuits), social (connections and networks) and symbolic (the legitimised recognition of capitals). He describes systemic mechanisms operating in society, which are 'aimed at controlling the official, direct transmission of power and privileges' (Bourdieu, 1986, p. 254). From a social justice perspective seeking to redress social inequalities and oppressions, Bourdieu's concept of capitals offers a helpful framework for conceptualising the powers and privileges held and perpetuated by classed systems and individuals. From a transcultural perspective, different systems of social stratification exist, such as 'caste systems' in India and some parts of Africa. Additionally, for some groups, one's social class may not feel as relevant compared to other social identities.

Similar to sex and sexism or race and racism, class and classism are co-constructs. This means one does not exist without the other (Liu & Colbow, 2017). Classism has received comparatively less attention in social justice literature however, which is evidenced by its absence in research and training (Smith, 2008). In the UK, this absence could be because class is not a protected characteristic in the 2010 Equality Act. Therefore, the concepts of class and classism are not commonly used or understood. Indeed, it has been claimed classism is the 'unseen prejudice' in the UK and the 'missing piece' in counselling, psychotherapy and psychology. Like racism, sexism, (cis)heterosexism and ableism, classism is always experienced intersectionally (see Lago, Chapter 3 this volume). However, social class and classism are largely ignored in intersectional research.

Classism is a form of prejudice, discrimination and oppression which functions 'so that poor and working-class people are systematically disadvantaged through our society's institutions (like health care); attitudes and stereotypes (like deficit models of homelessness); and policies, procedures, and economic structures' (Smith, 2008, p. 899). Several commentators claim classism can be enacted 'upwards' and 'laterally'. However, from a social justice perspective, it is argued classism can only be enacted 'downwards' from those with more class privileges towards those with less, because only dominant groups with more social, economic, cultural and symbolic capital are able to oppress others through prejudice and discrimination (Smith, 2008).

Three specific types of classism have been defined as *institutional*, *interpersonal* and *internalised*. Lott and Bullock (2007, p. 6) define *institutional* classism as 'the maintenance of low status and barriers to resource access by social institutions' and *interpersonal* classism as 'the related but independent dimensions of prejudice (negative attitudes), stereotypes (beliefs), and discrimination (distancing or denigrating behavior)'. Russell (1996) outlines *internalised* classism as a process which involves a member of the poor or working-class internalising classism and their negative classed experiences. A growing body of research also highlights classist microaggressions, which 'expose and reinforce a status quo that devalues working-class and poor people based on their social class and that undermines the psychological wellbeing of people who hold these class memberships' (Smith & Redington, 2010, pp. 269–270).

Subjective vs Objective Definitions of Class Membership

Traditionally, in the sociological and psychological literature, objective measures have been used to 'rank' individuals according to pre-determined stratified classifications. Objective measures classify individuals based on their income and occupational status, as seen in the UK's Office of National Statistics' Socio-Economic Classification (NS-SEC). Research has shown a more effective measure, in terms of impact on perceived wellbeing, is subjective social class. From a psychological perspective, understanding one's subjective definition of social class helps us gain insight into the phenomenological experiences of one's 'values, skills, social networks, physical and mental attributes, and behaviours associated with various social class cultures' (Liu & Colbow, 2017, p. 251). Consequently, an increasing number of psychological studies incorporate subjective measures of social class, including subjective self-definition.

The Widening Gap between Rich and Poor

The already-existing gap between rich and poor has increased since the 2008 global recession and has subsequently been exacerbated by the COVID-19 pandemic (OECD, 2021). Wealth inequality data in the UK now reveal the top 1% of households is 230 times wealthier than the lowest 10% (ONS, 2022). Furthermore, 22% of the UK population lives in poverty, 8.1 million of whom are working-age adults and 4.3 million are children (Joseph Rowntree Foundation, 2022). In the US, this figure stands at 11.4%, 38.1 million of whom are working-age adults and 11.6 million are children (United States Census Bureau, 2021).

Social Class Inequalities and Health and Wellbeing Outcomes

Social class and poverty are predictors of a range of health and wellbeing outcomes. Class-related health inequalities have been documented ever since Engels' (1892) observations of the conditions of the working-class in England during the Industrial Revolution, as he highlighted infant mortality amongst working-class women was significantly higher than that of the upper classes. The social health gradient persists today and shows the further down the socio-economic scale one ranks, the worse one's experiences of a range of outcomes are. When it comes to physical health, research demonstrates working-class and people in poverty experience increased risks to heart health, cortisol levels, back pain and quality of sleep. Regarding wellbeing inequalities, studies show working-class people and those living in poverty are more likely to experience and be diagnosed with mental health conditions. However, people from low socio-economic backgrounds are less likely to access therapy, and if they do, they are more likely to end therapy early and experience less successful outcomes (Delgadillo, 2018). Counselling and psychology research has historically individualised the roots of these health inequalities and often blamed working-class people and those living in poverty for their lack of hard work and their resultant deserving ill-health (Day et al., 2014). From a social justice perspective, it is imperative we challenge this view and shine a light on the systemic factors contributing to health and wellbeing inequalities between classes. The chapter now outlines three core principles for how we might consider working in a social justice informed way with issues of social class.

CORE SOCIAL JUSTICE PRINCIPLES FOR WORKING WITH CLIENTS FROM WORKING-CLASS COMMUNITIES AND THOSE IN POVERTY

Ending Class Blindness in Therapy

Despite the well-documented health and wellbeing outcomes associated with social class, class blindness persists in therapy (Ballinger, 2017). Class commentators have called for counsellor and psychologist training to include 'class-sensitive' approaches to therapy in curricula (Ballinger, 2017; Liu & Colbow, 2017). For Liu and Colbow (2017), this includes practitioners making radical changes to how we work with clients from working-class and poor backgrounds. They suggest rethinking the length and number of therapy sessions with clients and conducting 'extra-therapeutic advocacy work' (Liu & Colbow, 2017, p. 257), such as researching information online and calling services directly to support clients with referrals. For Ballinger (2017), class-sensitive counselling also includes examining barriers to access and increasing training content around class-based issues in therapy. However, few training institutions offer modules or content addressing issues of social class in counselling and psychotherapy. Several commentators have linked this lack of training to class blindness plus a sense of class being taboo, or too awkward for middle-class people to talk about. A significant exception to this exists within the American Psychological Association (APA) which has developed free online resources for psychologists and educators regarding the 'Inclusion of Social Class in Psychology Curricula' (APA, 2022). A link to this website is included in the references section of this chapter. Examples of classism will now be outlined, and considerations offered for the impacts of these different types of classism on individuals' health and wellbeing.

Institutional Classism

In the Great British Class Survey, Savage (2015) identified that 15% of Great Britain's population can be classified as belonging to a 'precariat' class. Savage (2015, p. 353) defines this group as people who are 'at the mercy' of the structural instability of a global market, which has given rise to low-paid and temporary jobs. This means those within this class tend to live precarious lives marked by unemployment, or zero-hour and temporary contracts. Due to precarious employment, this group is often denied workers' rights such as sick leave, holidays or protective legislation which are typically enjoyed by permanent employees. Through qualitative interviews conducted by working-class sociologist Lisa McKenzie, Savage's (2015) research also highlights how the precariat were hard hit by austerity measures that cut funding to local services and significantly reduced a range of benefits. For people whose lives revolve around unpredictable working hours and income, therefore, we can imagine they might experience a lack of autonomy regarding the choices they are able to make. We could also imagine uncertainty around being able to afford basic provisions such as food, electricity, transport and housing. Indeed, Savage's (2015) study found many participants experienced anxiety, fear and worry associated with not knowing when they would be employed, and whether they would be able to afford to keep living in their current accommodation. He summarises: 'their lives were filled with insecurities, from where they might get their next meal to where they would be living next week' (Savage, 2015, p. 345).

Whilst not all working-class people or those living in poverty have jobs which demand physical labour, many were and still are employed in the mining, construction or service industries. Research shows sustained physical labour can have a negative impact on physical health, with working-class people more likely to incur work-based injuries than middle-class workers. Additionally, many manual labour jobs expose workers to hazardous materials and chemicals which can result in skin and respiratory conditions, asbestosis or silicosis (associated with mining and quarry work). Occupations can also negatively impact mental health and wellbeing, with several studies linking lack of control at work and poor working conditions with reduced wellbeing, and increased anxiety and depression.

Although not all working-class people or those living in poverty experience challenges with their living conditions, it is estimated that 3.66 million people live in 'housing need' in the UK (Bramley, 2019). This includes people living in inadequate social rented accommodation that is damp, uninhabitable or overcrowded. Additionally, around 330,000 households experience forms of homelessness in the UK, including over 120,000 children in temporary accommodation (McHale, 2021). Research highlights housing instability is linked with lower levels of autonomy and self-efficacy, and higher rates of depression amongst adults. For children living in housing uncertainty, difficulties with school readiness, academic achievement, overall development and mental health challenges have been highlighted (McHale, 2021). Thus, a range of health and wellbeing inequalities are associated with the effects of institutional classism, which impact almost every sphere of an individual's life and development.

Interpersonal Classism

Although research into classist microaggressions is still a relatively new area for counselling and psychology, US-based studies in education have indicated the negative impacts classist microaggressions can have on wellbeing. Smith and colleagues (2016) highlight the lived experiences of college students from working-class and poor families in the US. Their research found students from poor and working-class backgrounds experience classist microaggressions from peers who use derogatory language about people from working-class communities. Classist microaggressions experienced include hearing peers describing working-class people as 'lazy' or asserting they live in poverty due to their own personal shortcomings. The study also notes the students' emotional responses to experiencing microaggressions, which often led them to hide their class background and feel their class identity had been invalidated.

Further examples of classist microaggressions include words used in popular culture to describe people from poor and working-class communities, such as 'trailer trash' in the US, 'bogans' in Australia, and 'chavs' in the UK. A range of sociological, film and media literature outline the ways popular media exacerbates and normalises this kind of classism. Programmes such as *Benefits Street* and *The Jeremy Kyle Show* in the UK, also known as 'poverty porn', feature mainly working-class people who are portrayed as 'benefits scroungers' or 'dysfunctional' as a form of 'entertainment'. Research also highlights the harmful impacts of experiencing all types of classism on one's self-esteem, self-concept, perceived self-efficacy, mental health and overall wellbeing.

A little-known but harmful interpersonal classist prejudice involves what Liu and Colbow (2017) have termed the upwards mobility bias (UMB). The UMB can be defined as assuming that everyone aspires to 'move up' and 'out' of their social class. Indeed, successive UK governments have driven an 'upwards social mobility' agenda based on this very premise since the 1990s (see UK Government Social Mobility Commission webpages). Many class commentators have critiqued the philosophy of the UMB for its underlying classism; firstly, for assuming the pursuit of happiness is based on material gains, as opposed to intrinsic self-worth and the search for fulfilment; and secondly for presuming working-class people want to 'better themselves' by moving out of their working-class communities. Instead, the case could be made for equality of housing, working conditions and health outcomes through social justice, rather than social mobility. Literature highlights the contexts in which interpersonal classism based on the UMB could negatively impact working-class people and those living in poverty, such as education and therapy. For example, in education, if a child or young person grows up hearing negative messages from teachers about certain jobs not being 'aspirational' enough, this could have a negative impact on their self-esteem and relationship with their working-class community. The chapter later discusses therapists' roles in perpetuating classism in the second core principle.

Internalised Classism

Very few studies explore the lived experiences of internalised classism, and therefore limited empirical literature exists regarding the impacts of internalised classism on working-class people and those living in poverty. In one of the first papers to conceptualise internalised classism, Russell (1996) draws upon her experiences as a therapist working with people from working-class communities. She describes internalised classism as 'the process by which a person's experience as a member of the poor or working-classes becomes internalized and influences her self-concept and self-esteem as well as her relationships with others' (p. 59). In many ways, internalised classism is unconscious and invisible and therefore rarely recognised by the client or therapist. It usually involves internalising interpersonal classist messages from the dominant middle- and upper-class (as outlined before), which tell working-class people and those in poverty that they are inferior, lacking or somehow flawed. Consequently, internalised classism can result in working-class people rejecting parts of their classed identity, and in some cases, rejecting their working-class communities of origin. This can manifest in working-class people changing the way they speak, look or dress, to 'fit in' with dominant middle-class norms. Russell (1996) highlights how working with internalised classism in therapy can result in feelings of grief and loss for the client's classed identity, plus anger at social unfairness, and shame at how they are relating to themselves and others in their community. Internalised classism therefore is a complex and often unconscious process resulting in difficult emotions and relational challenges for the client. From a social justice perspective, internalised classism can be seen as another mechanism of oppression which serves to maintain power over working-class people and those living in poverty.

Ending Therapy and Therapists Being Perpetuators of Classism

Counselling and psychology are perceived as middle-class professions, mainly occupied and accessed by those from middle-class backgrounds. Limited research explores the barriers around access to both training and therapy. However, financial costs could be seen as an obvious limitation for those from working-class backgrounds being able to train as therapists and being able to access private therapy. Consequently, there is very little class diversity and representation in the field of therapy. This could be one of the key contributing factors as to why class is not considered in many counselling and psychology training programmes. Indeed, Smith (2008) argues the very reason for class blindness in counselling and psychology is due to inherent and unacknowledged institutional classism within the helping professions.

Liu and Colbow (2017) highlight the ways therapists might propagate interpersonal classism against their clients. This includes maintaining classist stereotypes in therapy and inadvertently making class-based microaggressions towards clients from working-class backgrounds. Drawing upon the UMB concept, Liu and Colbow (2017) hypothesise unexamined social class biases could perpetuate classism in the therapeutic relationship. For example, if a middle-class therapist assumes 'upwards social mobility' is the goal of every client, they may view a client through a deficit lens if they fail to express ambitions in keeping with the UMB. Indeed, several studies have linked poorer therapeutic outcomes with class mismatches between client and therapist, with limited research indicating therapists can inadvertently oppress working-class clients with their social power and classist assumptions if left unchallenged. Countertransference has also been cited as a potentially damaging way in which therapists could perpetuate interpersonal classism.

This section has offered several possibly challenging points for reflection, in terms of how we as therapists and the profession could be perpetuating classism and class-based inequalities in therapy and beyond. The chapter concludes with specific questions for self-reflection and critical thinking which could offer potential ways to tackle these challenges.

Anti-Classist Therapeutic Practices

The intention of this final core principle is to start a conversation around what it could mean, and look like, to become anti-classist practitioners. It covers considerations for individuals, institutions and the discipline of therapy.

Starting the Conversation around Anti-Classist Therapy

If we are truly committed to social justice values of redressing social inequalities in all their forms, we must extend our efforts beyond 'class sensitivity' towards becoming anti-classist practitioners. Anti-classism begins with us, through acknowledging our own class privileges in terms of economic, social, cultural and symbolic capitals we hold and perpetuate within our own families, networks and communities. Becoming an anti-classist practitioner involves recognising and challenging the systemic roots of the damaging impacts of classism many of our clients will have experienced.

In our professional work, being an anti-classist practitioner means including clients' experiences of classism in our therapeutic formulations, reflections and interventions. It means sensitively and respectfully naming class differences in the therapeutic relationship and enabling the client to know it is safe for them to talk about their classed experiences without fear of being judged or shamed by their therapist. Indeed, research shows clients from working-class backgrounds are more likely to have positive and successful experiences with therapists who acknowledge class, even if the therapist appears to be of 'higher' class than the client.

Anti-Classist Therapy Training

When considering recruitment and diversity of new trainees, institutions could commit to anti-classism by ensuring they engage with potential applicants outside of typical middle-class domains. Crucially, information about funding and fees must be transparent. Plus, scholarships and reduced fees would be a step towards anti-classist access to training, thereby potentially increasing the number of people from working-class backgrounds entering the profession. To work towards ending class blindness, training institutions could take inspiration from the APA's (2022) free online resources and ensure social class and classism are integral parts of counsellor and psychologist training programmes.

Challenging Prejudices and Moving beyond a Deficit Model of Social Class

Finally, becoming an anti-classist therapist means moving beyond the deficit view of what it means to be working-class and living in poverty. This could involve taking time to acknowledge the rich history of working-class people, poetry, art, literature and music. Research highlights the many resources held by working-class people and communities, including collectivism, solidarity, compassion and kindness. To be an anti-classist therapist therefore means working with clients to understand some of these class-based resources which they may well possess, and which could help them in therapy.

CASE STUDY: ANNIE

This section of the chapter presents a fictitious case study vignette. It encourages you to study Annie's story and make notes of incidents of class-based inequalities, experiences of classism, and how you would begin to formulate working with Annie in therapy. For readers who are interested in considering what actions they could take as an anti-classist therapist, you are invited to think about interventions you could make within and beyond therapy. After the case study, you can read several reflections for consideration.

Annie

Annie is a white, heterosexual, able-bodied, working-class Mum-of-three in her early 40s. She comes from a large loving family in an ex-industrial town, and is very close with her Mum and five sisters. She has recently been through a long, drawn-out divorce from her husband of 19 years, who was, in Annie's words 'a mean, controlling man'. Her ex-husband has taken the car and their minimal savings, leaving Annie responsible for the rent on their three-bedroom council house and their teenage children. Annie is worried about keeping up payments on the house, and how to cover the increasingly expensive utility bills. After working for over 20 years as a part-time cleaner, a job Annie loves due to the friends and colleagues she has there, she is now wondering if it is more financially beneficial to take on full-time hours, or to enquire about applying for benefits to help supplement her income. Annie has never applied for benefits before and is worried about what people might think about her if she does. Annie was advised to go online to find out about government support, but feels she lacks confidence with technology. Although Annie has a smartphone, she does not have access to a laptop or Wi-Fi at home. Annie has spoken to her GP about how she is feeling. She was diagnosed with anxiety and depression and prescribed medication. She was not referred for therapy until her third visit to the GP when she found life was becoming more difficult to manage. In your first session together, Annie appears upset and angry about how she was treated by her GP. Annie shares with you that her GP asked her 'why don't you just move house?' if she is worried about keeping up the rent payments. When you speak with your service administrator about booking in Annie's next appointment, you hear Annie being referred to as 'that rough client who seemed like she had a bit of a temper'.

Some Reflections on Annie's Case Study

Whilst this is not a comprehensive list of the many observations you could have made whilst reading Annie's case study, below are a few ideas about how classism and social class inequalities could be considered if you were working with Annie in therapy.

1. Institutional classism

Digital technology inequalities: The assumption that everyone has access to Wi-Fi and a laptop, and the confidence to go online, to access services such as benefits and government advice, online therapy or resources.
Housing inequalities: The uncertainty faced by many families regarding their housing situation and ability to pay the bills.

2. Interpersonal classism

Classist microaggression: The assumption that Annie can 'just move house' to solve her worries.
Classist stereotype: The indirect classist comment regarding the 'rough' and 'angry' working-class person.

3. Internalised classism

Stereotype threat: Annie is concerned about what others will think if she applies for benefit support.

4. Resources

Collectivism and family support: Annie's family could be a great resource for her.
Annie's love of her job and colleagues.

What did you notice as you read Annie's case study? Did you have any thoughts, feelings or somatic reactions towards Annie, the GP, the service administrator? Did you recognise any classist prejudices or assumptions arising within you? What political actions could you consider taking in light of Annie's experiences?

CONCLUSION

The aim of this chapter was to shine a light on a much-neglected form of oppression in counselling, psychotherapy and psychology: classism. Framing social class through a social justice lens, it was suggested that classism can only be enacted 'downwards' from those with more class privilege and power towards those without. The chapter outlined some of the many social inequalities faced by people living in poverty and those in working-class communities, including precarious living, working conditions and housing insecurity. Three types of classism were outlined (institutional, interpersonal, internalised) and considerations of the deleterious impacts of classism were offered. A case study application invited readers to consider some of the ways classism could impact a client's life. Through offering several reflections on the case study, I encouraged readers to think about how they could formulate some of Annie's experiences in their work together, including how readers could take action as anti-classist practitioners. Recommendations for further reading and viewing are offered below, along with more questions for self-reflection and critical thinking regarding social class and classism in therapy.

REFLECTIVE AND CRITICAL THINKING QUESTIONS

1　How would you describe your own position or location regarding social class?
2　What assumptions or prejudices do you hold towards people who live in poverty and/or are working-class? Can you trace where your social class beliefs may have come from? How do you think these beliefs and assumptions manifest in your therapeutic work with people who are working-class and/or living in poverty?
3　What steps can you take to become more informed about class-related issues? (i.e., Do you understand how social housing, or the benefits system works? Do you know what the minimum wage is? Can you name a working-class writer or musician?)
4　How do the intersections of other oppressions, such as racism and ableism, impact people's lived experiences of classism?

RECOMMENDED READING AND RESOURCES

American Psychological Association. (2022). *Inclusion of social class in psychology curricula: Resources for educators*. www.apa.org/pi/ses/resources/publications/social-class-curricula
US-focused website offering free resources for educators, including class-based exercises and reading lists around issues of social class in counselling and psychology.

De Waal, K. (Ed.). (2019). *Common people: An anthology of working-class writers*. Unbound.
An invaluable collection of 34 working-class writers who share poems, memoirs and essays in celebration, not apology.

Loach, K. (2016). *I, Daniel Blake*. Sundance Selects.
A moving, raw and honest film shining a light on the systemic injustices faced by characters living precariously in austerity Britain in the twenty-first century.

Liu, W. M. (Ed.). (2013). *The Oxford handbook of social class in counseling*. Oxford University Press.
US-focused handbook presenting an in-depth and intersectional range of chapters on issues surrounding social class in counselling.

REFERENCES

American Psychological Association. (2022). *Inclusion of social class in psychology curricula: Resources for educators.* www.apa.org/pi/ses/resources/publications/social-class-curricula

Ballinger, L. (2017). Social class. In C. Feltham, T. Hanley, & L. A. Winter (Eds.), *SAGE handbook of counselling and psychotherapy* (4th ed., pp. 43–48). Sage.

Bourdieu, P. (1986). The forms of capital. In J. Richardson (Ed.), *Handbook of theory and research for the sociology of education* (pp. 241–258). Greenwood.

Bramley, G. (2019). *Housing supply requirements across Great Britain for low-income households and homeless people.* Research for Crisis and the National Housing Federation, Main Technical Report. https://doi.org/10.17861/bramley.2019.04

Day, K., Rickett, B., & Woolhouse, M. (2014). Class dismissed: Putting social class on the critical psychological agenda. *Social and Personality Psychology Compass, 8*(8), 397–407. https://doi.org/10.1111/spc3.12118

Delgadillo, J. (2018). Worlds apart: Social inequalities and psychological care. *Counselling and Psychotherapy Research, 18*(2), 111–113. https://doi.org/10.1002/capr.12168

Engels, F. (1892). The condition of the working-class in England in 1844 with preface written in 1892: By Frederick Engels. Translated by Florence Kelley Wischnewetzky. London: Swan Sonnenschein & Co. Paternoster Square.

Joseph Rowntree Foundation. (2022). *UK poverty 2022: The essential guide to understanding poverty in the UK.* www.jrf.org.uk/report/uk-poverty-2022

Liu, W. M., & Colbow, A. J. (2017). Social class in counselling psychology. In D. Murphy (Ed.), *Counselling psychology: A textbook for study and practice* (pp. 249–264). John Wiley & Sons.

Lott, B., & Bullock, H. E. (2007). *Psychology and economic injustice: Personal, professional, and political intersections.* American Psychological Association.

McHale, S. (2021). *An ecologically informed study of perceived emotional wellbeing in school-aged children experiencing family homelessness* [Doctoral thesis, University of Manchester]. https://ethos.bl.uk/OrderDetails.do?uin=uk.bl.ethos.843568

OECD. (2021). *Inequalities in household wealth and financial insecurity of households.* www.oecd.org/wise/Inequalities-in-Household-Wealth-and-Financial-Insecurity-of-Households-Policy-Brief-July-2021.pdf

Office of National Statistics. (2022). *Household total wealth in Great Britain: April 2018 to March 2020.* www.ons.gov.uk/peoplepopulationandcommunity/personaland householdfinances/incomeandwealth/bulletins/totalwealthingreatbritain/april2018tomarch2020

Russell, G. M. (1996). Internalized classism: The role of class in the development of self. *Women and Therapy, 18*(3–4), 59–71. https://doi.org/10.1300/J015v18n03_07

Savage, M. (2015). *Social class in the 21st century.* Penguin Books.

Smith, L. (2008). Positioning classism within counseling psychology's social justice agenda. *The Counseling Psychologist, 36*(6), 895–924.

Smith, L., & Redington, R. M. (2010). Class dismissed: Making the case for the study of classist microaggressions. In D. W. Sue (Ed.), *Microaggressions and marginality: Manifestation, dynamics, and impact* (pp. 269–285). John Wiley & Sons.

Smith, L., Mao, S., & Deshpande, A. (2016). 'Talking across worlds': Classist microaggressions and higher education. *Journal of Poverty, 20*(2), 127–151. https://doi.org/10.1080/10875549.2015.1094764

United States Census Bureau. (2021). *Income and poverty in the United States: 2020.* www.census.gov/library/publications/2021/demo/p60-273.html

9
SOCIAL JUSTICE INFORMED THERAPY AND VISIBLE AND INVISIBLE DISABILITIES

Esther Ingham

OVERVIEW

Disability, as a matter of difference and diversity, is a biopsychosocial construct of identity, unavoidably linked to issues of equality of opportunity, respect, social action and inclusion. It is a concept that packages together individuals with a broad range of differing impairments, who thereby become the cause of a common experience of marginalisation, discrimination and oppression from the dominant non-disabled community. Disability will inevitably enter any therapeutic practice, as it is a natural part of human existence that, should we live long enough, will affect us all. Yet, as an 'issue' it invokes a variety of (often powerful) feelings that can make it feel hard to engage with. This chapter outlines some of the dominant conceptualisations of disability, before going on to use my own experiences to illustrate how their mobilisation can significantly negatively impact the individual. I conclude with a section on how to integrate awareness of issues relating to disability into therapeutic practice.

CONTEXT

To explore how therapeutic practice can be informed by disability as an issue of social justice, it is necessary first to establish some clarity about the term. The International

Classification of Functioning, Disability and Health (ICF) (WHO, 2001) asserts that 'disability' refers to difficulties encountered in any combination of three areas of functioning: impairment, activity limitation and participation restriction. These difficulties can be physical and/or intellectual, congenital or acquired, visible or invisible, and can be temporary, permanent or intermittent.

All UK psychological practitioners are obliged to practise within the legal context of the 2010 Equality Act, which requires an awareness of disability issues – it is not just a matter for those working overtly in the field of disability. Yet, the therapist is as vulnerable as any other individual to unwittingly ingesting some, or even many, of the commonly held negative constructions and attitudes towards disability that permeate contemporary UK society. As a member of a profession that endeavours to align itself with the notion of social justice, however, the therapist also has an ethical obligation to embrace issues of inequality and discrimination in both practice and personal development, and to be able to question inequitable political, economic and social practices. Regarding issues concerning disability, this appears to have been left consistently unaddressed in counselling training and literature (Parkinson, 2006), and consequently unconscious assumptions can remain unchallenged, despite the widely acknowledged fundamental importance of a non-judgemental approach to counselling. Disability remains largely invisible in contemporary UK society through various forms of both hidden and overt segregation and discrimination, so many non-disabled people (therapists and clients included) may form their perceptions of disability through media portrayal, which tends to rely on negative and inaccurate stereotypes (Olkin, 2012). Without identifying and addressing the chasm between the (often absent and regularly oppressed) disabled and (prevalent and privileged) non-disabled communities, there is little or no chance for the non-disabled population (including therapists and clients) to begin to be able to comprehend some of the experiences of disabled people (Rosenberg, 2009).

It is always possible, of course, that an individual may come to therapy with issues unrelated to their experience of disability; however, as practitioners, we may not always properly identify it as such. Without some dedicated and specific consideration, there is a danger that therapists might either over-emphasise disability and make it the source of all issues, or ignore it altogether, which risks denying an integral part of the individual's experience of 'being-in-the-world'. Therapy that is specifically provided for disabled individuals is likely to involve some common issues of disability experience such as living with/managing pain and/or physical (or other) limitations or managing medical interventions. It is also important, however, to be aware of the potentially equally disabling and devastating effects of the experience of prejudice and discrimination, and possible internalised oppression that a disabled individual may well live with (Reeve, 2000). Despite the potential for struggle with any/some of these challenges on top of anything else a client might bring, therapists seem to have avoided the consideration that disabled people may require them to have some extra awareness regarding issues relating to social justice (Reeve, 2014). The paltry attention given to the subject area is perhaps less helpful than none; disability is predominantly presented in therapy literature as a gloomy, pathological issue of loss, depression and/or denial (Parkinson, 2006; Reeve, 2000, 2004). Or, worse, the disabled individual's struggle for autonomy and independent identity has been likened to problematic developmental issues in adolescence, asserting significant parallels with the infant/caregiver relationship (Wilson, 2003). This is, to my mind, an irrefutably dangerously patronising construction of disability. The voice of experience of those who know what it means to live with disability is, in this discipline, almost silent (Rosenberg, 2009), and so the dominant perspective remains one of non-disabled assumptions. There are a few notable perspectives from which to consider issues relating to disability that are not presented in mainstream therapeutic literature, such as from Shakespeare (1994), Reeve (2002), Parkinson (2006) and Olkin (2012) – all authors who themselves live with disability. From these perspectives, much of the challenge of living with disability is identified as managing the tensions caused by the various constructions of people as 'disabled'. Historically, British society has viewed disability as a tragic and incurable individual medical issue. Economically, the consequences of disability in capitalist society have reduced individuals to merely either needs- or work-based 'subjects', whilst aesthetically, the current cultural requirement for a specific version of physical 'perfection', as well as total independence, renders those living with any degree of physical otherness and/or need for supported living as utterly hopeless. Combined, these dominant constructions of disability comprehensively serve to brand disabled individuals in contemporary UK society as unattractive, undesirable, biologically inferior, socially devalued and fundamentally disempowered (Shakespeare, 1994).

CORE PRINCIPLES

Models of disability are used to understand and define some of the implications of living with disability. They bring to light the many ways in which society limits and/or enables integration and provide a framework from which we can gain a better understanding of the power play that exists. A working awareness of various models of disability can mobilise insight into some of the attitudes, perceptions and prejudices of society that (usually unconsciously) inform institutions, organisations and individuals about how we relate to, engage with and discriminate against people who live with the experience of disability. Consequently, I briefly outline an overview of the most dominant models of disability currently prevalent in the UK for us to consider our own unchallenged personal attitudes, assumptions and prejudices.

Moral/Religious Model

This model of disability is usually associated with belief systems where presence of impairment or 'otherness' is seen as the embodiment of evil, a punishment from God or, at the very least, an embodied representation of an absence of morals and/or faith.

It is the oldest bias, and requires the disabled individual to exhibit stoic, patient endur-
ance, resilience and strength of moral fibre to be tolerated. It is a fearful and superstitious
construction of disability that places sole responsibility for any issue with the affected
individual and sets in motion a judgemental assessment of personal issues of worth,
value and ability that are directly linked to faith, mindset and effort. In short, to 'solve'
issues of disability as seen through this lens, the disabled individual must overtly work
hard to become 'better' (less frightening/problematic), or risk total rejection/ostracisa-
tion from their community until they eventually die.

Medical Model

The medical understanding of disability is one that assumes any sort of biological
'otherness' to be a defective abnormality of the bodily system that necessarily causes
some disadvantage and must be treated in order to 'fix'. In this context, the expert
medical professional has total power to objectively pathologise and dehumanise the
affected individual by reducing them to a categorisation, dependent on diagnosis, to
determine their future 'treatment'. The model frames disability as a medical devia-
tion and subordination from 'normal' and is often felt to be a 'model of limitations'
where the focus is on the 'defective', and a dependency on professionals is encouraged
(a 'good *patient*'). This medical conceptualisation consequently constructs disability
as something fundamentally disempowering as it denies potential for choice, control
and independence – rendering the affected individual as forever 'in-valid' and trapped
within a medical context and establishment.

Charity/Tragedy Model

This most commonly mobilised model (along with the medical model) constructs disabled people as victims of tragic circumstance, who are to be pitied for their inevitable
suffering. There is an assumption of unhappiness, grief and inevitable loss accompany-
ing the experience of disability, as well as a notion that there is a perpetually unob-
tainable desired quality of life forever out of reach due to the limitations of disability.
The model identifies the non-disabled community as more privileged, and consequently
appeals to their philanthropy to minimise the tragic circumstances of the disabled vic-
tim. Whilst this positioning can be successful in providing much-needed resources/
services not funded by the state, it also perpetuates an often misrepresentative and
offensive stereotype of inevitably helpless and hopeless disabled individuals in need of
care/patronisation and unable to support themselves. Positioning disability as a tragic
issue requiring charity also risks perpetuating the assumption that survival requires segregation and institutionalisation of the individual, rather than properly supported community integration.

Social Model

In an attempt to reclaim some sense of power by challenging the fundamental individualistic focus of all the above models, the social model (the first to be developed by disabled people) highlights the negative impact of the social and physical environment when it fails to accommodate the needs of disabled people. Through this lens, disability has become redefined socio-politically as the detrimental consequence of a society that views limitations caused by impairments as flaws that lead to social devaluation. The social model expressly identifies and seeks to address the socially created 'barriers of participation' that are the result of various ableist environmental factors, and it is through such a lens that disability becomes an overt issue of social justice (Swain & French, 2008). For some non-disabled people, this conceptualisation of disability can be challenging as it necessitates a change in basic assumptions from 'cure of individual' to 'care in community' and a focus on empowering and enabling those who have previously been constructed as defective and fundamentally problematic. For many people living with the experience of disability, however, the model has been a liberating recognition of how context and environment are significant factors in the experience of being dis-abled.

Human Rights Model

The increasingly mobilised disability model centred around human rights moves beyond an illustrative conceptualisation of disability into dynamic activism that offers a theoretical framework for disability public health, focusing on dignity from a human rights perspective (Degener, 2017). It employs a political discourse to shift the focus from dependence to independence by rejecting the privileging of 'normal' over 'abnormal', validating individual differences and needs, and maintaining the importance of cultural identification.

CASE STUDY: ESTHER

The chapter will now explore some personal experiences to help integrate awareness of issues relating to disability for the practitioner and move towards formulating distress as manifestation of conflict between the processes active within an individual, but also the turbulence caused by dynamic conflict between the individual and their environmental/social factors. This then points towards a holistic approach to therapy as best practice.

My Experience

After a road traffic collision some years ago that resulted in my classification as an 'incomplete tetraplegic', I found myself the subject of assessment for therapy. After a long series of questions, the therapist cheerily declared, 'Well, as far as I can tell, you only have two problems'. I was a self-employed, single mother of three small children, and I was trying to recover some semblance of self, life and physical ability from being unable to move from the neck down. As far as I could see, I had more problems than I had ever encountered previously, and all within a personal framework of pressing urgency and fundamental, existential importance... I couldn't imagine what two things he thought were most significant and was keen to know. I asked as much, and his answer changed everything for me: 'You are intelligent and articulate'. I had no idea what this 'expert' could possibly mean by this statement, but I did know that to focus on these things in such a negative way was painfully hopeless-feeling and was totally wrong and destructive. It has taken me some dedicated time to fully understand why this moment felt so offensive and oppressive, and, more importantly, how it could be that someone in his position could feel it would be an okay thing to say.

I will use moments from my existence in subsequent years that have helped my understanding to formulate this case study. My experience is one of acquired disability that has become less impactful and 'visible' as time has gone on: I feel I regularly straddle the divide between identifying, or being identified as, disabled, and non-disabled. I was able-bodied, then dis-abled, and now I can feel I am (and can be seen to be) either, dependent on the context, my body and my frame of mind. It is one perspective only, but also one that has and does shift according to these three primary factors – how it feels (in a situation/moment) to exist, how it feels to (have capacity to) engage, and the context (what expectations are there). These factors are all clearly interconnected and not at all exclusively related to issues of disability. However, they are all constantly impacted by the presence of disability in my life. By identifying and illustrating some pivotal moments, I hope that I might provide an opportunity to challenge each of our embedded assumptions and prejudices and become more aware of some of the perpetuated oppression that surrounds and ensnares disability.

My induction into the world of being disabled occurred over the months I spent in a specialist Spinal Injury Rehabilitation Unit. It quickly became apparent that we (the patients) were all acutely aware of how vulnerable we had become, but less consciously aware of what we were vulnerable to. Whilst we knew we were all in quite different circumstances, we had all been thrown together into a (disparate) group and yet it was here, amongst ourselves, that many of us seemed to find a sort of comfort, understanding and unity that we could find nowhere else. We all wanted and needed to talk about what had and was happening to us, and yet the specific elements of the common topics of conversation were different for each of us, as well as the same. There was one subject however that we were all absolutely in agreement on; whilst the attention to our physical needs was dedicated and comprehensive, our psychological and emotional wellbeing was hardly even acknowledged, let alone addressed. This is no slur on the medical attention we received, which was specialist and excellent and necessary – rather, it starkly illustrated to us that how we felt and what we wanted to communicate and address were not important or even relevant in this environment.

Within an institution that consists of a hierarchy of a specific form of medicalised knowledge, the authorities of such knowledge determine how power is exercised through surveillance and discipline. Such a hierarchy is clear; the individual needing care is at the bottom, consultants at the top, and family, nursing staff and other practitioners at various points in between. On a practical intervention level, this organisational system is often entirely appropriate, yet it can also create psychological tension and distress when the person requiring care and help with functional implications of their physicality feels that decisions are being made on their behalf, seemingly for their own good, and sometimes even contrary to their wishes. I have had experience of being told I was stupid to have opened a window when I was hot (I would apparently get too cold), I was reckless to go to the toilet when I needed to (I would have apparently been at risk), I was causing problems for staff (I didn't feel I needed any pain relief at the moment I was meant to apparently need it) and that I was difficult (I didn't want to participate in a disabled sporting activity that was apparently good for me) as a few (of very many) examples. The effect of such a powerful and persistent paternalistic attitude was fundamentally destructive and disempowering as I began to question my own judgement and became aware of a risk of becoming increasingly disconnected from my own sense of self. Such an attitude denied my maturity in experience, age and cognitive capacity – infantilising me even in relation to taking charge of my own physical needs, functions and, ultimately, lifestyle. The subsequent sense of powerlessness over what happened, when, and even how, to my body (let alone my environment) had a significant negative impact on my sense of worth, value and pride. A sub- or unconsciously adopted paternalistic attitude and medicalised understanding in family members who become implicated in addressing physical needs by having the role of 'carer' thrust upon them can create and perpetuate further power imbalance and lack of agency for the disabled individual who then moves back into the home. Such persistent medical objectification, infantilisation and depersonalisation across environments can erode self-identity and personal strength and leave instead a fearful chasm of vulnerability, dependence and invalidity.

It was in the first months after I returned home that I began to recognise some of the enduring socially constructed effects of disability. Whilst in 'rehabilitation', I had felt more that I was injured than I was disabled – a significant difference in my mind, perhaps, as injury alludes to potential for repair and consequently also hope for 'validity' again. It wasn't until I returned home that I realised that my life was going to be physically forever different. The current welfare state in the UK locates disability on a scale of need rather than productivity, which practically translates into the disabled individual being 'awarded' certain rights and 'privileges' to aid their living at a significant cost of potential loss of autonomy/independence and privacy. It was only when I was first going through the process of a PIP (Personal Independence Payment) assessment (Gov.uk, 2018) that I began to feel angry at this. Without being aware at that time of any specific discourses of disability and oppression, it was still clear to me that there was a covert power being asserted over me under the guise of 'offering' something that was ostensibly enabling. I felt a confusing fundamental disconnect between my experience of disability as something absolutely contextual and ever-changing according to many (often external) factors, and the hostile, rigid, pathological individual-focused criteria that had to be met in order to achieve the unenviable position of being granted financial assistance in recognition of being 'disabled enough'. To qualify for any financial assistance with living and mobility, I first had to surrender my entire private life to the scrutiny of the State via an extensive and invasive questionnaire that focused only on personal deficiency, inability and incapacity, before attending an assessment to determine if what I claimed was my experience was plausible (to a non-disabled assessor). To my shock this included my having to 'prove' that I can't stand on one leg. The stigma of 'scrounging' infused this process, and any relief felt by being awarded such a benefit was offset by significant feelings of failure, loss and diminution.

Most individuals who identify themselves as having a disability in the UK will likely have, at some point, gone through this (or some similar bureaucratic) process of having to 'declare' their disability at the risk of segregation, as well as a perception of humiliation, to receive a degree of practical assistance. For some, this is a case of absolute necessity and there is no choice, but for me, as time has passed, I sometimes now wonder if it might be better to 'hide' my disability and 'manage' – to take on personal responsibility for potentially enduring levels of physical hardship that are not necessary, rather than accept the cost of a level of submission to a more powerful, prejudicial 'other'. Obviously, this choice also brings issues and challenges, not least of which are feelings of isolation and the increased risks of lowered resilience, tolerance and capacity to fully engage in life to the best of my ability.

These moments of having to weigh the costs against the benefits of declaring disability (like in every job or educational course application, for example) also highlight the situational dependence of the question, and the potential for the environment to be the disabling factor. If the social environment is accessible and considerate of issues relating to disability, then the individual is far less likely to feel or be dis-abled. A simple illustration of the many everyday examples of this that I encounter repeatedly is the presence of pedal-controlled bins in disabled toilets. For those of us who cannot always control or move our feet, the lack of thought that has resulted in such a circumstance creates a significant but totally unnecessary issue for me to negotiate, where the disabling factors are the design of the bin and the absence of consideration. Stairs pose a similar issue for me – if I have a meeting to attend that is accessible, then I truly don't consider myself to be disabled; if it is up three floors and there is no lift, I am not only disabled by my environment, but I also feel defeated, humiliated, ostracised and thwarted before the meeting has even begun. On the occasions I have dared allow myself to voice my anger at these situations, I have been accused of 'giving people with disabilities a bad name', 'being unrealistic and demanding' and even being 'a health and safety problem'; the clear message has been that I am the issue, not societal ignorance and/or discrimination.

And, finally, the words of apparent kindness often offered to me, that always disturb me: 'I don't consider you to be disabled'. In this simple exchange, the speaker reveals their (usually subconscious) belief that to be disabled is something so negative as to be almost unthinkable, and certainly something to be pitied. It asserts a position of authority that suggests the relationship encapsulates a task for the non-disabled individual through which to bestow the generous 'gift' of mercy to justify the existence of the relationship. Simultaneously, in the denial of the existence of disability and all the challenges that go with it, the speaker of the statement also acts to silence and invalidate my lived and felt experiences. Such (misguided) charitable benevolence has a painful impact on my self-esteem as in those few words, my validation, authority and worth as an equal human have been threatened and/or denied.

So, returning to the start of this case study, when the expert therapist identified my problems as being 'intelligent and articulate', what he really meant was that I was going to work out that the way society was going to construct and treat me as dis-abled and in-valid was wrong, and that he did not want to be the one to either hear about it or be held accountable.

THERAPEUTIC PRACTICE

Informed awareness of the potential relational interplay of clients' inner and outer worlds demands attention to phenomenological experience and a holistic approach to therapy. The essential commitment of the therapist is to recognise and give value to their client's (inter)subjective experiencing of the world in order to help facilitate their empowerment and actualisation of potential, whilst also appreciating and recognising the forces of their social context (Strawbridge & Woolfe, 2014). By establishing a therapeutic relationship that is overtly equal and collaborative (rather than expert–patient), the well-informed therapist can hand control and power to the disabled individual, thus acknowledging that they have both responsibility and choice. In recognising and valuing their client's subjective experience of both life and disability, the therapist illustrates their awareness that the client cannot be reduced to their disability, or any other singular component part. Also, that their client's emotional reactions to circumstance are all valid and to be respected.

'Third wave' therapies (e.g., mindfulness-based cognitive therapy, dialectical behavioural therapy) are values-, mindfulness- and acceptance-based methods which deal holistically with topics traditionally embraced by humanistic philosophy. Of these, acceptance and commitment therapy adheres to a health model (Hayes et al., 1999), and acknowledges the historical (as well as situational) context of the individual and their distress, making therapy in this vein an absolutely holistic and contextual task. By making a holistic co-constructed formulation of understanding of a client's distress, central focus can be given to that which has been previously obscured by pathology; the operation and consequence of power, the wider social, political and cultural contexts; and the attempts at meaning-making and agency of those who are struggling to survive/live/thrive within their embodied environments. In terms of therapeutic approaches then, a 'bespoke' integrative application of therapeutic formulations co-constructed with the client would be the most privileged when working with disability, and ideally preferring those that take a holistic and values-based approach.

CONCLUSION

I have tried to make use of my own positioning as fluctuatingly (dis)abled to inform all aspects of the chapter as usefully as possible. The experiences outlined above are representative of the consequences of current common attitudes towards disability throughout the UK and can be understood as constructions of disability that are embedded in religious rhetoric, medical practice and cultural representation. It is my feeling that much of society does not realise the level of discrimination and negativity directed at disabled people, in part because it is so deeply ingrained that it has become practically invisible, and certainly infrequently challenged on a personal level. I acknowledge that therapeutically, there can be no simple model or 'easy answer' – instead, in contrast to the simplistic assessments and formulations found in much of the existing literature relating to disability, I suggest that it is only with a holistic, in-depth awareness of forces acting both upon and within a disabled individual that therapists can satisfactorily meet the needs of clients, and potentially avoid ignorantly perpetuating oppressive and prejudiced attitudes and behaviours. It is perhaps easier to slip into using long-established subject discourses in practice; yet the competent, ethical and effective therapist has an obligation to meet any client with awareness of (their own and the client's) self and context.

REFLECTIVE AND CRITICAL THINKING QUESTIONS

1 What informs my personal understanding of disability?
2 What are my assumptions about disability?
3 Do I feel comfortable talking about disability? If not, why not, and what can I do about it?
4 How much/often do I consider my environment from a disabled perspective?
5 Is my therapy space accessible? Does it have parking and appropriate toilet facilities?
6 Have I ever talked about disability with a client?

RECOMMENDED READING AND RESOURCES

Wong, A. (2020). *Disability visibility: First-person stories from the twenty-first century.* Penguin.
Compiled by activist Alice Wong, this is a vibrant collection of well-informed personal essays written by disabled people that gives insight into the vast diversity of disabled experience. With voices representing a broad spectrum of disabilities, it fiercely documents some of the difficulties encountered in everyday life, whilst also celebrating disability culture in our current society. A good starting point for engaging in disability discourse.

Oliver, M. (2009). *Understanding disability: From theory to practice.* Palgrave Macmillan.
Written by a leading academic in disability studies and respected activist, this is an important collection of essays discussing current and enduring theories and policies that affect disabled people. It combines a mixture of personal experience and theoretical exploration and development across disciplines that provides excellent perspective for anyone seeking to understand key issues relating to disability.

Marks, D. (1999). *Disability: Controversial debates and psychosocial perspectives.* Routledge.
Written by a psychotherapist who has been director of the MA in Disability Studies at Sheffield University, this book comprehensively reviews and critically engages with debate around the social construction of disability. It provides a clear analysis of disability as it has been both historically and culturally constructed, and physically experienced.

REFERENCES

Degener, T. (2017). A new human rights model of disability. In V. Della Fina, R. Cera, & G. Palmisano (Eds.), *The United Nations convention on the rights of persons with disabilities* (pp. 19–44). Springer. https://doi.org/10.1007/978-3-319-43790-3_2

Gov.uk. (2018). *Personal independence payments.* www.gov.uk/pip

Hayes, S. C., Strosahl, K. D., & Wilson, K. G. (1999). *Acceptance and commitment therapy: An experiential approach to behavior change.* Guilford Press.

Olkin, R. (2012). *What psychotherapists should know about disability.* Guilford.

Parkinson, G. (2006). Counsellor's attitudes towards disability equality training (DET). *British Journal of Guidance & Counselling, 34*(1), 93–105.

Reeve, D. (2000). Oppression within the counseling room. *Disability & Society, 15*(4), 669–682.

Reeve, D. (2002). Negotiating psycho-emotional dimensions of disability and their influence on identity constructions. *Disability & Society, 17*(5), 493–508.

Reeve, D. (2004). Psycho-emotional dimensions of disability and the social model. In C. Barnes & G. Mercer (Eds.), *Implementing the social model of disability: Theory and research* (pp. 83–100). Disability Press.

Reeve, D. (2014). Counselling and disabled people: Help or hindrance? In J. Swain, S. French, C. Barnes, & C. Thomas (Eds.), *Disabling barriers – enabling environments* (3rd ed.) (pp. 255–261). Sage.

Rosenberg, M. (2009). Harm, liberty, and disability. *Disability Studies Quarterly, 29*(3), 8.

Shakespeare, T. (1994). Cultural representation of disabled people: Dustbins for disavowal? *Disability and Society, 9*(3), 283–299.

Strawbridge, S., & Woolfe, R. (2014). Counselling psychology: Origins, developments, and challenges. In R. Woolfe, S. Strawbridge, B. Douglas, & W. Dryden (Eds.), *Handbook of counselling psychology* (3rd ed.) (pp. 3–22). Sage.

Swain, J., & French, S. (2008). *Disability on equal terms.* Sage.

Wilson, S. (2003). *Disability, counselling, and psychotherapy: Challenges and opportunities.* Palgrave Macmillan.

World Health Organization. (2001). *ICF: International classification of functioning, disability and health.* World Health Organization.

10
SOCIAL JUSTICE INFORMED THERAPY AND NEURODIVERSITY

Stephanie Petty, Lorna Hamilton, Brett Heasman and Natasha Fiberesima

OVERVIEW

This chapter illustrates important social contexts for psychological therapists working with neurodivergent clients. We set out some core principles for working in a social justice informed way, considering the potential for oppression of minoritised clients and what it means to move beyond a deficit-coloured lens. In Chapter 1, social justice is characterised by honouring notions of fairness, equal opportunity and equitable outcomes for social problems. To work with neurodivergent clients in a just way, practitioners must adopt a neurodiversity framework (Pellicano & den Houting, 2022). The term 'neurodiversity' refers to the natural variation in human brain development that underpins the different ways in which individuals experience and interact with the world. We encourage you to think of 'differences' without falling into using the language of 'deficit' or 'disorder' (although these terms are widely used in diagnostic manuals and much of the research literature). Neurodiversity captures a range of neurodevelopmental differences, which are complex in their origins, lack clear biological markers and are therefore largely defined by behaviours. Such differences include autism, attention deficit hyperactivity disorder (ADHD), dyslexia, developmental language disorder, dyscalculia, developmental co-ordination disorder and Tourette's syndrome. Accurate assessment of these, and subsequent support planning, is complex. There is considerable heterogeneity in behaviours and cognitive profiles between individuals with the same diagnosis, and overlap across diagnoses. For example, people with diagnoses of autism and/or ADHD often experience executive skill difficulties, such as planning and cognitive flexibility, which impact on aspects of engaging with psychological therapy.

Dual diagnosis of autism and ADHD has increased sharply in recent years and is newly supported by the updated diagnostic criteria. And yet, practitioners must be able to specialise their practice and demonstrate understanding of what specialised working means (NICE, 2016). Currently, specialism is best understood as learning ways to adapt therapies for individual 'disorders' (for example, Cooper et al., 2018; Spain & Happé, 2020; Young & Bramham, 2012). There is thus a difficult balance to strike between staying apprised of the latest developments in therapeutic working and having confidence to understand individual clients' experience of neurodivergence more holistically than by diagnostic label alone.

In this chapter, we focus on ways of working with autistic clients. This focus is a means to share recommendations for good practice, building on the attention that autism has received in the therapeutic research literature, relative to other types of neurodivergence. However, many of the principles discussed are applicable to neurodevelopmental 'conditions' more broadly as noted throughout to help inform your practice.

CONTEXT

Historical and political contexts continue to shape our work with autistic clients. Autism was originally used as a term to describe a form of schizophrenia. Though this language has since been revised, expectations for an autistic client to prefer being alone, in their own world, without meaningful social relationships continue to prevail. Early studies by Kanner focused on young boys with significant verbal impairments, resulting in an ongoing diagnostic bias towards autism in young boys. As a result, clients belonging to other demographic groups (e.g., adults; women and girls) may report narratives of being missed and misunderstood because of not fitting with these original definitions. Furthermore, with each transformation of definition, autism is presented as a 'static, decontextualised "thing" discoverable by science' (Verhoeff, 2013, p. 444). Even now, the psychiatric diagnostic label determines who can identify as autistic. Autistic people who come to psychological services are, therefore, mostly understood through a lens of being disordered and compared unfavourably with a majority group.

The neurodiversity movement has sought to move away from a pathologising conceptualisation of autism and other experiences. Instead, neurological differences are understood as a core aspect of human diversity and, while impairment and distress are acknowledged, so too are individual strengths and human rights. The advance of the neurodiversity movement has met criticism, especially on the grounds of its potential to promote unhelpful binary reductionism, such as 'neurodivergent' vs 'neurotypical' (Russell, 2020). Nonetheless, we argue that neurodiversity-informed and neurodiversity-affirming therapies are vital and an appropriate form of psychological formulation of lived difference.

Importantly, what has been omitted from our inherited definition of autism – a definition that is then held to be true by many autistic people themselves and their families – are autobiographical accounts. That includes the 'real' experiences of being autistic (Pearson & Rose, 2021). It also includes theoretical work by autistic scholars who have powerfully highlighted the dangers of excluding autistic voice from research, which scale up to societal-level discrimination. One influential example is the 'double empathy problem' (Milton, 2012), a disjuncture that occurs when people hold different norms and expectations of each other, making it hard to establish common ground; hence 'double', because the empathy problem flows in both directions. In the case of different neurotypes, these challenges can be pervasive due to different communication styles, sensory sensitivities to one's environment, and stereotypes about the condition itself. The key to addressing double empathy barriers is reflecting on one's own assumptions and expertise. We therefore demonstrate ways to be curious about the experiences of difference and marginalisation of neurodivergent clients.

This perspective has led to a new influx of language, designed to address the stigmatising way that autism has historically been objectified. In this chapter, we use identity-first language, referring to an 'autistic person', rather than a 'person with autism'; we describe diagnoses as 'co-occurring' rather than 'comorbid' (Bradshaw et al., 2021). Considering your language use is an impactful change that you can make.

Key Terms

Neurodiversity: a noun to describe neurological diversity across a population.
Neurodivergent: an adjective to refer to an individual with a neurodevelopmental difference.
Non-autistic: to describe populations that do not have a diagnosis of autism; however, this reflects a problematic binary autistic/non-autistic distinction grouping. Other types of neurodivergence may exist within this group.
Neurotypical: to describe populations that represent a 'normative neurotype'. We have particular concern with the implied 'typical' neurotype.

The personal meaning of these terms varies widely. Terms in everyday usage, such as 'on the spectrum', are generally not used within the autistic community. We do not recommend any correct use and we advise you to discuss preferred language with the people you are working with.

CORE PRINCIPLES

Consider the different, sometimes conflicting, ambitions of healthcare professionals working with autistic clients (note that we focus on autistic clients rather than therapists, but much of what we say is important to considerations of autistic therapists). There is tension for practitioners and a temptation to simplify the heterogeneity of autism to reduce the complexity of providing health and social care to a growing group of neurodivergent people. However, a social justice perspective reminds us that our conceptualisation of autism must incorporate *real* complexity and the experiences of all. It does not maintain a narrow expectation of what autism should look like. Autism applies to women or those with neutral or marginalised gender identities, adults who did not have the opportunity to be diagnosed in childhood, people who have co-occurring mental ill-health, co-occurring neurodiversity, those who are from minoritised ethnic groups and those with any and all intellectual abilities (Hull et al., 2020).

We live in a world where there are paradigmatically different ways of viewing autism. Some people see it as a disorder with an underlying pathology and identifiable symptoms that require treatment. Other people, notably within autistic-led scholarship and commentary, see autism as central to one's being and indivisible from identity. In this conceptualisation, autism represents meaningful difference in aspects of cognition and behaviour but is not 'worse than' the neuro-normative majority.

Psychological practitioners have the capacity to tolerate complexity and to use the available tools and frameworks to reach a meaningful narrative of understanding for each client. As a practitioner, asking an individual how they define autism is a central part of initial trust-building interactions. Being curious about preferred language and the implications for identity is a valuable starting point in psychological practice.

MENTAL HEALTH AND WELLBEING: CURRENT STATUS AND DEVELOPMENTS

Put simply, a neurodiversity paradigm frames our practice with autistic clients in two important ways. First, we approach our clients without assuming deficit. Second, we work with clients without simply using 'add-ons' to traditional therapeutic approaches.

We first consider what it means to provide psychological assessment, diagnostic and therapeutic services for autistic clients without assuming deficit.

ASSUMING DEFICIT: THE DOUBLE 'DISORDERS' OF AUTISM AND MENTAL HEALTH

Autistic adults are more likely to receive a mental health diagnosis than their non-autistic peers, with particularly high co-occurrence of anxiety and depression (Lever & Geurts, 2016). Further concerns relate to high estimates of loneliness, reduced quality of life and increased suicidality associated with being autistic (Hedley et al., 2018). A challenge faced by many practitioners is how to reach clarity for their autistic client as to whether there are inherent vulnerabilities of being autistic that predispose mental ill-health, or whether we have a flawed way of understanding their experiences.

Consider that some descriptions of mood overlap with descriptions of autism, such as social withdrawal or sleep problems. When describing behaviours using checklists of symptoms, we contribute false positives, whereby an autistic person is considered depressed in mood, or lonely, when they may not be. Similarly, symptoms such as sensory exhaustion and social fatigue can be mistakenly assumed to be evidence of anxiety. Although anxiety is not a core feature of autism, it is the most common co-occurring diagnosis. Anxiety is often better understood in practice than sensory exhaustion or social fatigue. The predominant medical model allows practitioners to assign a diagnostic label of depression or anxiety as an explanation for the difficulties being described. These misunderstandings become part of a person's identity and come to be used to explain times of feeling different, by the person themselves, their friends, family, teachers, employers and wider society. Thus, something that is neurodivergent becomes disordered.

Mood disorders, or emotions, are seemingly experienced and expressed differently by autistic people (Bearss et al., 2016; Uljarević et al., 2018), who are more likely to describe depressive thoughts than they are depressive emotions; emotions can escalate rapidly from limited awareness and take time to be processed. Ways of coping with emotional distress described personally by autistic adults also show differences from neuro-normative assumptions, for example autistic clients first seek reprieve from social and sensory stressors (Petty et al., 2022). Research exploring anxiety experienced by autistic children suggests how our templates for understanding mood can be revised (Rodgers et al., 2016).

The important point here is that scales assessing mood are designed for and normed with non-autistic samples. Autistic people who come to psychological services are often understood via this majority group. A revised starting point in socially just practice is to wonder whether autistic lived experiences are different. First, is there emotional distress? Second, how have experiences of difference contributed, with good reason, to low mood or anxiety, much as we would understand themes of vulnerability or trauma contributing to distress in later life. When presumed different in a negative way, a person's identity takes on strain from having carried an unrecognised burden of marginalisation.

Co-occurrence of diagnoses is a red flag to clinicians. It tells us of likely worsened outcomes for our clients, including reduced wellbeing and increased support needs from society. Other concerns include prolonged prescription of psychiatric medications, diagnostic overshadowing and personal confusion (Maddox et al., 2020). The cost to individual wellbeing is easily seen. The additional costs are to society, to subsequent individuals inferring the meaning of difference or inclusion, perpetuated misunderstandings in research and the misapplied investment of healthcare resources.

WORKING WITH MEANING INSTEAD OF DEFICIT

Personal descriptions of emotions and the development of assessment tools with neurodivergent participants are beginning to offer practical solutions to psychologists who attempt to better understand the important links between neurodiversity and wellbeing. These include placing more emphasis on emotion psychoeducation. Also, consider difficulties in imagining future scenarios, being upset by rules and justices being broken and an accumulation of stress and fatigue from incoming sensory information and social expectations.

A formulation of emotional distress should account for neurodivergent differences in thinking, which interact with the person's unique culture and life-learning. We should ensure that an individual's experience of marginalisation is heard and understood. For those expressing emotional distress, there will be specific interactions to explore, such as the meaning that has been assigned to being different, or the conditions under which the person is able to be themselves. Practitioners need also to consider the vulnerability to traumatic and adverse experiences that can occur with autism (Griffiths et al., 2019). Currently psychological formulation relies upon the clinician's skill in working across different therapeutic models.

WORKING WITHOUT DISCREDITING DIFFERENCE

Chapter 1 introduced the concept of testimonial injustice, which occurs when a client is unable to share their experiences within therapy because being different is decentred or discredited. A temptation when working with neurodivergent clients is to emphasise the shared nature of difference, the spectrum, the relatable experiences. While this is an understandable attempt to avoid deficit-thinking, in our experience it is an unhelpful stance. It has the potential to discredit the often-prolonged experiences of difference when an individual's lifelong experience has been of negotiating dominant expectations of how to think and behave.

From a young age, many autistic people learn to 'mask' autistic behaviours to meet others' normative expectations, for example by limiting talk about topics of focused interest or maintaining eye contact even when uncomfortable (Pearson & Rose, 2021). Young people negotiate conflicting, and often stigmatising, societal discourses about autism as they make sense of themselves (Mesa & Hamilton, 2021). Erasing natural behaviours can come at significant personal cost, both to a person's wellbeing, and to late or missed diagnosis. There are challenges of self-acceptance and self-understanding for many autistic people, notably for those who are neither neurotypical nor 'typically autistic'. Harmens et al. (2022) explored personal narratives of wellbeing and autism diagnosis for females. They described exclusion from being autistic because of the predominant, narrow understanding. Therefore, it is important to hear the personal meaning of both being and becoming autistic. Neurodiversity intersects with other aspects of identity – age, gender, sexuality, socio-economic status, intellectual ability, race and ethnicity – to influence experiences of marginalisation (Botha & Gillespie-Lynch, 2022). Understanding this diversity of autistic experience, alongside the impact of cumulative 'minority stress', is vital for us as clinicians.

Winter and Charura (Chapter 6) invite a principle of collaboration, of working with and having power with, rather than doing to or having power over. Guiding notions are curiosity and willingness to learn. We cannot discredit the experience of difference for the sake of simplicity or ease. Social justice means we must be aware of the personal cost to many people who face significant barriers to understanding themselves, their place in society and their strengths.

PSYCHOLOGICAL PRACTICE WITHOUT 'ADDING ON'

Given the timeline we have had for innovation it might seem uncomplicated to provide person-centred psychological therapy to neurodivergent clients. In fact, this is ambitious.

Though cognitive behavioural therapy (CBT) has been increasingly applied with autistic clients (Spain & Happé, 2020), and clients with ADHD (Young & Bramham, 2012), there are concerns about the many modifications being made to the original therapy, which can be inconsistently applied across services, on an ad-hoc basis, with limited evidence or clinical guidance (Ainsworth et al., 2020). This reflects the latest best practice guidance for psychologists working with autistic clients, which prioritises psychological formulation across therapeutic modalities and clinician judgement, without a clear steer for adhering to theoretical models. Psychologists are asked to modify, rather than design. Furthermore, the availability of only CBT as a psychological intervention does not offer the repertoire of therapies available for non-autistic clients, such as trauma-informed therapy and multidisciplinary interventions including occupational therapy. A helpful stance towards psychological practice can be to ask what the unspoken expectations are of an autistic person when the default assumption is neurotypical. Finally, how we evaluate the effectiveness of therapy needs more scrutiny. What measures would indicate meaningful outcome? And whose voice is being heard?

Designing Inclusive Psychological Therapy

Examples of psychological services designed for a neurodiverse population are lacking. Difficulties in doing so include the inheritance of buildings, processes and protocols, busy-ness and the piecemeal way in which clinicians and organisations come together at the point of service delivery. Tell-tale signs of this reality include buildings without appropriate sound proofing and too many over-subscribed multi-use spaces. Petty and colleagues (2021) provide an example of how to adopt full-service thinking about the needs of autistic clients, including consideration of how to first anticipate an appointment, travel, and the social, sensory, emotional and thinking demands of a psychology appointment. Before arriving, clients know what will happen, who they will interact with, where they can sit and what facilities there are. Service systems allow for gender-neutral pronouns across all interactions. Some clients choose to wait outside the clinic or go ahead to the therapy room alone before an appointment. Waiting areas are free from potentially distracting sensory details including in the décor and choice of seating. No clocks tick. Clinicians avoid wearing perfume or jingling jewellery. There are different and adjustable lighting options including lamps and blinds and music that can be turned up, down or off by the client without need for an interaction. Possible changes that can be tailored to each client include omitting expectations of sharing eye contact, sitting still or answering in a back-and-forth conversation exchange. Some of these details might seem simplistic, but they demonstrate flexibility in working with neurodivergent clients: an assumption of diversity and not an expectation for a client to adapt to a neurotypical default.

When autistic clients and practitioners have agreed priorities for psychological thera-pies, these include psychoeducation around emotions, practical ways to reduce sensory and environmental demands, ways to reduce social expectations, ways to increase cer-tainty around what to expect, more sessions, longer to process change and an emphasis on practising skills learning. These do not fit together neatly within any one psychologi-cal therapy model. These are the beginnings of psychological therapies being designed by stakeholders. However, the design of psychological therapies to best suit the needs of autistic clients is still woefully lacking the voice of autistic clients themselves.

Autistic Service User Voice

A critical overview of the research literature shows that the perspectives of autistic service users are given too little attention (Pellicano et al., 2014). It is typically parents, clinicians and researchers who are most frequently asked to define wellbeing. Research needs to be led by autistic people setting priorities. We must also employ meaningful, inclusive research prac-tices (Fletcher-Watson et al., 2019). Importantly, when asked about priorities for research, autistic people have asked for research into how a neurotypical society might change.

Across autism science there is a growing interest in using 'participatory action research', an umbrella term for a range of methodologies seeking to promote autistic voice (Nicolaidis et al., 2019). Such approaches take a critical stance on issues including use of terminology and valuing lived experience (i.e., autistic expertise) as a counterbal-ance to traditional psychological expertise. Research practices become more creative.

Emerging research topics explore personal narratives of wellbeing and autism: positive coping strategies used within the day-to-day lives of autistic people, including reading to learn socially and for immersion, transportation, and escape (Chapple et al., 2021). Also, online gaming and sharing interests within relationships can be positive relational expe-riences (Umagami et al., 2022). We intend to contribute to a wealth of up-and-coming creative and participatory research outputs.

CASE STUDY: ALEXANDRA

Here we share an anonymised case study written by an autistic adult to give personal voice to central ideas introduced in this chapter, of difference, marginalisation and iden-tity. We encourage you to listen for similar stories in your own practice.

My autism diagnosis came as a surprise to me at the age of 14. Prior to receiving my diagnosis, my GP diagnosed me with anxiety and depression, and this was my only way of understanding why I was different to the people around me. I thought I was just a 'nor-mal' person who did not share the positive attributes that the popular pupils at my school had; I had no concept of how to keep up with them in conversation and I spent most of my time at school alone. My journey to getting a diagnosis came after being bullied out of school. At this stage of my life, I knew there was something different about me, but I had no tangible sense of what made me different beyond comparing myself unfavourably to my peers. I soon started going to hospital frequently for discussions with the mental health team and one day of education per week. Several months later, I remember my mother informing me that the mental health team thought I might be autistic. I knew very little about autism before my diagnosis. I have never felt disappointment at receiving an autism diagnosis; instead, it was a relief. My diagnosis allowed me to approach life with a different way of creating meaning, and to reflect on the struggles I'd had up to this point.

The aftermath of receiving a diagnosis was tough. I expected to access further support to help me make sense of the world around me following my diagnosis, and to do further work on untangling the damaging messages I had received as an undiagnosed autistic person. However, I was given no such support and I was left to cope with the many complex feelings that come from receiving an autism diagnosis alone. When I told some of the other pupils in school about my diagnosis, I was met by disbelief due to how 'normal' I look, and I continue to be met with similar responses now. Sharing my diagnosis with others can feel jarring at times as I have faced numerous communication and sensory challenges in life that have been missed by others, but I am also questioned by others because I do not fit into their idea of what an autistic person should be like, or they dismiss my autistic quirks as behaviours that can be attributed to anyone. Being around fellow autistic people or neurotypical allies has been affirming and validating. Being afforded with the opportunity to be listened to without being judged through a neurotypical lens is valuable. I do not believe autistic people's voices are heard and supported enough in mental health interventions and research, and some therapeutic interventions for autistic people continue to prioritise autistic people learning to appear more neurotypical as opposed to learning about their frame of reference and prioritising the goals that are important to them. Learning how to value myself in the face of microaggressions due to my differences has been my most valuable lesson following my diagnosis. The negative self-worth I held prior to this shifted as I realised that I am not a flawed, lesser version of a neurotypical person; I am a first-rate neurodivergent person, and this is a perspective that I hope will become more widely known as opposed to perceiving autism as a deficit.

CONCLUSIONS

As psychological practitioners working with neurodivergent clients, we must hold in mind 'the social'. This means understanding the historical context and current, rapidly shifting understandings. It means being curious about and centring personal narratives of difference. Holding in mind the social also means framing the 'problems' of difference as existing within a particular context. Therapy might include meaning-making alongside social change, rather than aiming to change the individual towards fitting with the majority. We invite you to be curious about language use around neurodiversity and the implications for identity, to be open and willing to learn about personal meaning and the cumulative toll of marginalisation, to consider neurodivergence as an alternative to disorder, and to begin with an assumption of diversity, designing practice with consideration of the unspoken majority expectations of the neuro-normative.

REFLECTIVE AND CRITICAL THINKING QUESTIONS

1 How might your delivery of therapy have been unintentionally stigmatising – how do power, opportunity, wealth, privilege, rights and ease of access determine who you work with?
2 How can we repair the social memory for older neurodivergent people given the turbulence and stigma of past definitions?
3 Does the neurodiversity movement include all autistic people when the voice of people with learning disabilities is rarely heard?

RECOMMENDED READING AND RESOURCES

British Psychological Society. (2021). *Working with autism: Best practice guidelines for psychologists*. British Psychological Society.
This text gives comprehensive guidance to psychological practitioners in their working with autistic clients.

Pellicano, E., & den Houting, J. (2022). Annual research review: Shifting from 'normal science' to neurodiversity in autism science. *Journal of Child Psychology and Psychiatry*, *63*(4), 381–396.
This article critically engages with debate around concepts of normal science, and thus provides an analysis of neurodiversity and a social justice approach.

REFERENCES

Ainsworth, K., Robertson, A. E., Welsh, H., Day, M., Watt, J., Barry, F., Stanfield, A., & Melville, C. (2020). Anxiety in adults with autism: Perspectives from practitioners. *Research in Autism Spectrum Disorders*, *69*. https://doi.org/10.1016/j.rasd.2019.101457

Bearss, K., Taylor, C. A., Aman, M. G., Whittemore, R., Lecavalier, L., Miller, J., ... & Scahill, L. (2016). Using qualitative methods to guide scale development for anxiety in youth with autism spectrum disorder. *Autism*, *20*(6), 663–672. https://doi.org/10.1177/1362361315601012

Botha, M., & Gillespie-Lynch, K. (2022). Come as you are: Examining autistic identity development and the neurodiversity movement through an intersectional lens. *Human Development*, *66*(2), 93–112.

Bradshaw, P., Pickett, C., van Driel, M. L., Brooker, K., & Urbanowicz, A. (2021). 'Autistic' or 'with autism'?: Why the way general practitioners view and talk about autism matters. *Australian Journal of General Practice*, *50*, 104–108.

Chapple, M., Williams, S., Billington, J., Davis, P., & Corcoran, R. (2021). An analysis of the reading habits of autistic adults compared to neurotypical adults and implications for future interventions. *Research in Developmental Disabilities, 115*, 104003.

Cooper, K., Loades, M. E., & Russell, A. (2018). Adapting psychological therapies for autism. *Research in Autism Spectrum Disorders, 45*. https://doi.org/10.1016/j. rasd.2017.11.002

Fletcher-Watson, S., Adams, J., Brook, K., Charman, T., Crane, L., Cusack, J., Leekam, S., Milton, D., Parr, J. R., & Pellicano, E. (2019). Making the future together: Shaping autism research through meaningful participation. *Autism, 23*(4), 943–953. https://doi.org/10.1177/1362361318786721

Griffiths, S., Allison, C., Kenny, R., Holt, R., Smith, P., & Baron-Cohen, S. (2019). The Vulnerability Experiences Quotient (VEQ): A study of vulnerability, mental health and life satisfaction in autistic adults. *Autism Research, 12*(10), 1516–1528.

Harmens, M., Sedgewick, F., & Hobson, H. (2022). The quest for acceptance: A blog-based study of autistic women's experiences and well-being during autism identification and diagnosis. *Autism in Adulthood, 4*(1), 42–51.

Hedley, D., Cai, R., Uljarević, M., Wilmot, M., Spoor, J. R., Richdale, A., & Dissanayake, C. (2018). Transition to work: Perspectives from the autism spectrum. *Autism, 22*(5), 528–541. https://doi.org/10.1177/1362361316687697

Hull, L., Petrides, K. V., & Mandy, W. (2020). The female autism phenotype and camouflaging: A narrative review. *Review Journal of Autism and Developmental Disorders, 1*, 1–2.

Lever, A. G., & Geurts, H. M. (2016). Psychiatric co-occurring symptoms and disorders in young, middle-aged, and older adults with autism spectrum disorder. *Journal of Autism and Developmental Disorders, 46*, 1916–1930.

Maddox, B. B., Crabbe, S., Beidas, R. S., Brookman-Frazee, L., Cannuscio, C. C., Miller, J. S., Nicolaidis, C., & Mandell, D. S. (2020). 'I wouldn't know where to start': Perspectives from clinicians, agency leaders, and autistic adults on improving community mental health services for autistic adults. *Autism, 24*(4), 919–930.

Mesa, S., & Hamilton, L. G. (2021). 'We are different, that's a fact, but they treat us like we're different-er': Understandings of autism and adolescent identity development. *Advances in Autism*. https://doi.org/10.1108/AIA-12-2020-0071

Milton, D. E. (2012). On the ontological status of autism: The 'double empathy problem'. *Disability & Society, 27*(6), 883–887.

National Institute for Health and Care Excellence (NICE). (2016). *Autism spectrum disorder in adults: Diagnosis and management* [CG142]. www.nice.org.uk/guidance/cg142

Nicolaidis, C., Raymaker, D., Kapp, S. K., Baggs, A., Ashkenazy, E., McDonald, K., Weiner, M., Maslak, J., Hunter, M., & Joyce, A. (2019). The AASPIRE practice-based guidelines for the inclusion of autistic adults in research as co-researchers and study participants. *Autism, 23*(8), 2007–2019. https://doi.org/10.1177/1362361319830523

Pearson, A., & Rose, K. (2021). A conceptual analysis of autistic masking: Understanding the narrative of stigma and the illusion of choice. *Autism in Adulthood, 3*, 52–60.

Pellicano, E., & den Houting, J. (2022). Annual Research Review: Shifting from 'normal science' to neurodiversity in autism science. *Journal of Child Psychology and Psychiatry*, *63*(4), 381–396.

Pellicano, E., Dinsmore, A., & Charman, T. (2014). What should autism research focus upon? Community views and priorities from the United Kingdom. *Autism*, *18*(7), 756–770.

Petty, S., Bergenheim, M.-L., Mahoney, G., & Chamberlain, L. (2021). Adapting services for autism: Recommendations from a specialist multidisciplinary perspective using freelisting. *Current Psychology*. https://doi.org/10.1007/s12144-021-02061-3

Petty, S., Trickett, A., Thompson, K., Garbutt, R., & Saunders, M. (2022). Revising our understanding of emotional distress for autistic adults; call for research. *Current Psychology*. https://doi.org/10.1007/s12144-022-03254-0

Rodgers, J., Wigham, S., McConachie, H., Freeston, M., Honey, E., & Parr, J. R. (2016). Development of the anxiety scale for children with autism spectrum disorder (ASC-ASD). *Autism Research*, *9*(11), 1205–1215.

Russell, G. (2020). Critiques of the neurodiversity movement. In S. Kapp (Ed.), *Autistic community and the neurodiversity movement* (pp. 393–410). Palgrave Macmillan. https://doi.org/10.1007/978-981-13-8437-0_21

Spain, D., & Happé, F. (2020). How to optimise cognitive behaviour therapy (CBT) for people with autism spectrum disorders (ASD): A Delphi study. *Journal of Rational-Emotive & Cognitive-Behavior Therapy*, *38*. https://doi.org/10.1007/s10942-019-00335-1

Uljarević, M., Richdale, A. L., McConachie, H., Hedley, D., Cai, R. Y., & Merrick, H. (2018). The hospital anxiety and depression scale: Factor structure and psychometric properties in older adolescents and young adults with autism spectrum disorder. *Autism Research*, *11*. https://doi.org/10.1002/aur.1872

Umagami, K., Remington, A., Lloyd-Evans, B., Davies, J., & Crane, L. (2022). Loneliness in autistic adults: A systematic review. *Autism*. https://doi.org/10.1177/13623613221077721

Verhoeff, B. (2013). Autism in flux: A history of the concept from Leo Kanner to DSM-5. *History of Psychiatry*, *24*(4), 442–458.

Young, S., & Bramham, J. (2012). *Cognitive-behavioural therapy for ADHD in adolescents and adults: A psychological guide to practice*. John Wiley & Sons.

11

SOCIAL JUSTICE INFORMED THERAPY AND GENDER

Lynne Gabriel

OVERVIEW

Injustice anywhere is a threat to justice everywhere. (Martin Luther King, Jr, 1963)

This chapter focuses on key issues, concepts and practices for working with gender in therapeutic contexts and considers embedding socially just and informed approaches in therapeutic work associated with gender. This topic is seldom covered in any depth or detail on counselling or therapy training courses, yet it is central to human beings' lived experiences and perspectives and is a core area of human mental health and well-being. In recent years, gender work has taken on compelling, complex and conflicted dimensions, with increasing focus upon marginalised gender minorities, and in particular transgendered people. In sociology and psychology, gender is now recognised as a complex psychosocial construct (Levitt, 2019) and this chapter conveys both the complexities of gender and the injustices experienced by those who represent a range of gender identities. In terms of defining gender, the World Health Organization describe it as:

> characteristics of women and men that are socially constructed, while sex refers to
> those that are biologically determined. People are born female or male but learn to
> be girls and boys who grow into women and men. This learned behaviour makes
> up gender identity and determines gender roles. (World Health Organization, 2002)

Whilst this definition hints at nuanced concepts of gender, it excludes inter-sexed people. Other exclusions include those who identify as non-binary and those who are transgendered. Notably, WHO published an updated International Classification of Diseases (ICD11) in 2018, in which transgender was no longer classified as a mental disorder. To support deeper understanding of how people express their gender identity, practitioners can seek definitions and descriptions that offer inclusive, non-oppressive, psychosocial definitions that have value and meaning for both clients and their therapists. There is agreement that pre-existing definitions do not capture gender and recent studies have sought to generate frameworks for diverse gender identities, including sexual configurations theory (Abed et al., 2019) which offers a more inclusive biological and cultural understanding of gender and has been valued and well received in studies with gender and sexual minorities; however, it requires further research with those who identify as heterosexual. This chapter presents content to support working with gender, poses questions for reflection and invites reflexive practice. It also provides resources and signposts helpful materials, with the aim of providing support for practitioners to develop their *practice toolkits* for working with gender. The term *practitioner* is used here to denote a range of distinct roles within helping professions including *counsellor, psychotherapist, therapist, counselling psychologist, supervisor, researcher* and *trainer*.

CONTEXT

Concepts of Gender

Gender is a concept that conveys an aspect of human identity. It impacts all humans. At the core of human life are organising systems and protocols, gender and sexual identities and norms, and heterosexual or LGBTQI+ relationships that play out in the context of patriarchal and heterosexual cultures. The patriarchy has been described as a system of inequality that has features and dynamics like racism or classism (Hartsock, 1983). Gender roles of 'woman' and 'man' predominate. However, a male/female gender binary, rooted in invidious colonial concepts, no longer adequately captures, or represents, changes in how gender is perceived and enacted in global cultures across recent decades (Lindqvist et al., 2021). Moreover, a binary system excludes those who see themselves outside of or between the usual gender dichotomies. Whether intentional or unintentional, this excludes those who do not sit within a male/female dichotomy (Lindqvist et al., 2021), including people who are non-binary or who are biologically inter-sexed.

External and internalised discriminatory attitudes and behaviours – *whether known and intentional or edge of awareness/out of awareness* – can elicit negative assumptions or microaggressions related to gender. For example, I have lost count of the number of times people have presumed that my life partner is a man; I am married to a woman. My wife and I have been together for over thirty years. My own encounters and connections with gender and the evolution of ways of expressing my gender and sexuality have shifted across the decades. I am contented in my life, as a woman, married to another woman. I eschew personal 'labels' such as lesbian, whilst also recognising that for many, 'labels', or gender and sexuality identifiers, are an important part of social, relational, community, cultural and political identities. I have researched with, worked with and counselled people from LGBTQ+ communities, as well as people who identify as heterosexual or inter-sexed, and my lived experiences reflexively inform my personal and practitioner conceptualisations of gender.

Although gender expression and sexual preferences may be protected in law (UK), discriminatory and oppressive situations continue to be common occurrences for gender minorities. A prime example occurred recently in the UK. The government demonstrated potentially oppressive decision-making when it excluded trans people from new legislation banning conversion therapies (The Guardian, 2022). This represents an important area of gender identity, yet it is essential that non-discriminatory and inclusive evidence-based research and informed decisions contribute to bringing about appropriate change and protection.

Gender Injustices

The notion of *justice for gender* is central to this chapter. Gender injustices prevail across multiple gendered contexts including, for example, women and men as victims of domestic violence, women having less workplace opportunities, and women from black and ethnic minority groups who face intersecting and interlocking injustices associated with female gender, misogyny and racism. These examples raise social, cultural and political dimensions that have sat in uneasy alliance with the world of counselling and psychological therapies. Yet clients, by the very nature of their citizenship and lived experiences, bring the external world into consulting rooms. Practitioners need to be alert to how their clients encounter, or are subjected to, gender injustices and microaggressions.

Issues associated with gender equality, diversity and inclusion exist across cultures and countries. Parmenter et al.'s (2021) research on LGBTQ+ and people of colour (PoC) highlights interlocking forces that intensify discriminatory or heterosexist behaviours and experiences. Their project found that LGBTQ+ PoC felt excluded from predominantly white queer communities and did not experience the benefits of solidarity, group identity, belonging and kinship that can accrue through being part of minority LGBTQ+ communities.

Researchers have explored multiple and complex issues associated with gender, yet few pragmatic practice solutions have been identified. To provide a research context conducive to inclusive engagement with gender minorities Levitt and colleagues (2022) used creative writing to elicit LGBTQI+ peoples' perceptions and experiences of injustice, exclusion and discrimination. The writing activities took place within a non-pathologising, accepting and facilitative context, enabling more authentic and meaningful engagement. Provision of an inclusive, non-discriminatory clinical and research environment is likely to be a core condition that can contribute to successful therapy.

Intersectionality

Complex intersecting and interlocking forces can impact peoples' perceptions of and attitudes towards gender, within both therapeutic contexts and wider society.

Intersectionality identifies multiple factors of advantage and disadvantage (see Chapter 3). Examples of these factors include gender, sex, race and ethnicity, class, sexuality and disability.

The concept of *intersectionality* was first introduced by a feminist law scholar in the late 1980s (Crenshaw, 1989). Kimberlé Crenshaw identified and explored interlocking factors that disadvantaged women. Crenshaw's work identified multiple interlocking systems of power and pervasive oppression faced by women who were members of black and minority ethnic groups. Such interlocking systems of oppression can also operate to further disadvantage individuals whose gender identity is more fluid than the dichotomous male/female binary (Collins & Levitt, 2022; Levitt, 2019; Parmenter et al., 2021). The more interlocking factors and forces there are, the more oppressive and limiting it is for persons subjected to them, and the greater the need for practitioners who can facilitate inclusive and collaborative practices.

Critical Praxis

When developing an understanding of how interacting forces or factors might influence clients presenting for psychological therapies and mental health support, it is helpful to critique any limiting or excluding contexts and processes. Essentially, *critical praxis* (Kridel, 2010) involves the critical and reflexive 'unpacking' and critiquing of protocols and practices. This cultivates a way to remain informed and up to date. Fostering an inquisitive and critical inquiry approach when working with people who present with gender issues or challenges will provide a fertile context in which factors and experiences can be collaboratively explored.

CORE PRINCIPLES

This section considers ways of working that embed justice and facilitate compassionate, collaborative and constructive decision making during therapeutic work associated with gender. Table 11.1 below sets out key knowledge and skills to support working with gender. The knowledge, skills and ways of working are derived from key authors and papers noted in this chapter, as well as from principles and practices derived from relational ethics (Gabriel & Casemore, 2009) and pluralistic approaches (McLeod, 2017; Smith & De La Prida, 2021).

Additional explanatory narrative, to illustrate content from the table, is provided. This is offered in the spirit of an approach to working with gender that is non-discriminatory, inclusive, dialectical, and brought into being and experiencing through the practitioner and client/person intentionally working in co-productive ways. This approach is followed in the case study below, to exemplify key aspects of working with gender in a psychological therapies context.

Table 11.1 Key aspects of working with gender in therapeutic contexts

Meta-components for working with gender	Competencies
Knowledge and understanding	• Reflexivity as a *way of being* • Knowledge that genders are fluid, not fixed; there are multiple gender identities • Understanding that seemingly intractable and contradictory factors, forces or variables co-exist in states of oppression or intersectional disadvantage • Intentional practice to actively build cultural competency • Open to learning from clients with lived experience • Understanding of internalised oppression, discrimination or injustice • Awareness of rights groups and political, cultural, social and community influences in relation to gender • Recognition and understanding of women, gender and wellbeing • Recognition and understanding of men, gender and wellbeing • Recognition and understanding of LGBTQI+ gender identities and wellbeing • Knowledge of people who are biologically inter-sexed • Understanding that people may be defensive and feel unable to share, because of past experiences of pervasive oppression, discrimination, exclusion or 'gaslighting' and multiple microaggressions • Knowledge of specialist charities and organisations for networking, referrals and client access
Skills	• Practitioner reflexivity • Relational skills including compassionate presence, authenticity, congruence, being non-judgemental, relationship building and communication skills • Creation and co-creation of a helping context that is conducive to collaborative conversations and open to exploration of gender and sexual identity matters • Create a supportive therapy environment and relationship for clients to share their current gender/sex identity • Able to explore gender if the client wants to, or feels able to • Develop dialectical discussions – identify opposing forces, conflicting or troubled content, people and events, and generate mediating and enabling conversations in collaboration with the client • Able to facilitate collaborative, co-produced decision making between practitioner and client • Capacity to challenge own and client's internal and external injustices through compassionate conversations • Able to share relevant information in the spirit of positive dialectical discussion within a therapeutic context
A pluralistic framework for working with gender	• A collaborative, dialogical, co-produced and compassionate way of working with gender • Co-created contracting and decision-making throughout therapy • Identification of client preferences to build client participation, ownership and agency in the helping process • Use of reasoned and deliberate practice, in dialogue with clients • Use of meta-communication throughout therapy work • Development of therapeutic concepts and theoretical choices, decisions and practices in collaborative dialogue with the client

Essentially, the information offered here can be construed as *practitioner toolkit* materials. Having a literal or imaginary toolkit bag can be a great practice aide. My own toolkit bag is real, in the form of a beautiful large carpet bag full of artefacts, creative materials, and objects that I have used in practice across three plus decades.

Knowledge and Understanding

Practitioner reflexivity is central to all helping work. It can be both embedded in a practitioner's way of being, and perceived as a skill that can be engendered as appropriate to the clinical or mental health context. Reflexivity is essential when working with the complexities of gender and associated identities, enabling organic, fluid and compassionate critique of helping practice. Ethical reflexivity also provides 'scaffolding' that supports both practitioner and client in flexing therapy process, content and relationship (BACP, 2021). This is important, as some perceive and experience gender as a fluid and dynamic state, not a fixed entity. For those questioning their identity, there are multiple gender identities that could be involved in their processes of exploration. Working reflexively also supports practitioners to work with paradoxical, seemingly intractable, contradictory factors, or forces, which can co-exist in states of oppression or intersectional disadvantage.

Knowledge to inform your intentionality and associated actions as a reflexive practitioner continues to build over years, as information, abilities, skills and practice hours are accrued. When first working with gender in a helping context, aim to explore intentional practice and build cultural competency. Research the subject of gender through professional texts, research papers, reports and, importantly, actively listen to and learn from people with lived experience. Enhance your knowledge and understanding of gendered roles, societal perceptions of binary gender stereotypes of 'man' and 'woman', as well as LGBTQI+ people, and those who are inter-sexed.

As part of generating a conceptual understanding of gender work, build your awareness of local or national rights groups and political, cultural and social influences operating in and influencing communities and societies in relation to gender. To support reflexive and informed practice, build networked 'communities of courage' that can influence dissipation of discrimination and oppression. Identify potential referral pathways or portals, including supervisory contexts in case you encounter aspects of gender that are outside your competence or comfort zone, and you need to seek information or support. Aim to build 'networks for courage' – that is people with whom you can discuss or challenge concepts, ideas, instances or events when working with gender. For example, this network could include your supervisor, as well as colleagues in specialist agencies, or practitioner colleagues in a professional support group.

Skills

Alongside knowledge and understanding, practitioners' core skills of compassion, care, authenticity, congruence and being non-judgemental sit well with relationship and communications building abilities to create a context conducive to collaborative conversations. Whatever a practitioner's core training or education, these skills can prepare the therapy context for therapeutic work where the client can be invited to share their gender and any associated issues or injustices in an inclusive and supportive space. It is possible to challenge internal and external injustices through compassionate conversations.

In therapy work with gender, it can be helpful to develop *dialectical discussions*. In essence, a dialectical discussion within the context of a supportive therapy space provides a reasoned and relationally ethical way of exploring opposing forces, or conflicting content, people or events that are contributing to a client/person's issues or situation. In some therapy approaches this can translate as 'parts' work, with intentional work with different 'voices' or 'parts' representing conflicting internalised material being presented by the client. Dialectical discussion can in turn inform the generation of mediating and enabling conversations and narratives. See Shapiro's (2016) helpful publication on working with ego parts.

Skills of value for generating dialectical discussions include having a well-developed *repertoire of interpersonal skills* to support the therapeutic holding of opposing content and processes within therapy sessions. Importantly, the process can involve *distress tolerance skills*; working collaboratively with the client to identify resources, activities and points of support during difficult moments. These might include people and places of support, as well as self-soothing activities.

Using a Framework to Support Practice

A pluralistic approach offers a collaborative way of working with gender. Given that people presenting in therapeutic settings with gender issues are likely to have encountered multiple injustices, a pluralistic approach, which holds social justice central to therapy concepts and practices, provides an effective way of framing the work and relational processes. You can use a range of evidence-based interventions and approaches commonly included in a pluralistic framework for therapeutic practice, including the following:

- *Case formulation* – working with the client to identify therapy aims and ways of working, including which therapy approaches could be integrated into the therapy content and process.
- *Working with client preferences* – the conditions and activities that clients want or prefer.
- *Collaborative decision-making* – begins from the beginning of therapy and remains through to completion, involving both client and therapist in making decisions about therapy content, process and progress.
- *Meta-communication* – in essence, communication about what and how client and therapist are communicating; a reflective and reflexive process that can richly deepen the meaning-making potential of the therapy.

See Cooper and McLeod (2010), Cooper and Dryden (2016), McLeod (2017) and Smith and De La Prida (2021) who offer a range of excellent texts on working pluralistically, and their publications provide accessible practitioner resources.

Those working within the psychological professions will encounter gender in multiple ways – whether as a known/unknown, or intentional/unintentional aspect of the therapy content and process. Some practitioners may find it a challenging prospect to explore a person's gender and it is likely that not all practitioner training courses will provide adequate content on working with human gender, leaving practitioners inadequately equipped.

Increasingly, gender minorities are likely to consider entering the psychological professions as a means of providing accessible therapy. It is essential that the professions can provide adequate training, as well as representation of minorities within an education and clinical context. Of contemporary significance, and thus by necessity front and centre for professional bodies and practitioners from the psychological professions, is the challenge faced by trans people. This is a professional and societal challenge that will continue to play out in the next few years and one that practitioners cannot ignore. Additionally, other LGBTQI+ clients will continue to experience discriminatory societal attitudes and access to supportive psychological therapies will be important for many. As noted earlier in the chapter, challenges faced by women in patriarchal cultures will continue to be presented in clinical contexts. Additionally, archaic and toxic colonial attitudes will continue to be challenged as we advance our theoretical, conceptual and pragmatic frameworks for effective work with gender.

The case study below provides a clinical example and links the client experience to chapter content, to exemplify working with gender in a therapy context.

CASE STUDY: DEBORAH

Deborah presented for counselling for depression and anxiety in a community counselling service where clients could access up to 20 sessions of therapy. Early in the counselling work, Deborah disclosed that they were a transgendered woman and were struggling to adjust to the loss of their marriage and the associated family and friendship relationships. Their wife was unable to accept Deborah's presentation and presence as a woman and had left the marital home, taking their three children. Longstanding friendships with cis and heterosexual couples they had previously socialised with were fast disappearing. Hostile responses from family members meant that Deborah was feeling excluded and isolated. They worked as an accountant and for the past year had been living and working as a woman. Some colleagues shunned Deborah; several seemed ok with their new gender identity and did engage in the workplace, although did not include them in any social activities. Increasingly Deborah was feeling alone and isolated and hoped that counselling could help them move forward in life.

For years they had felt like they were 'in the wrong skin' and to shift their public and private identity from Martin to Deborah was a phenomenally fraught experience. Their transition from male to female was traumatising, yet they felt driven to be the person they wanted to become. Their wife initially supported Deborah's exploration of their gender, but swiftly became antagonistic when they realised their partner seriously questioned their gender identity and was serious about wanting to transition from a male to female identity.

Deborah's counsellor, Sarah, identified as a heterosexual woman and used the pronoun 'she'. Sarah had experience of working with people from diverse sexual identities and knew Heidi Levitt's psychosocial conceptualisation (Levitt, 2019) of therapeutic work with gender minorities. Levitt's model identifies four key domains of significance for work with trans people: psychological, cultural, interpersonal and sexual. Each of these plays a part in the lived experience and perceptions of gender minority people. For Deborah, the psychological impact of recognising that their identity was not male but female was both heart-breaking and ground-breaking.

In working with Deborah, Sarah shared in therapy how working with the four domains identified by Levitt's research could provide a helpful framework for Deborah and Sarah to explore aspects of gender and identity; in particular, how these manifested and were lived and experienced by Deborah. Working through the psychological, cultural, interpersonal and sexual domains brought new understandings and insights for Deborah, who came to realise that transitioning to being a woman was a central aim. Deborah and Sarah explored internalised shame and oppression, stigma in work and relational contexts, building new connections and relationships, and recognition of the sexual dimensions of transitioning, including sexual preferences as well as Deborah's physical presentation. Throughout the therapy, Deborah and Sarah worked collaboratively to make decisions on therapy content and process and, over time, Deborah found learning about and encountering new concepts and ways of working in the secure therapeutic setting could be transferred to connections and interactions outside of therapy.

Deborah found dialectical discussions and associated creative parts work a helpful 'tool' to challenge internalised shame and oppression, as well as to build confidence in their life and gender choices. Deborah and Sarah worked together for a year, following which Deborah was planning future surgery to support their complete transition to living as a woman. Additionally, with Sarah's encouragement and affirmation, Deborah was networking and socialising with LGBTQI+ people and building a sense of belonging and community, as well as competence and confidence to be authentic and congruent in their lived life as a woman.

In this case study the therapist, Sarah, was a compassionate, competent and conscientious presence for the client. They were aware of potential implications of political decisions taken by a government – that is, the UK government decision not to include transgendered people in their bill to protect people from conversion therapies. This generated significant tension and anxiety for the therapist and raised the challenging question of how they could influence political and professional actions in relation to people from gender minorities. The client had already received treatment and was awaiting surgery. For others who have not transitioned yet, the climate could be less conducive to positive and proactive gender transitions. Whilst professional bodies have a responsibility to lobby and campaign for humane actions for transgendered people, lobbying groups and individual practitioners too are called to action. Transgender issues are politically, socially and culturally contended, as well as emotionally charged and divisive. Acknowledging multiplicity and flexibility is essential, along with awareness of internal and external biases or discriminatory attitudes (West et al., 2021). In this respect, practitioner reflexivity and the judicious use of supervisory contexts are essential to support good practice and to minimise unintentional or intentional injustices.

CONCLUSION

Gender is a richly complex and diverse aspect of human existence and one that continues to evolve over time, particularly in relation to trans identities and societal and political oppression. It is evident that human gender and sexual expression are complex representations of personal and relational preferences and understandings, and perspectives and therapeutic approaches will continue to evolve over time. A pluralistic approach, with its overt vision and aims of challenging injustices and working collaboratively to co-produce therapeutic content and processes, offers an excellent framework for working with gender. Materials to support this work have been highlighted in the chapter and are included in the reference list.

The chapter has provided key content to utilise when working with gender in a therapy context. A core takeaway message is the importance of remembering the value of utilising an organising framework for work with gender – one that values justice and foregrounds co-produced, collaborative ways of working. Table 11.1 provided components to inform the work and in the sections above offered explanatory narratives and ways of working that can be utilised individually, or in seminars, training or supervision contexts.

The final sections below signpost further reading and resources, as well as key questions to inform good practice in working with gender. These could helpfully be explored in a training or supervisory context to support development of competencies and appropriate ways of being when working with gender.

REFLECTIVE AND CRITICAL THINKING QUESTIONS

1 What impact might internalised oppression have on clients from gender stigmatised, gender non-conforming and LGBTQI+ communities?
2 How might external oppression and disenfranchisement impact people from gender stigmatised, gender non-conforming and LGBTQI+ communities?

3   What therapeutic approach(es) might best fit working with clients on matters or content associated with gender?

4   How can I keep my knowledge and understanding of human gender and associated matters up to date?

RECOMMENDED READING AND RESOURCES

GIRES – Gender Identity Research & Education Society – Improving the Lives of Trans People (gires.org.uk); a UK charity who provide support for trans people as well as resources for those working in the field.

Generate (generateuk.org); a UK based charity that provides support for people questioning their gender identity, as well as information to inform those who work with people questioning their identity.

ManKind Project UK and Ireland (mankindprojectuki.org); a UK and Ireland charity who provide practical, emotional and psychological support to men, as well as resources of value for those working with gender.

Women's Aid UK (womensaid.org.uk); a UK charity who provide support to women and children, as well as crisis accommodation.

REFERENCES

Abed, E. C., Schudson, Z. C., & Gunther, O. (2019). Sexual and gender diversity among sexual and gender/sex majorities: Insights via sexual configurations theory. *Archives of Sexual Behaviour, 48*(5). https://doi.org/10.1007/s10508-081-1340-2

BACP. (2021). *GPiA044. Ethical decision-making in the counselling professions*. BACP.

Collins & Levitt ref to add in: Kathleen M. Collins & Heidi M. Levitt (2021). Healing from heterosexism: A discovery-oriented task analysis of emotion-focused writing. *Journal of Gay & Lesbian Mental Health*. doi: 10.1080/19359705.2021.1876805

Cooper, M., & Dryden, W. (2016). *The handbook of pluralistic counselling and psychotherapy*. Sage.

Cooper, M., & McLeod, J. (2010). *Pluralistic counselling and psychotherapy*. Sage.

Crenshaw, K. W. (1989). *Demarginalizing the intersection of race and sex: A black feminist critique of antidiscrimination doctrine, feminist theory and antiracist politics*. Columbia Law School.

Gabriel, L., & Casemore, R. (2009). *Relational ethics in practice: Narratives from counselling & psychotherapy*. Routledge.

Hartsock, N. (1983). *Money, sex and power: Toward a feminist historical materialism*. Longman.

King Jr, M. L. (1963) Letter from a Birmingham jail. *Birmingham News*.

Kridel, C. (2010). Critical praxis. In *Encyclopedia of curriculum studies* (Vol. 1, p. 151). SAGE Publications. https://dx.doi.org/10.4135/9781412958806.n90

Levitt, H. (2019). A psychosocial genealogy of LGBTQ+ gender: An empirically based theory of gender and gender identity cultures. *Psychology of Women Quarterly, 43*(3), 275–297.

Levitt, H., Collins, K. M., Maroney, R. M., & Roberts, T. S. (2022). Healing from heterosexist experiences: A mixed method intervention study using expressive writing. *Psychology of Sexual Orientation and Gender Diversity, 9*(2), 152–164. https://doi.org/10.1037/sgd0000478

Lindqvist, A., Gustafsson Sendenb, M., & Renstrom, E. A. (2021). What is gender, anyway: A review of the options for operationalising gender. *Psychology and Sexuality, 12*(4), 332–344. https://doi.org/10.1080/19419899.2020.1729844

McLeod, J. (2017). *Pluralistic therapy: Distinctive features* (Psychotherapy and counselling distinctive features). Routledge.

Parmenter, J. G., Galliher, R. V., Wong, E., & Perez, D. (2021). An intersectional approach to understanding LGBTQ+ people of color's access to LGBTQ+ community resilience. *Journal of Counseling Psychology, 68*(6), 629–641.

Shapiro, E. (2016). *Easy ego state interventions: Strategies for working with parts.* Norton.

Smith, K., & De La Prida, A. (2021). *The pluralistic therapy primer: A concise introduction.* PCCS Books.

The Guardian. (2022, April 4). LGBT groups quit UK conference over failure to ban trans conversion practices. *The Guardian.* www.theguardian.com/society/2022/apr/04/lgbt-groups-quit-uk-conference-failure-ban-trans-conversion-practices

World Health Organisation. (2002). *Integrating gender perspectives in the work of WHO.* WHO Gender Policy.

West, A., Wada, K., & Strong, T. (2021). Authenticating and legitimizing transgender and gender non-conforming identities online: A discourse analysis. *Journal of LGBTQ Issues in Counseling, 15*(2), 195–223.

12
SOCIAL JUSTICE INFORMED THERAPY AND SEXUALITY

Silva Neves

OVERVIEW

Gender, sex, sexuality and relationship diversity (GSRD) is misunderstood in the fields of psychology and psychotherapy mostly because clinical trainings in these areas are often (though not exclusively) poor or non-existent. Furthermore, traditional theoretical models are dominated by the thinking of white, middle class, heterosexual and cisgender clinicians serving the same populations, and thus informing practice methods that do not fit the specific needs of LGBTQ+ clients (lesbian, gay, bisexual, transgender and Queer, to name a few, amongst other sexuality minorities), and worse, can harm them. The history of LGBTQ+ people and psychiatry is problematic. In the past, people engaging in consensual same-sex sexual activities and relationships were considered to have a mental illness and a sexual perversion. The *Diagnostic and Statistical Manual of Mental Disorders* (DSM) removed 'homosexuality' as a mental health disorder in 1973 (Drescher, 2015) but the *International Classification of Diseases* (WHO, ICD) did not remove it until 1990 (Cochran et al., 2014). 'Homosexuality' was also deemed to be a criminal offence until 1967 in the UK. Thankfully, the field of sexology, the study of human sexuality, grew and provided evidence in arguing that LGBTQ+ people are not diseased people (Neves, 2023). As you will read in this chapter, the ethical position to normalise gender, sex, sexuality and relationship diversities largely comes from a commitment to social justice. This commitment also involves staying updated with the current language. Words are important as they can be used to either dismiss or affirm someone's existence. The language continues to develop at a fast pace with the expansion of our diversity awareness, which means that adopting an inclusive language is an ongoing careful consideration. At the same time, humankind is so diverse that it is not always possible to get it right for everybody. For example, many people embrace the term 'Queer' as an empowering and inclusive identity while others hate this term because it reminds them of homophobic attacks. With this in mind, I aim to use the most inclusive language in this chapter, while also respecting differences and committing to cultural humility in continuing to learn to be more and more inclusive. The essence of the acronym GSRD refers to the broad range of diversities, including heterosexual people. However, in this chapter, I will focus on people who identify as LGBTQ+ as it is relevant to social justice.

This chapter will argue that it is difficult to provide good and effective therapy to LGBTQ+ clients without paying attention to social justice. In fact, social justice needs to be one of the core components of the psychotherapeutic dialogue for optimum healing. Social justice informed therapy for LGBTQ+ people is to frame clients' distress in the historical and current context of homophobia (dislike of or prejudice against gay people), biphobia (dislike of or prejudice against bisexual people), transphobia (dislike of or prejudice against trans people), cisgenderism (the assumption that being cisgender is the normal and everything else is a pathology), heteronormativity (the assumption that heterosexuality is the norm and everything else is alternative or strange) and mononormativity (the assumption that monogamy is the norm and everything else is bizarre). Indeed, traditional psychotherapy tells us that mental health problems are generally considered problems with the self, but with a social justice informed frame, we can begin to help clients identify that the source of distress is not always lodged in the self but rather coming from the impact of oppression and hate. In other words, it is to move away from 'I am broken' to 'I am reacting to a toxic environment'. To work effectively with LGBTQ+ clients, clinicians need to be aware of the specific difficulties people who are not heterosexual, cisgender or monogamous face just by living in a heteronormative, cisgenderist and mononormative world.

CONTEXT

There are several aspects of the overall context in which LGBTQ+ clients live that can negatively impact on their wellbeing: the world, the therapeutic space and the self. The following section outlines the context in those three elements.

The World

I hear people say that because LGBTQ+ people have rights in liberal countries, we should stop seeing this population as 'victims' and there is no more need for Pride events. Sadly, this mindset is informed by the privilege of heterosexuality. The reality is quite different. Stonewall (n.d.) reported on their website page 'LGBTQ+ facts and figures' some disturbing information about the lives of LGBTQ+ people in the UK today:

1   One in eight LGBT people (13%) have experienced some form of unequal treatment from healthcare staff because they're LGBT.
2   Seven in ten trans people (70%) report being impacted by transphobia when accessing general health services.
3   Only half of lesbian, gay and bi people (46%) and trans people (47%) feel able to be open about their sexual orientation or gender identity to everyone in their family.
4   More than a third of LGBT staff (35%) have hidden that they are LGBT at work for fear of discrimination.
5   Almost half of LGBT disabled students (47%) have been the target of negative comments or conduct from other students.
6   One third (34%) of Black, Asian and minority ethnic LGBT people have experienced a hate crime or incident in the past 12 months, compared to one in five white LGBT people (20%).

Charity organisation Just Like Us (justlikeus.org) released a 2021 report *Growing Up LGBT+* and found that 68% of young people say their mental health has got worse since the pandemic, compared to 49% of their non-LGBT peers. Also, LGBT+ young people are twice as likely to contemplate suicide than non-LGBT+ young people, and Black LGBT+ young people are three times more likely.

These facts and figures reveal an uncomfortable truth that not all is well in a country deemed as 'liberal'. Despite laws protecting LGBTQ+ people in the UK, the reality of their lives is quite different. Moreover, a report made by Galop (Hubbard, 2021) found that over nine in ten respondents to the survey were negatively impacted by their experiences of anti-LGBT+ violence and abuse (94%). Eight in ten of the respondents who accessed LGBT+ specific support were satisfied with the service they received (80%), compared to only 1 in 4 respondents who accessed generic support (38%). This reflects an urgent need for support services such as mental health and advocacy services to improve their trainings in working with LGBTQ+ people.

Homophobic, biphobic and transphobic hate crime attacks are traumatic events. LGBTQ+ people also experience vicarious trauma by being exposed to homophobic, biphobic and transphobic contents, or witnessing other LGBTQ+ people being attacked or murdered, whether it is witnessing it in the same geographical location, on social media or on the news (Kort, 2018).

In 2022, the UK government excluded trans people in the ban on conversion 'therapy' despite evidence that they are severely harmed by this unethical practice. The law on the ban of conversion 'therapy' has not yet passed at the time of writing this chapter (May 2023), after several years of promise that a ban would be implemented. The 2022 World Cup was hosted in Qatar putting on the world stage a country that has some of the worst anti-LGBTQ+ laws, imposing the death penalty on people engaging in consensual same-sex sexual behaviours. At the time, the UK foreign secretary James Cleverly asked the general public to make a compromise with Qatar, which was short of asking us to ignore the issue, another example of the wellbeing of LGBTQ+ people being either dismissed or de-prioritised. In the USA, another country that is seen as liberal, the Supreme Court overturned Roe v. Wade taking away abortion rights. Florida approved the 'Don't Say Gay' bill, which prohibits discussions of sexual orientation and gender identity. There is also a growing movement to ban Drag performances (but not guns). This causes a real fear amongst the LGBTQ+ communities that this might be just the beginning of other damaging political decisions, including the very real possibility of the overturning of Lawrence v. Texas which could re-instate the criminalisation of same-sex sexual behaviours. The political dismissal and oppression of the LGBTQ+ people in recent years comes from a long history of homophobia, biphobia and transphobia. For example, in the UK, Section 28, a law prohibiting the 'promotion of homosexuality' was introduced by Margaret Thatcher in 1988 and stayed until 2000 in Scotland and 2003 in England and Wales. The impact of this law meant that LGBTQ+ people had to self-censor and education on sexuality diversity was forbidden. The traumatic echo of Section 28 is still felt today in the therapeutic space when clients describe feeling a deep sense of shame for speaking up about their Queer lived experiences.

The world also includes countries that actively oppress and harm LGBTQ+ people with their laws. According to the Human Dignity Trust (www.humandignitytrust.org), there are 67 countries that criminalise private, same-sex, consensual sexual activity. Out of those, 11 countries impose the death penalty, and 32 of those are Commonwealth jurisdictions. This is a bleak picture for LGBTQ+ people. Much of the worldwide LGBTQ+ populations fear for their lives daily, and many do get murdered.

The Therapeutic Space

The therapists who live and work within the privilege of heterosexuality may be well-meaning but they may be confronted with blind spots because of inadequate trainings on sexology and GSRD. I sometimes hear therapists say: 'sexuality doesn't matter, I treat everyone the same'. These kind of statements are indeed well-intentioned however they are also problematic as they erase the very specific issues that LGBTQ+ people face that are not relevant to the lives of heterosexual people. For example, the very simple gesture of holding a partner's hand in the street is significant for LGBTQ+ people (Rohleder et al., 2023), yet it is something that heterosexual people do all the time without ever needing to think about their safety. For same-sex partnerships, it is an act that can result in attacks so LGBTQ+ people have to seriously consider and scan their environment for signs of potential threats before holding hands. For some LGBTQ+ people, holding hands is an act of defiance and social justice. It is easy for heterosexual therapists to miss this simple yet crucial aspect of the lives of their LGBTQ+ clients. Treating everyone the same needs to refer to offering the same safe space and respect regardless of the sexual orientation or other identities of clients, but it does not mean offering the same therapy, because LGBTQ+ clients have specific needs that require the therapeutic process to be adapted to their needs, not for them to fit in therapy modalities originally informed by theories for white, heterosexual, cisgender, monogamous people.

The Self

LGBTQ+ individuals often report experiences of homophobia, biphobia and transphobia prejudice in their childhood. For example, severe bullying at school is a common occurrence. There is also much oppression on how people 'should' show affection to others. In the UK men tend to be socialised not to hug or kiss other men as these behaviours are perceived as 'gay'. Some boys and men can be ostracised or attacked for showing such affection. Some LGBTQ+ people learn from their upbringing that they can only be worthy of their parents' love if they are heterosexual. These types of events, which are often 'the normal' in LGBTQ+ people's childhood, can result in lasting psychological disturbances such as poor self-esteem and self-worth, shame, depression, suicidal thoughts, anxiety, substance misuse, hating their sexual orientation, hiding and concealing who they are, to mention only a few.

Many LGBTQ+ clients report growing up in homophobic households, for example, hearing parents make insulting comments when an LGBTQ+ character appears on television or being explicitly told by parents they would be rejected if they turned out to be gay: *'I'd rather have a dead son than a gay son'* is, sadly, a phrase many LGBTQ+ people hear from their parents. This type of childhood can cause major psychological disturbances. Feeling unsafe with the very people that are supposed to love and care for them, especially when they rely on that attachment figure to survive when they're children, is a complex relational trauma precipitating significant attachment disruptions.

When experiences of oppression and conditional love wrapped in homophobia, biphobia and transphobia happen early in life, it creates the phenomenon termed internalised homophobia, biphobia and transphobia, which means that people develop negative core beliefs about themselves and other LGBTQ+ people based on their sexual orientations and/or gender identities. For example, it is common to hear a gay man say: *'all gay men are sluts, they're not interested in love'* or *'I hate camp men'*; or a transgender person say: *'I hate being trans, it's so hard on everybody, I hate upsetting my family, I wish I could be normal'*. Many LGBTQ+ people struggle to accept their sexuality and gender identity and wish they could be heterosexual, cisgender and monogamous, making them vulnerable to being offered conversion 'therapy' and be further harmed.

Post-Trauma and Ongoing Stress

Therapists working with LGBTQ+ people will likely work with clients with both post-trauma and ongoing stress; therefore, it is important to be trauma-informed. Post-trauma may include a history of being bullied at school or growing up in a homophobic household, as mentioned above, which could impact on the client's here-and-now adult life with battling against internalised homophobia, and/or post-trauma stress symptoms. It may also include history of sexual assaults or having been in a previous relationship with domestic violence, being the survivor of conversion practices and so on. Ongoing stress is the continuous minority stress and micro-aggression (Meyer, 2003) that is felt daily just by being LGBTQ+ in a heteronormative, cisgenderist and mononormative world.

Every micro-event of prejudice and oppression is associated with survival (scanning for safety, for example) and it is felt in the body and the nervous system which contribute to psychological disturbances. The ongoing minority stress and micro-aggression has the same effect psychologically and somatically as a traumatic event, but because it is micro, it is often dismissed and not addressed, allowing the stress to build up slowly, until there is an overload. It is no wonder why LGBTQ+ people are over-represented in mental health services, and drug and alcohol misuse services. As a clinician working with LGBTQ+ people, it is important to make the difference between post-trauma and ongoing stress because post-trauma can be addressed with various trauma therapy methods (somatic trauma therapy, EMDR, trauma-informed CBT, etc.) but ongoing stress is best acknowledged and addressed with social justice informed therapeutic interventions.

CORE PRINCIPLES

The need for social justice informed therapy with LGBTQ+ is urgent as there are currently too many clients who are let down by their mental health professionals, and unfortunately, are often caused harm by them. In my opinion, addressing harm done in therapy is part of the overall social justice commitment that we need to adopt. I believe we don't discuss this topic often enough in our mental health professions because it is an uncomfortable topic. We need to keep learning from each other.

Here are some brief vignettes to illustrate how the absence of GSRD knowledge can harm LGBTQ+ people:

1 Lesbians are often a forgotten population in clinical discourse. The myth of the 'lesbian death bed', which means that lesbians stop having sex as soon as they commit to each other, is unhelpful and only encourages the erasure of their sex lives and discourages appropriate help such as sex therapy.

2 Gay men are often harmed in therapy when their sexual behaviours are deemed as 'unhealthy' because the therapist thinks the frequency and/or sexual activities are problematic (using the dubious pseudo-diagnosis of 'sex addiction'). The industry of 'sex addiction' is traditionally rooted in heteronormativity, mononormativity and religious morality (Neves, 2021). It is important to note here that the study conducted by the UK government (2021) reported that some survivors of conversion practices were offered this harmful so-called 'therapy' by being told that they had 'sex addiction'.

3 Bisexual people are also being erased. Often bisexual people are accused of being 'gay in the closet', being 'greedy' or can't make up their mind. If a bisexual person chooses to be in a monogamous relationship with the same gender, they will be perceived to be gay. If they choose to be in a relationship with a different gender, they will be perceived to be heterosexual. However, they always remain bisexual.

4 Transgender people's very existence is often debated by people who hold gender critical views (the view that gender is binary and determined by genitals and physical characteristics, arguing against gender diversity). Some transgender people are being

traumatised on a regular basis for having their very own lived experience denied. Some feel acute shame for their gender expressions and may delay seeking gender affirming therapy, increasing psychological distress, poor mental health and suicidal ideations.

5   Queer is an identity that means different things to different people. For some it means 'gay', but for others it may mean 'non-monogamous', 'non-binary' and/ or 'kinky'. For each of them, it usually means identifying with something that is outside of 'the norm'. Queer people tend to report regular micro-aggression with overt and/or covert prejudices. For example, a non-monogamous person may be told that they are so because they have an avoidant attachment style, and they would be monogamous if they were more secure. Kinky people may be told that they are into that 'stuff' because they were sexually abused as a child, and they would enjoy vanilla sex if they healed their trauma.

6   Asexual people also face discrimination on a regular basis. They are perceived as 'childish' or 'immature' for not wanting to have sex. They can often be unduly pathologised by theories that tell us their lack of sexual interest is because they were sexually abused in childhood, and if they healed their trauma they would have 'normal' sexual desire. Some asexual people are 'diagnosed' with the ghastly term 'sexual anorexic'. As a result, asexual people are vulnerable to being offered conversion practices by forcing them to be sexual with their partner either through a Sensate Focus programme (a sex therapy programme designed to facilitate sexual desire and arousal for the purpose of intercourse), or through irrelevant trauma theories.

GSRD Therapy

GSRD therapy is an emerging modality first pioneered in the UK by Dominic Davies and Charles Neal with the ground-breaking first UK textbook *Pink Therapy* series on LGBT therapy in 1996 and 2000. More recently Davies and Neves (2023) outline the six core principles of GSRD therapy:

1   Practice a commitment to social justice
2   Demonstrate cultural humility and cultural competence
3   Understanding of the specific adverse effects of oppression
4   Trauma-informed care
5   Gain knowledge of contemporary sexology
6   Integration of core GSRD theories

A commitment to social justice is one of the core components of effective therapy with LGBTQ+ clients. GSRD therapy requires not only working with the client's self, but also incorporating the impact of the context and the world into the client's clinical formulation. The book *Queering Psychotherapy* (Czyzselska, 2022), taking social justice seriously, reminds us: '*know your history*' to keep paying attention on how heteronormativity, mononormativity and cisgenderism have influenced our psychotherapy theories and how these types of thinking keep infiltrating our profession. Dunlop and Lea (2022) encourage us to be more curious in *'understanding broader systemic variables, and the impact these have on individual mental health'*. Understanding about privilege and oppression helps us to not replicate a sense of power imbalance and oppression in the therapeutic space.

Knowledge in contemporary sexology is important not to unduly pathologise clients. For example, being aware that the notion of 'sex addiction' and 'porn addiction' are not clinically endorsed diagnoses, or knowing that there isn't a direct association between kink and childhood trauma, or that asexuality is a sexual orientation like any other. The field of sexology in itself is based on a commitment to social justice. In the UK, Havelock Ellis was one of the first clinicians to develop sexology, motivated by social justice in challenging the thinking of his time on pathologising 'homosexuality'. Sexology in its history has a tradition of promoting human sexual health rights.

CASE STUDY: SIMON

This case study is fictional based on a composite of different anonymised client vignettes.

Simon identifies as a gay cisgender man. He is 40 years old. He came to therapy presenting with various issues: acute anxiety, feeling low, finding it difficult to start and maintain an intimate relationship, struggling with unreliable erections, poor body image, excessive use of the gym. Although this seems like a long list of complaints, it is not uncommon amongst gay men to present with this kind of combination of struggles.

Simon grew up in a rural Northern town in England. From as far back as he can remember, he felt 'different' and 'weird'. He was often criticised by his parents who compared him with his younger brother. Simon was labelled 'too sensitive' and 'awkward' because he didn't like doing the boisterous things that other boys, including his brother, liked doing. He loved playing with his older sister's Barbies but he knew that he had to do so in secret because it was prohibited. He resented his brother because he was perceived as the 'successful' one and therefore Simon was the 'failure'. He remembers hearing so often from his parents: *'Why can't you be more like your brother?'*

He grew up in a religious household. Both his mother and father were overtly homophobic. At school, he was often verbally abused by his peers with homophobic name-calling, punching and kicking. Sometimes, his school uniform would be torn, or he would have a visible bruise on his face. Returning from school in this state prompted more criticisms at home from his parents. His father and mother would scold him for the torn uniform, and they would frequently say: *'Why can't you defend yourself, like a real boy?'*

Thankfully, he was good at maths, so he left the rural town as soon as he could to go to a London University on a scholarship. When he arrived in London, he was excited to meet other gay men and finally found people who wouldn't be homophobic. He loved hanging out in Soho, where he didn't have to conceal or hide his sexual orientation, which was a relief.

When there was enough geographical distance between him and his parents, he came out to them. His parents instantly responded with disgust. They told him he was no longer welcome at home as he brought shame to the family.

In Soho, he was disappointed to see that many gay men were in competition with each other, and the gay scene was quite a harsh and rejecting world too. To keep up with the demands of the gay scene, he started going to the gym as often as possible to become as desirable as possible. It worked. He was popular when he went out. He had a large number of one-night-stands or brief encounters, preferring to be bottom to hide his unreliable erections. After his university years, he started to have a full life in London, working, making money and going out even more, always in the hope of meeting 'the one'. He found himself becoming 'obsessed' with Grindr and other dating apps, hoping he would find a person to have a long-term relationship with. But, for various reasons, he never managed to find anyone. On a few occasions, he was called 'needy' by potential dates. Not being able to hang on to a relationship reinforced the message his parents instilled in him: he was worthless because he was a gay man. His mother's voice echoed in his head: '*You will always be alone and you will die young if you choose to be gay*'. As the years went by, he started to doubt if indeed he could be happy as a gay man. The more he felt 'broken', the more he attended the gym. He believed that if only he could become more 'perfect' he would somehow be loved. But despite all his efforts, his anxiety increased, his low moods became longer episodes, his unreliable erections persisted, and he was losing hope in finding a lasting relationship. As he was reaching his 40s, he became more aware of his decreased desirability because the gay scene can be ageist. He felt alone in the world. Suicidal thoughts crept in, and it was then that he sought therapy.

Sadly, Simon's story is a common one. A social justice informed therapy approach is to help Simon make sense of his struggles through the lens of his past trauma and ongoing stress because of homophobia in the world: overt homophobia with his family and school, internalised homophobia, intra-community stress in the gay scene (Pachankis et al., 2020) and covert homophobia in society. All of those contributed to his ongoing minority stress experiences. Reframing his various symptoms of psychological distress as a reaction to the heteronormative world, rather than something about him that was 'broken' was not only an important first step but also a theme to maintain throughout therapy. Encouraging Simon to find his 'tribe' was pivotal in his therapy. For example, rather than enduring the harsh world of hook-up apps, how about meeting other gay men through different apps? Perhaps one based on special interests? He was amazed to see that there were many LGBTQ+ communities out there that weren't focused on hook-ups, like gay men interested in hiking, theatre, music, tennis and book clubs. It somehow reduced his internalised homophobia and he felt relief that he no longer had to work so hard in fitting into the gay scene.

Many of Simon's core beliefs about himself were created by his experiences of past homophobic trauma. Slowly, using some classic psychotherapy tools such as CBT, Gestalt chairwork, person-centred therapy and mindfulness, Simon developed new thoughts and feelings about himself, and started to connect with others differently. He was able to identify that despite being 'out there' he was also 'hiding', making relation-ships more difficult to maintain. In therapy, he understood that the 'hiding' was a com-mon survival strategy for gay men navigating the homophobic world, and perhaps was no longer needed when with peers.

In recognising that Simon lived with ongoing stress too because of the heteronorma-tive world, part of his therapy was to help him build up resilience and the awareness that ongoing self-care was needed.

Towards the end of this therapy, his self-worth grew enough for him to volunteer for an LGBTQ+ charity organisation. He reduced the gym and increased his pleasure of living, which helped with being more assertive in expressing his sexual needs with partners, which, in turn, improved his erections. He met a man through the charity work, they became sexual and romantic partners, and he was able to maintain the rela-tionship. One of the central parts of his therapy was to understand the role of shame (instilled by the heteronormative world and his upbringing) and how perfectionism was his way to mitigate shame. When he was aware of this, he became kinder to himself. He no longer had suicidal ideations, and, for the first time in his life, reported thriving.

CONCLUSION

It is not possible to offer effective therapy for LGBTQ+ people without a social justice informed practice because it is at the core of helping clients understand the actual source of their distress. The LGBTQ+ populations have been unduly pathologised for a long time, where simply being themselves was a criminal offence or described as a mental health dis-order. LGBTQ+ people were harmed by psychiatry, politics and the law. These populations are still harmed today in the UK, but more covertly, the ongoing intrinsic homophobia, biphobia and transphobia are still palpable on our streets and on social media. In some other countries, homophobia, biphobia and transphobia are still overt and encouraged by their laws. It is therefore imperative for therapists to guide conversations for clients to become aware that they are not 'broken', despite many historic attempts by society to make us believe so, and instead they are reacting to the impact of hate and oppression, which has negative consequences on their mental health. Placing the source of the distress in the world rather than in the self and helping clients heal their past trauma, as well as building up resilience for the ongoing stress of living in a heteronormative, mononorma-tive and cisgenderist world is usually a good combination for positive outcome in therapy.

REFLECTIVE AND CRITICAL THINKING QUESTIONS

1   Out of the LGBTQ+ people, what population do you feel the least knowledgeable about? What about the one(s) about whom you have the most assumptions/ prejudices? Do you know why?

2   How might you integrate the concept of minority stress into the formulation of LGBTQ+ clients' presenting issues and interventions?

3   How would you reframe the traditional theories on mental health and dysfunctions with the social justice lens?

4   What was the most surprising part of this chapter for you? How might it influence your practice and your continuous professional development?

RECOMMENDED READING AND RESOURCES

Dunlop, B. J. (2022). *The queer mental health workbook: A creative self-help guide using CBT, CFT and DBT*. Jessica Kingsley Publishers.
This is an LGBTQ+ affirming and helpful resource for people identifying as Queer, offering exercises to work through common difficulties and reframe some of their maladaptive thoughts and behaviours.

Harding, D. (2022). *Gay man talking: All the conversations we never had*. Jessica Kingsley Publishers.
This is a thought-provoking and modern book on the lived experiences of gay men.

Barker, M. J., & Iantaffi, A. (2022). *How to understand your sexuality: A practical guide for exploring who you are*. Jessica Kingsley Publishers.
This is a helpful book for readers to explore their sexuality in a compassionate way, with invitations for self-reflection and thought-provoking information.

Barker, M. J. (2018). *Re-writing the rules: An anti-self-help guide to love, sex and relationships* (2nd ed.). Routledge.
This is a wonderful guide challenging heteronormativity, mononormativity and cisgenderism, inviting readers to explore who they are and how they love, moving away from binary norms.

REFERENCES

Cochran, S. D., Drescher, J., Kismödi, E., Giami, A., García-Moreno, C., Atalla, E., Marais, A., Vieira, E. M., & Reed, G. M. (2014). Proposed declassification of disease categories related to sexual orientation in the International Statistical Classification of Diseases and Related Health Problems (ICD-11). *Bulletin World Health Organization, 92*(9), 672–679. https://doi.org/10.2471/BLT.14.135541

Czyzselska, J. C. (2022). *Queering psychotherapy*. Karnac Books.

Davies, D., & Neves, S. (2023). Gender, sex and relationship diversity therapy. In T. Hanley & L. A. Winter (Eds.), *The SAGE handbook of counselling and psychotherapy* (5th ed.). SAGE Publications.

Drescher, J. (2015). Out of DSM: Depathologizing homosexuality. *Behavioral Sciences, 5*(4), 565–575. https://doi.org/10.3390/bs5040565

Dunlop, B. J., & Lea, J. (2022). It's not just in my head: An intersectional, social and systems-based framework in gender and sexuality diversity. *BPS Psychology and Psychotherapy*. https://doi.org/10.1111/papt.12438

Hubbard, L. (2021). *The hate crime report 2021: Supporting LGBT+ victims of hate crime*. Galop.

Just Like Us. (2021). *Growing up LGBT+*. Retrieved November 20, 2022 from www.justlikeus.org/wp-content/uploads/2021/11/Just-Like-Us-2021-report-Growing-Up-LGBT.pdf

Kort, J. (2018). *LGBTQ clients in therapy: Clinical issues and treatment strategies*. W.W. Norton & Company.

Meyer, I. H. (2003). Prejudice, social stress, and mental health in lesbian, gay, and bisexual populations: Conceptual issues and research evidence. *Psychological Bulletin*, *129*(5), 674–697. https://doi.org/10.1037/0033-2909.129.5.674

Neves, S. (2021). The religious disguise in 'sex addiction' therapy. *Sexual and Relationship Therapy*. https://doi.org/10.1080/14681994.2021.2008344

Neves, S. (2023). *Sexology: The basics*. Routledge.

Pachankis, J. E., Clark, K. A., Burton, C. L., Hughto, J. M. W., Bränström, R., & Keene, D. E. (2020). Sex, status, competition, and exclusion: Intraminority stress from within the gay community and gay and bisexual men's mental health. *Journal of Personality and Social Psychology*, *119*(3), 713–740. https://doi.org/10.1037/pspp0000282

Rohleder, P., Ryan-Flood, R., & Walsh, J. (2023). Holding hands: LGBTQ people's experiences of public displays of affection with their partner(s). *Psychology & Sexuality*. https://doi.org/10.1080/19419899.2023.2185533

Stonewall. (n.d.). *Facts and figures*. www.stonewall.org.uk/media/lgbt-facts-and-figures

UK Government. (2021). *Conversion therapy: An evidence assessment and qualitative study*. www.gov.uk/government/publications/conversion-therapy-an-evidence-assessment-and-qualitative-study/conversion-therapy-an-evidence-assessment-and-qualitative-study#what-forms-does-conversion-therapy-take-1

13

SOCIAL JUSTICE INFORMED THERAPY WITH REFUGEES AND ASYLUM SEEKERS

Anne Burghgraef

OVERVIEW

The forced migration of people displaced from their homes whether young or old, alone or with family to seek sanctuary in a country not their own has increasingly become one of the global challenges of the 21st century (The Guardian, 2012).

Until the plight of refugees crossing seas in overcrowded vessels was exposed by photojournalist Nilifur Demir with the image of two-year-old Syrian Alan Kurdi lying lifeless on a Turkish beach in 2015, this world was largely hidden from the majority. This was the year journalists recorded the largest ever movement of people across boundaries and when it was first widely recognised that Europe had a refugee crisis. Analysing the media trends covering this crisis, the Council of Europe (2017) concluded that:

> The sympathetic and empathetic response of a large proportion of the European press in the summer and especially early autumn of 2015 was gradually replaced by suspicion and, in some cases, hostility towards refugees and migrants.

This summary captures the challenge psychotherapists face when offering psychological therapy to asylum seekers and refugees. Do they perceive them as victims of injustice or unwanted intruders? What is their role and what in their knowledge base, skill set, or values could help? Informed by media sound bites alone, the psychotherapist may be overwhelmed with stories of loss and violence or the complexities of seeking asylum. Some will draw upon their available resources, but others may conclude that they 'aren't ready' for therapy or they 'failed to engage'.

In this chapter, social justice informed psychotherapeutic practice with refugees will be explored by considering the complexities of refugee legal and mental health difficulties. A culturally sensitive, multi-dimensional model of psychotherapy will be outlined to support social justice informed practice with refugees.

CONTEXT

Western psychotherapy developed within a modernist scientific, individualist paradigm, which is reflected in the dominant models that have become embedded in UK institutional practices including variations of psychoanalysis, cognitive-behaviour therapy and person-centred counselling. With the emergence of post modernism, it has become increasingly recognised that therapeutic modalities are informed by the worldviews and socio-political contexts of their time and place (Van Belle, 2014).

Comparisons of the use of specific therapeutic modalities when working with refugees has been limited aside from Vander Veer (1998) who compared the advantages and limitations of various approaches. Instead, adapting to a model of best practice with refugees has been emphasised, which now includes being trauma informed. Refugee research studies have focused upon specific mental health disorders such as depression, anxiety or post-traumatic stress disorder (PTSD), and the efficacy of such treatments as narrative exposure therapy (Schauer et al., 2011), cognitive behaviour therapy or eye movement desensitisation reprocessing therapy (EMDR) (Acarturk et al., 2015). While some showed limited improvement in PTSD symptoms or mood, the outcomes of single model approaches were often inconclusive (Kronick, 2018). The literature suggests a consideration of the multiple contexts which frame the refugee experience is needed for effective therapeutic support (Blackwell, 2005; Vander Veer, 1998).

Numbers of people forced to migrate continue to escalate with The United Nations High Commission for Refugees (UNHCR) concluding that by mid 2022, over 100 million people were forcibly displaced with about half of those their country of origin. Two decades earlier, the numbers were half as much. In 2023, 75 per cent of refugees had fled from just five countries including Syria, Venezuela, Ukraine, Afghanistan and South Sudan, demonstrating the impact global conflicts are having on patterns of migration. The majority (75%) are hosted in neighbouring, usually low-income countries, with the UK hosting 1% (Refugee Council, 2023).

Legal Context

Recognising that people seek asylum because their lives are under threat with no assurance of protection from their governments puts the legal framework in the foreground of their existence. For millennia, people have crossed borders in search of safety, food or other opportunities; however the current global refugee situation is unique. Following the Second World War, when millions were displaced, the United Nations established the Convention relating to the Status of Refugees in 1951 to resettle the one million Europeans who were left homeless. While intended to be temporary, this convention was recognised as an effective legal structure with universal applicability so it was retained and modified with the 1967 Protocol. To date 114 states throughout the world, including the UK, are signatories to this convention. The UNHCR who oversees it expects all signatories to have fair and just systems for assessing refugee applications, however they do not specify how in practice it should be done. According to the convention, a refugee is defined as:

> A person who owing to a well-founded fear of being persecuted for reasons of race, religion, nationality, membership of a particular social group or political opinion, is outside the country of his nationality and is unable or, owing to such fear, is unwilling to avail himself of the protection of that country; or who, not having a nationality and being outside the country of his former habitual residence as a result of such events, is unable or, owing to such fear, is unwilling to return to it. (UNHCR, 2023)

Thus, a refugee is legally defined by an authority, either the UNHCR or a country which has granted them protection within this framework. Someone who has submitted an application that has not yet been concluded is known as an 'asylum seeker'. Once accepted, they are granted refugee status and entitled to all the usual rights and benefits, however some may be granted other forms of temporary status that include restrictions and hidden costs. UK legislation impacting the lives of asylum seekers and refugees includes the Human Rights Act (1998), Asylum and Immigration Act (1999), the Nationality and Borders Bill (2022) and the Equality Act (2010) which prohibits discrimination on the grounds of sex, race, disability, religion or belief or sexual orientation (https://www.legislation.gov.uk/ukpga/1998/42/schedule/1). In 2022 the UK government passed the Nationality and Borders Act, which radically changes the system and penalises those who arrive in the UK via irregular means, which may mean a higher burden of proof is required with fewer protections. The implications of this bill continues be debated, highlighting the contentiousness of the debate with respect to asylum and refugee policy.

Despite these protective legal frameworks, a gap between what is legislated and its implementation often exists. The processes used to determine who qualifies as a refugee and those responsible for decision making are critical, as legal and social justice can be facilitated or frustrated. Being recognised as a refugee is a matter of legal justice, while access to such rights as food, shelter and participation within one's society involves social justice. With refugees, it is impossible to have social justice without legal justice.

To obtain legal justice, asylum seekers are subject to a complex and difficult process, which psychotherapists need to understand to facilitate justice through signposting or working with refugee sector colleagues to obtain expert legal advice and assistance to navigate the system along with the therapeutic support. Being fully present to and standing in solidarity with someone who has experienced cruelty at the hands of others whether torture, enslavement or abuse is a powerful act of 'bearing witness'. It does not mean you make a determination about someone's status, but you take a human rights stance against such inhumanity. Therapists have tremendous power to document what refugees and asylum seekers have experienced and what they continue to endure. They are not country experts or expected to comment upon the veracity of someone's disclosure, however they can describe the difficulties someone is experiencing and how they are responding in therapy. For example, it is possible to detail someone's trauma symptoms and to give a view whether there is a fit between their symptoms, their responses and the nature of what you understand them to have experienced.

Determining whether an asylum seeker will be granted protection is often dependent upon their credibility, as few will have objective evidence of their persecution. Therefore, they are dependent upon their story, and whether a Home Office official or judge believes it to be true. The criteria used to determine the veracity of the account is based on a modernist view of truth which does not recognise the complexities of human memory, and the particular difficulties people who are highly stressed and traumatised have in giving a coherent narrative of their experience. Psychotherapists who understand these issues can promote justice by preparing asylum seekers to give a clear account and helping decision makers to understand these issues through report writing or verbal testimony. Unlike other professionals, psychotherapists are uniquely positioned to promote justice in this way and are encouraged to develop their knowledge and skills further (Burghgraef, 2021). These therapeutic reports are not Medical Legal Reports (MLR), which are prepared by medical and legal specialists according to the Istanbul protocol, however they can facilitate access to them if needed.

High levels of emotional distress amongst refugees and asylum seekers have regularly been documented as noted by Aspinall and Watters (2010), who concluded that they are five times more likely to have mental health needs and that 61% experience serious mental distress. As many find it difficult to access mental health services, an understanding of their unique issues is needed by practitioners but also the managers so services can be adapted to be accessible, engaging and effective.

All refugees and asylum seekers have experienced being uprooted from their home and dislocated from their community following an experience or threat of persecution (Papadopolous, 2005; Vander Veer, 1998). Pre-migration experiences vary with some being caught up in protracted wars as in Syria while others may be subjected to organised violence without government protection. Some may be political activists and be forced to escape suddenly without their families while others have time to plan. Many women flee gender-based violence including forced marriages, honour killings and not following expected community practices (Storkey, 2015). This exodus always carries multiple losses, which will include familiar cultural patterns, social structures, relationships and possibly the separation or death of family and friends. Whether in the foreground or the background, whether spoken or implicit, these losses will be present like an underwater current, sometimes barely perceptible and at other times pulsating with an overwhelming power.

Many will have suffered in prisons, prolonged torture, rape, enslavement by traffickers, abuse by families and communities or witnessed the ravages of war. Sexual violence and witnessing bodily harm to loved ones can be especially difficult to live with. Extreme emotions of fear and terror, anger and rage, shame, humiliation and guilt may be overwhelming, or they may be repressed and cut off as someone slides into a state of hypo-arousal of deadness and passivity. Along with disturbing memories and re-living experiences will be the chronic and acute uncertainty of the future. For some who are already outside their country of origin when they realise their lives are under threat, it is their imagination of what could happen to them that is a source of terror; as in the case of a pharmacist who was wanted by the authorities because his medicines were found in the hands of a so-called terrorist group, which re-awakened in him traumatic scenes of torture.

As it is impossible to apply for asylum from within one's own country, all need to travel irregularly often with false documents. The journey which may last months or years tends to be uncommonly stressful as it is easy to become separated from families, exploited by agents or to experience traumatic events. Upon arrival, many may spend years navigating an unforgiving asylum system. Resettlement refugees arrive with status granted to them by the UNHCR, usually after many years of displacement.

The challenge of rebuilding one's life in an alien country in the context of uncertainty can be overwhelming. Given Britain's prominence in the world and the ubiquity of the internet, most will have some preconceived ideas of what life will be like. Some will encounter kindness and generosity while others may experience indifference or hostility, the sharp end of racism; particularly as a deliberate policy to deter people from seeking asylum in the UK became official policy in 2013 and was reinforced by the 2022 UK Nationality and Borders Bill including the proposal to house asylum seekers in offshore facilities. In contrast the City of Sanctuary movement and the refugee sector advocate on behalf of refugees, fight for their rights and strive to create a culture of welcome. Those who are given the right to remain relatively quickly with some support to rebuild their lives will usually go on to successfully integrate and become financially independent (Papadopolous, 2005). But those enduring years of refused applications, court appearances, destitution or periods of detention before gaining some right to remain are likely to experience an increase in physical and mental health difficulties.

By traversing two or more worlds, one's worldview and sense of self are called into question. Assumptions about what it is to be human and expectations about life will be undermined and for some completely overturned. Responses can vary from existential crises and confusion to embracing the new or clinging to the old ways. How one manages depends upon available support as well as personal resilience. Being confronted with the reality of human evil existentially through witnessing or experiencing acts of human cruelty can precipitate major disturbance and overturn one's ability to cope leading to dissociative experiences, making it even more difficult to manage. It is in the crucible of human relationships that embodies the opposite of this within an ethos of mutual respect that someone can pick up the jagged shards of their broken existence and begin to reform their world and identity.

CORE PRINCIPLES

Given these unique challenges, it may be tempting to refer on to an expert, however keeping in mind some useful principles will help to facilitate the best possible outcomes.

Multiple Contexts

The multiple cultures and systems refugees engage with need to be understood, especially the asylum process. They are also places where our minds dwell, so being aware of these contexts will sensitise us to possible conflicting demands and loyalties experienced by refugees and asylum seekers. While physically present, their thoughts may be anxious ones about the future or preoccupied with events in their country of origin and the people left behind. Many will worry about asylum claims, signing on at the Home Office, being detained or becoming destitute.

Power and Privilege

These are inherent in the role of psychotherapist and how they are exercised is always an ethical responsibility, but when someone's vulnerability is multiplied by virtue of being dislocated or being a visible minority, it has additional salience. If an asylum seeker is struggling with feeling misunderstood or treated unfairly by legal processes, they need to know you are not allied with those authorities, but that you are committed to justice and their welfare.

Diversity and Difference

Working therapeutically across cultural backgrounds, worldviews and lifestyle practices poses unique challenges. Not all therapeutic trainings prepare people to reflect upon their own cultural background and how it impacts the way they approach and position themselves with people who are unlike themselves. Systemic practitioners have cultural competence embedded within their training (Thomas, 2011); however others may be more focused upon their specific methodologies. In that case training in working with diversity and anti-oppressive practice to enhance sensitivity and awareness would be encouraged (Charura & Lago, 2021). As it is impossible to have a working knowledge of all countries and cultures, cultivating a stance of therapeutic curiosity will go a long way to building bridges and affirming the expertise of the refugees you want to engage with. The Social GGRRAAACCEEESSS acronym (Burnham, 2013), referring to gender, geography, race, religion, age, ability, appearance, class, culture, ethnicity, education, employment, sexuality, sexual orientation and spirituality, can be helpful, as these categories can aid exploration and reflection upon perceptions and hidden influences.

Global and Historic Awareness

Developing a critical awareness of global and historical issues including the role of Western governments in subjugating nations and the imposition of cultural values is an integral part of being a social justice informed practitioner. Imperialism and colonialism have left a legacy of oppression and injustice that continues as was evident in the Windrush scandal when there was an attempt to force many black Britons who had lived in the UK for decades to move to the Caribbean (The Guardian, 2022). Being open and attending respectfully to the perspective of those seeking sanctuary will offer insight into the diversity of experience globally and demonstrate solidarity with those who have suffered the negative impact of colonialism.

Media Messages

Given the power of the media to shape perceptions of refugees, becoming media literate is to be aware of the worldviews of journalists and their organisations along with the impact of political agendas, racism and the use of language. Too easily refugees can absorb negative views, and as they feel dismissed by others, they may dismiss themselves. Thus, challenging false or distorted representations with accurate information is integral to being a social justice informed psychotherapist in practice and in the public square.

Racism

As all have perceptions of those who are different from themselves in some ways, ethical practice requires therapists to be self-reflective, about their own racist attitudes and the impact upon their language and actions. Reflective practice supervision or groups may provide contexts to consider the factors influencing our attitudes and to increase sensitivity (Charura & Lago, 2021). Racism is not just an individual matter but can be embedded in policies and institutions, as was evidenced in the discussions about systemic racism in the Metropolitan Police Force (The Guardian, 2021). Understanding the negative impact of institutional racist practices can strengthen your practice as well as challenge public policy and provide a counter narrative in the media.

Language

As most psychotherapies are verbal, attending to the meaning embedded in language and the use of words, phrasing and metaphors requires nuanced attention. Rather than using technical mental health language, everyday speech to describe experience or dif-ficulties is preferred. For equitable access, using trained interpreters is essential for most non-English speakers, thus investing in interpreters and training them to work in a mental health setting is advisable (Boyles & Talbot, 2017).

SOCIAL JUSTICE INFORMED PSYCHOTHERAPY IN PRACTICE

As no single modality can address the multiple psycho-social needs of refugees, consider-ing what is essential to our humanity is a useful starting point. Most accept the universal needs for food, clothing and shelter but may differ on other aspects that are important for human flourishing. Some worldviews will prioritise the collective needs of society with little attention to individuals while others may assert the necessity to remain in one's position in the social order. Maslow's hierarchy of needs, beginning with basic needs and ascending to self-actualisation, a form of creative self-fulfilment that will be familiar to many psychotherapists, is useful but is limited by its Western individualism. For example, refugees will prioritise safety over food and shelter and there are those who choose to forego human relationships to have a transcendent experience of the divine.

In contrast The Human Givens approach (Griffen & Tyrell, 2003) identifies ten central human needs, believed to be fundamental to mental wellbeing, including: security in all major spheres of life, having and giving attention to others, having some control, being connected to a wider community, and having at least one close relationship as well as having privacy, achieving and feeling competent in one area of life with some recognised status, and lastly being stretched in a way that is meaningful. While not explicitly addressing the need for justice or fair treatment, it recognises the multi-faceted nature of wellbeing including the need for respect and recognition as well as a sense of meaning and purpose that some modalities may ignore. Modal aspect theory, developed by Dutch philosopher Herman Dooyeweerd (Kalsbeek, 1975) as a way of distinguishing the different dimensions of human functioning and their integral connections, offers some fruitful insights as noted in Table 13.1 which connects therapeutic models to the various aspects.

While this table is broadly indicative and debatable, it demonstrates how therapeutic modalities focus upon a few aspects while side-lining others. As modal theory recognises the interconnections and reciprocal influences amongst the aspects, all require consid-eration. The juridical mode is integral to being human, thus without justice, humans suffer. Unfair treatment can easily embitter, enrage or discourage people as well as under-mine social solidarity. Considering how your therapeutic approach reckons with justice

Table 13.1   Therapeutic modalities and their focus

Modal aspect	Meaning	Example of therapeutic model addressing this modal aspect
Faith	Worldview – beliefs about life	Faith based, existentialist, human givens, narrative and systemic
Ethical	Norms for human relationships	Feminist, systemic, group, transactional analysis, attachment
Juridical	Justice, rights, responsibilities	Human rights approaches, feminist and community psychology, narrative
Aesthetic	Imagination, playful	Creative therapies, narrative, hypnotherapy and guided imagery
Economic	Just use of resources, value	Person centred, Marxist approaches, just therapies
Social	Interaction, patterns	Psychodynamic, systemic, gestalt, interpersonal therapies
Linguistic	Communication, symbolism	Psychodynamic, systemic, bibliotherapy, narrative, hypnotherapy
Formative	Capacity to create, shape	Existentialist, human givens, psychodynamic, coaching
Analytical	Thinking, conceptualising	Cognitive behaviour therapies, systemic
Sensitive	Feeling, emotion, sensing	Psychodynamic, person centred, gestalt, attachment
Biotic	Growth, life and vitality	Body based, somatic experiencing, eco therapies
Physical	Energy, matter	Sensory motor, energy therapies
Kinematic	Movement	Dance, body therapies
Spatial	Continuous extension	
Numerical	Quantity	

or issues of faith, which are often neglected, is a useful exercise. Existentialist, narrative and systemic therapies engage more directly with beliefs, values and the meaning of life, so they can offer rich resources for refugees who have lost a sense of direction.

The oppression of particular groups is connected to the ethical and juridical modes as they are treated unjustly simply because of who they are. Community psychology, feminist, narrative and systemic therapists may find engaging with such groups easier as their perspectives recognise the impact of socio-political issues (Reynolds, 2022). While creative arts therapies work directly with the aesthetic and sensitive mode, the imagination is also used explicitly by narrative therapists to re-author lives (Denborough, 2014) and hypnotherapists to visualise their preferred futures. In other therapies, it tends to function implicitly.

Although human connection is integral to all therapeutic relationships, systemic therapies work explicitly with relationships in families, groups and institutions, thus including the sensitive, social and ethical modes. The lingual mode is foundational to most therapies, however neuro-linguistic programming and relationship therapies focus more explicitly upon patterns of communication. Shaping the world and engaging in meaningful activities is intuitively recognised as significant by most psychotherapists but more overtly by psychodynamic, creative and human givens therapies. Likewise, the analytic mode is an aspect of many therapies, but cognitive behaviour therapies focus upon it by identifying and challenging negative or self-defeating thought patterns. Person-centred therapists focus upon the sensitive mode by being fully emotionally present but may also include psychoeducation and other therapeutic techniques. Psychodynamic therapists utilise the crucible of the relationship to work out emotional and relational issues, while neuropsychological modalities ranging from somatic experiencing to various trauma tapping techniques and EMDR therapy address the biological, physical and kinematic modes.

While this brief foray into modal theory and psychotherapy cannot do justice to the richness of modal theory (see Strauss, 2015) or the diversity of psychotherapies, it has hopefully stimulated reflection on developing more multi-faceted, justice-sensitive and integrated approaches for refugees. In practice, such an approach would be comprehensive and collaborative, emphasising client choice. A relationship characterised by empathic understanding, respect, acceptance and genuineness with a hope for change is a precondition as refugees will disengage when faced with indifference and unresponsiveness. Working together with other health care professionals, case workers and voluntary sector agencies that offer support through befriending or language classes is essential for holistic care. With recent arrivals, sharing knowledge of how systems operate and available resources can be empowering.

As high levels of bodily stress and trauma symptoms are widespread and disturbing, psychoeducation with strategies to calm the body and regulate powerful emotions can enhance self-efficacy. Broken trust and fractured relationships are endemic in the refugee experience; thus, group therapies can help to heal the social aspect by fostering new connections and rebuilding community. Fundamental to social justice is understanding one's rights, so helping refugees understand and access what they are entitled to is indispensable.

As social justice and wellbeing are integrally connected, psychotherapists have a unique role in promoting social justice for individual refugees through direct practice as well as by witnessing and report writing. At a systemic level, psychotherapists can draw upon their knowledge by campaigning and speaking out against refugee injustice in the public square. While justice alone cannot restore the lives of refugees as they try to forge a new way forward, without it, they will struggle just to survive.

CASE STUDY: JOSEPH

Joseph aged 35 fled from a central African country following arrest, imprisonment and beatings for demonstrating against his government. After escaping to the UK, he was unable to communicate with his family. When appeal rights were exhausted, Joseph was transferred to a detention centre, where he was sexually assaulted by an official leaving him further traumatised. Destitute and homeless, he struggled to survive daily. At our first meeting, Joseph wept loudly and deeply, feeling overwhelmed, helpless and hopeless. We addressed his legal status, home culture, community in exile as well as his psychological functioning. His priorities included the injustice done to him by the sexual assault, his lack of refugee status and his emotional recovery.

Joseph was enabled to obtain solicitors for both the sexual assault and his asylum issues, and then was able to explore his complex feelings including humiliation about his sexual assault and shame about his inability to provide for his wife and children. He learned to manage his feelings and reconnect with his beliefs. We used EMDR to process his traumatic experiences and utilised guided imagery to rebuild his confidence and vision of the future. Eventually Joseph was reunited with his wife and children, received £20,000 in compensation, and became a popular taxi driver, welcoming all to his taxi with a broad smile.

CONCLUSION

As mental health support and psychotherapy is offered in both the statutory and voluntary sectors, the structure of the services and the therapy provided need to fit the particular exigencies of asylum seekers and refugees. A 'trauma informed' framework, including safety, trustworthiness, collaboration, empowerment and choice along with a sensitivity to cultural diversity, increasingly recognised as good practice, is a good starting point (Scottish Government, 2021). Additionally, knowledge of the legal systems and local resources along with the ability to work with refugee sector colleagues is essential to a social justice informed approach.

As not all mental health practitioners will have the time or inclination to develop the knowledge and skills needed, a system of 'refugee and asylum seeker champions' is recommended. A member of the therapeutic team with an interest to support refugees could be designated as a champion and equipped to fulfil that function. As well as understanding the global and local context, asylum and resettlement processes, they would need training in effective social justice informed psychotherapy with refugees, including the writing of reports. See recommended resources below. The champion would also be a resource to their teams and an advocate for refugee mental health in their locality. To support the champions, a peer support network and specialist supervision would be recommended. This network can have a unique role in enabling the public and the policy makers to understand refugee mental health difficulties and the consequences of legislative practices. Together with the refugee sector, they can promote social justice and uphold the rights of refugees and asylum seekers and encourage their flourishing as they seek to rebuild their lives.

REFLECTIVE AND CRITICAL THINKING QUESTIONS

1   What draws you to working with refugees and asylum seekers and what would you find difficult?

2 Describe your own worldview and how it relates to your therapeutic practice with people different from yourself?
3 What strengths does your therapeutic modality offer to refugees and what else might you draw upon for a more multi-modal and social justice informed practice?

RECOMMENDED READING AND RESOURCES

Maloney, C., Nelki, J. & Summers, A. (2022). *Seeking asylum and mental health: A practical guide for practitioners*. Cambridge University Press.
A multi-professional handbook on supporting asylum seeker mental health including the legal aspects and report writing.

Boyles, J. (Ed.). (2017). *Psychological therapies for survivors of torture: A human rights approach with people seeking asylum*. PCCS.

Solace Surviving Exile and Persecution: www.solace-uk.org.uk/new-free-e-learning
Free accessible e-learning courses on understanding refugee mental health and effective therapeutic practice. Also see Solace Professional Papers.

REFERENCES

Acarturk, C., Konuk, E., Cetinkaya, M., Senay, I., Sijbrandij, M., & Cuijpers, P. (2015). EMDR for Syrian refugees with posttraumatic stress disorder symptoms. *European Journal of Psychotraumatology, 6*, 1–9. https://doi.org/10.3402/ejpt.v6.27414

Aspinall, P. J., & Watters, C. (2010). *Refugees and asylum seekers: A review from an equality and human rights perspective*. Research Report 52. Equality and Human Rights Commission. www.equalityhumanrights.com/sites/default/files/refugees_and_asylum_seekers_research_rep

Blackwell, D. (2005). *Counselling and psychotherapy with refugees*. Jessica Kingsley.

Boyles, J., & Talbot, N. (2017). *Working with interpreters in psychological therapy – The right to be understood*. Routledge.

Burghgraef, A. (2021). *Truth, trauma and testimony solace monograph*. Solace UK. www.solace-uk.org.uk/wp-content/uploads/2021/05/No-3-Truth-Trauma-and-Testimony-Anne-Burghgraef-FINAL.pdf

Burnham, J. (2013). Developments in social GGRRAAACCEEESSS: Visible-invisible, voiced-unvoiced. In I. E. Kraus (Ed.), *Cultural reflexivity* (pp. 91–103). Karnac.

Charura, D., & Lago, C. (Eds.). (2021). *Black identities + white therapies: Race, respect + diversity*. PCCS Books.

Council of Europe. (2017). *The state of democracy, human rights and the rule of law in Europe: A shared responsibility for democratic security*. https://rm.coe.int/1680706b00

Denborough, D. (2014). *Retelling the stories of our lives: Everyday narrative therapy to draw inspiration and transform experience*. W.W. Norton & Co.

Griffen, J., & Tyrell, I. (2003). *Human givens: A new approach to emotional health and clear thinking.* HG Publishing.

The Guardian. (2012, October 16). Forced migration in the 21st century: Urbanised and unending. *The Guardian.* https://www.theguardian.com/global-development/2012/oct/16/forced-migration-21st-century-urbanised-unending

The Guardian. (2021, December 12). UK police leaders debate public admission of institutional racism. *The Guardian.* www.theguardian.com/uk-news/2021/dec/12/uk-police-leaders-debate-public-admission-institutional-racism

The Guardian. (2022, May 29). Windrush scandal caused by 30 years of racist immigration laws – report. *The Guardian.* www.theguardian.com/uk-news/2022/may/29/windrush-scandal-caused-by-30-years-of-racist-immigration-laws-report

Kalsbeek, L. (1975). *Contours of a Christian philosophy: An introduction to Herman Dooyeweerd's thought.* Wedge Publishing.

Kronick, R. (2018). Mental health of refugees and asylum seekers: Assessment and intervention. *Canadian Journal of Psychiatry, 63,* 290–296. www.ncbi.nlm.nih.gov/pubmed/29207884

Papadopolous, R. K. (2005). *Therapeutic care for refugees: No place like home.* Tavistock Clinic.

Refugee Council. (2023). https://www.refugeecouncil.org.uk/information/refugee-asylum-facts/the-truth-about-asylum

Reynolds, V. (2022). *Justice doing: At the intersections of power.* Dulwich Centre Publication.

Schauer, M., Neuner, F., & Elbert, T. (2011). *Narrative exposure therapy: Short-term intervention for traumatic stress disorders after war, terror or torture.* Hogrefe & Huber Publishers.

Scottish Government. (2021). *Trauma-informed practice toolkit Scotland.* www.gov.scot/publications/trauma-informed-practice-toolkit-scotland/pages/4/

Storkey, E. (2015). *Scars against humanity: Understanding and overcoming violence against women.* SPCK.

Strauss, D. F. M. (2015). *Herman Dooyeweerd's philosophy.* www.allofliferedeemed.co.uk/Strauss/DFMS2015Dooyeweerd.pdf

Thomas, L. (2011). Bloody foreigners here: Gender and culture – Working with refugees and asylum seekers. *Context, 113,* 5–8.

United Kingdom Legislation. https://www.legislation.gov.uk/ukpga/1998/42/schedule/1

UNHCR.(2023). *United Nations High Commission for Refugees.* https://www.unhcr.org/what-refugee#:~:text=The%201951%20Refugee%20Convention%20is,group%2C%20or%20political%20opinion.%E2%80%9D

Van Belle, H. A. (2014) *Explorations in the history of psychology: Persisting themata and changing paradigms.* Dordt College Press.

Vander Veer, G. (1998). *Counselling and therapy with refugees and victims of trauma* (2nd ed.). John Wiley & Sons.

14

THERAPY IN THE SHADOW OF THE CLIMATE AND ENVIRONMENTAL CRISIS

Martin Milton

OVERVIEW

In this chapter we meet Harry and his therapist Dr Leah Taylor (a fictionalised client and therapist). Their work explores the impacts of the climate and environmental crisis (from here on simply referred to as 'the crisis') on people, and the personal and social justice dimensions of the work. The story draws on common themes, outlined in research and writing, as an attempt to think about possibilities of meaning, of engagement and of practice.

Meeting Harry

Harry woke, that nauseating sense of unease there again. Bad dream? No, he realised, nothing like that, just the dystopian reality of life since early November, and that disappointing outcome of Cop26. He couldn't escape the profound sense of disappointment and despair.

It was this that brought him to therapy.

Harry put his phone in his pocket as he handed Dr Leah his self-referral form.

Continued

After acknowledging why they were there, Leah noted Harry seemed a little on edge, but … many clients were. It's never easy meeting a therapist for the first time, a stranger to talk to precisely about what distresses you.

'Fill me in, how can I help?'

Harry hesitated. 'It's since Cop26'.

'The climate meeting?'

Harry nodded. He explained his mood had plummeted since then, and he couldn't help but wonder what the point of anything was. 'It's dire, we know we gotta do something, but no one gives a shit'.

Harry's on-edgeness made sense.

'But, it's not just that', he explained. He told her about his regular bouts of low mood and, he said with worry in his voice, he was angry – about plans for the woods near where he was born, about people allowing their dogs to terrorise waterfowl near where he lived, and about the fact that whatever we thought of Cop26, London's air pollution, permits for more fracking or tax breaks for aviation, 'we get platitudes - not enforceable mitigations. Roger Hallam''s right, "we're fucked"'.

Leah sensed his desperation and heard his impotence. Was his mood a temporary thing? she wondered, or was it more deeply rooted? He sounded American, was he homesick perhaps? Or had a history of anxiety or trauma maybe?

Harry explained he'd listened to a therapist on a mental health podcast, and they'd suggested people try to be calm about the crisis, things 'will be what they will be'. He'd bristled at that, and more so when the presenter said anxiety could lead us to being overly controlling, adding stress in the face of things which are beyond our influence.

Why so angry? Leah wondered. The podcast had merely utilised a model of how one's thinking affects one's feeling and had advised him that worrying doesn't help.

'You have something more original than that for me, don't you?' Harry asked pointedly. Had he sensed the direction Leah's mind had started to go.

Did she? Leah wondered. Even if the point hadn't been well made, it was a principle that guides many therapies, obviously CBT, but it's embedded in other approaches too. It was a good question he was asking, and it got her wondering why she'd been so quick to think of 'other' reasons to explain his distress, why hadn't she considered Harry's own explanation first?

'We've only just started talking' – she hoped she wasn't avoiding the question, but she didn't understand enough to offer a formulation yet. 'Maybe you can fill me in more broadly so I can get a wider picture and *then* we can think about what you need and whether I might be the person to help?'

Notes

1   Taylor (2018)

CONTEXT AND ASSESSMENT

There's long been a concern as to how we understand the relationship between personal trauma and the impact of real-world events (see Cohn, 1989; Milton, 2018), and this has come to the fore again as therapists face growing numbers of clients experiencing 'eco-anxiety'.

Climate change isn't just happening in the environment, it's something we're *aware* of; it carries meaning and affects us in different ways. It's been discussed in the public domain since at least 1986 when the US Senate had its hearing on '*Ozone depletion, the greenhouse effect and climate change*' (Mooney, 2016). It, and other environmental devastations, give rise to land loss, drought, wildfires, species extinction and more (IPCC, 2014). People are becoming distressed as they recognise the damage the crisis is doing – to the physical environment, to people and to animals.

There are questions as to whether eco-emotions should be included in diagnostic manuals, or whether such terms are simply the latest manifestation of common or garden anxiety? The debate has the potential to be polarising, with eco-anxiety seen as *either* an indication of individual fragility, *or* a reasonable response to global calamity. Yet intersectional work shows much distress can be understood as a response to social inequality (see Johnstone & Boyle, 2018; Marshall, 2021; and for our purposes Lawrance et al., 2021).

The crisis, and its link to racial, gendered and other inequalities, demonstrates the importance of moving beyond artificial binaries. Assumptions such as 'self being separate to other', or the personal being the realm of the therapist, the political being irrelevant to our work, is stymying our understanding of people and their distress.

Harry's Assessment

Once Harry had outlined his initial thoughts, Leah asked about some of the issues he'd raised. This included many of the usual questions that a therapist asks when first meeting a client:

'How old are you, Harry?'

'21'.

'What can you tell me about your family and your upbringing?'

'I'm a New Yorker, born and raised. Mom and Dad are still together, I'm one of two'.

'And what do you do for work?'

'I'm studying ecological sciences'.

Leah heard that Harry was dating Clay, and that was going well. Leah asked about previous medical and psychiatric history, to which Harry didn't add a great deal. He'd had Covid but while it had been horrible for a couple of weeks, he wasn't left with any sense of long Covid and he'd had no major illnesses before. 'I expect we'll get more though, it's

Continued

inevitable the more we trash the earth, isn't it?' In terms of his health, Harry was mainly concerned about his recent anxiety and low mood.

Harry returned to the 'dismissive' tone of the podcast and Leah felt he was making a request for her to take his worry seriously. Help him find a way to be with a world under attack. And to help him decide what to do about it. Ignoring these issues, being upbeat, perky and positive, helping him distract himself may have *some* place she supposed, but not if it meant ignoring the trashing of the environment. Don't try to make this about him. At least, not in isolation.

Harry had done a lot of thinking. He described grief at the recent sell-off of a summer camp he'd attended every year since he was eight. He'd only stopped, age 15, to visit a friend in Southern Africa. That hadn't felt like a loss at the time as he'd traded the Catskills for the Cedarberg, another remote part of the world. He'd considered returning to the 'counsellors in training' programme but in the end decided to avail himself of more targeted conservation opportunities.

But maybe that'd been a mistake; it looked like he'd never be able to return. The camp was being sold. 'How can they just sell it off?' he asked. 'What's gonna happen to the city kids who depend on this facility for possibly their only non-urban experience? And what was going to happen to the woods? The deer, racoons, bats and fish when some corporation buys it? They've promised not to "overdevelop" it' - he used air quotes and a sneer to indicate his mistrust of those who'd made the statement, 'but clearly they're going to - it'll destroy it'. His pain was evident. 'Once you put condos on a lake, you are going to want a boat, once you have boats, you're not going to want beavers damming up the streams, are you? They'll go soon - either of their own accord or they'll be 'relocated' - to a zoo of some kind. And this is being replicated all over the state - the country too'.

Despite being a significant distance away, Leah realised Harry's experience of environmental vandalism left him feeling unsafe and despairing. The camp was a personal loss, and indicative of the way we treat wild places. Harry was familiar with the multitude of studies that show our ecology can only take so much destruction before it collapses. Only so many bees can be lost before food becomes scarce, only so many people can march across common land before it becomes denuded, only so many dogs can be allowed to chase wildfowl before the birds move on - but to where? Without the birds, the fish overwhelm the ponds until they suffocate...

'So, when you think about these possibilities -' Leah started, but Harry cut her off.

'They're not *possibilities*. They're happening'. He told her of plastics suffocating the rivers, and the air quality in London being so bad it kills over 9000 a year[2].

Leah nodded. 'OK right, yes. So that's what *is* going on, but tell me, what's the impact on you?'

Harry described physical and emotional reactions, nausea, worry and powerlessness. Anxiety would rise and he wouldn't know what to do. Distraction sometimes helped, as

Continued

did drinking too much, but he recognised that wasn't the answer, he didn't want to go down that route.

Leah was relieved to hear he was managing his drinking and there was no thought of self-harm, nor any other overt, immediate risks. However, the absence of risk doesn't mean someone is thriving.

As the first session drew to an end, Leah moved from 'what is the problem' to 'what might help?' To do that, she shared her initial formulation.

Formulation

'So maybe what's happened is something like this? You grew up in the city, but despite that, you had a great affinity for nature, for the wilds and for other species. This wasn't just some idea out *there*, but with access to the park and to summers spent in the woods you got to *experience* this, you *felt* the benefits, at a visceral level. It wasn't just theoretical; it became part of your existence'.

Harry nodded.

'So, it makes sense that when the space that you know so well is threatened, it would affect you. Anxiety is often an understandable reaction to unseen, or hard to deal with threats. Part of the problem is that the place under threat is not only *personally* very special to you, but you know it's happening everywhere, your social media remind you every day, several times a day of what is happening. So, you seldom get respite, get very little space to calm again'.

He nodded and smiled. 'Yes, I think so. But...'

'But what?'

'What do I do about it?' he asked.

That was the question. Psychotherapy is not something that magically changes the world out there, but nor is it any longer limited by an exclusive focus on the internal world. Many approaches have evolved to bridge the gap, to recognise the internal world is related to the 'real world'. In doing so it's possible to manage our encounters with the world less defensively and with greater attunement.

Notes

2   London Councils (2018)

PRINCIPLES

The crisis is resulting in somatic problems (Escobar et al., 1992), post-traumatic stress disorder (Galea et al., 2005) and depression. The experience of unusual weather events and uncertainty about the future is associated with poor mental health (APA, 2009). Changing landscapes, increased temperatures, and the viewing of images of environmental degradation create psychological distress (Doherty & Clayton, 2011). Albrecht et al. note that landscape alteration leads to feelings of solastalgia, a sense of helplessness and lack of control over the unfolding process (2007), and grief is associated with loss of the environment and uncertainty of the sustainability of life on Earth (Randall, 2009).

People respond to events that *have* happened, crises that *are* happening and to our awareness of what *may* happen. One factor is a sense of impotence when personal efforts to mitigate the effects of climate change do not bring immediate relief to the crisis (Kennedy-Woodard & Kennedy-Williams, 2022). Constant awareness of damage to the environment leads to anxiety about the future of the planet (Searle & Gow, 2010).

Assessment and formulation allow for a personalised view of the client, *and* their experience of the world. Relational understandings allow modern psychotherapies to consider the relationship between the client's inner world *and* the crisis. So rather than seeing Harry's dilemma as *either* an external issue (in relation to which neither he nor Leah have any immediate solution) or exclusively an issue of Harry projecting his own anxieties (which he had warned Leah off thinking), ongoing formulation allows space for both. Psychotherapy's attention to parallel processes, transference messages and the place of stories allows us to keep more than one thing in mind and in doing so avoid thinking in binary ways.

When the focus is on our relationship to the natural world therapists should consider what contexts could be best for the therapeutic work. Going beyond 'environmentally aware therapy' (Milton, 2010), therapists might consider a 'nature prescription' as an adjunct to the work (Dose of Nature, 2020); or maybe undertake some – or all – sessions outdoors in nature (see Harkness, 2019; Jordan, 2015).

Therapy

Harry was relieved to start therapy and Leah began to get a rounded picture of him, his life and his background. She could see this bright, compassionate young man had a lot of potential if he could tolerate his anxiety and navigate the world around him.

A dilemma arose when Harry and his boyfriend were arrested while protesting.

'For what?' Leah asked. 'Why'd they arrest you?'

'Criminal damage and aggravated trespass?' Harry said disdainfully. 'Really, it was for hanging out on the Bridge and chalking signs on the street. How is that outlawed when fossil fuel companies pollute the air every day and deliberately undermine science for decades?'

Leah heard powerlessness and recognised how the system benefits some more than others, the scales of justice are calibrated unfairly, and right now, Harry could not accept this. It got Leah thinking, maybe she and her colleagues shouldn't either.

Leah also had a more personal worry. The professional bodies were not clear on how therapists should support activists. The UKCP position seemed to suggest that involvement and arrest called into question a therapist's suitability to be on the UKCP register[3]. This is how systems work, disempower individuals and professions and bolster the status quo.

Continued

After the session Leah investigated further, finding that regulators expected that reg-istrants report cases of *therapist* arrest and have subjected members to investigatory panels to review competence/fitness to practise after involvement in non-violent pro-tests[4]. Thankfully the lengthy and distressing process resulted in a 'no case to answer' judgement, but it was hardly reassuring.

The BPS, the professional home of psychologists, and Leah's 'key' home were surpris-ingly quiet on the matter, saying little more than 'it was difficult'.

Leah worried whether there was an implicit expectation that she would be required to pass on information? But no, not as far as she could see.

Such questions may arise when working with material relating to all sorts of social justice issues - and has become increasingly complex with the *Police, Crime, Sentencing and Courts Act* (2022), aiming as it does to outlaw much social justice activism under the guise of noise and disruption interfering with 'normal business'[5]. This was something for Leah to explore in supervision and with her legal resources.

Notes

3   Cox (2020)
4   Jones (2020)
5   Liberty (2022)

There are times when psychotherapy has seemed to limit itself to the interpersonal aspect of people's distress, forgetting that systems create chaos, manipulate and abuse. Therapists therefore should not *limit* themselves to understanding the crisis as a per-sonal issue; instead, climate change should be understood as a distressing matter in its own right.

Counselling and psychotherapy have not offered as much to the crisis as they might. Institutionally, they remain embedded in contemporary political and economic perspec-tives that view humans through a dichotomous/binary lens resulting in us being seen as separate from nature (Kesebir & Kesebir, 2017).

This is not to say our professions offer nothing to the debate. Many schools of therapy take a useful relational stance; existential therapy focuses on being-in-the-world, systems theory on the impact of communication and interactional power on members of a system, and some psychodynamic theorists outline in detail the psy-chic damage that occurs in relation to environmental trauma. Searles challenged the over-reliance on internal formulations noting that too often psychotherapy 'relegates the world to being a mere backdrop' (1972). Samuels noted the profound relationship we have to place (1993), and Blair (2011) and Rust (2004) show how physical and mental health is intimately linked to nature and a healthy environ-ment. Psychology has a significant role to play in the amelioration of the crisis (Uzzell, 2021).

Therapy progresses

Once Harry trusted that Leah could see the world the way he did, he was able to engage with her otherness too. They accepted that Leah was less informed about some of the specifics of climate change, and this allowed Harry to clarify things for himself when he 'corrected' Leah's assumptions. Harry started to realise his distress could possibly be linked to *both* social and very personal matters.

Leah helped Harry look at the immense disappointment he felt after the watered down Cop26 declaration was made. As they explored this, Harry saw that he'd long been affected by those that failed to deliver; this was the case whether it was the camp authorities, or teachers who had failed to spot homophobic and biphobic banter at school.

Differences arose in the relationship too. There was an occasion when Leah was late. She couldn't help it, one of the bridges was closed with a fossil fuel protest; Harry was disappointed but seemed to minimise his experience.

'But how *was* that for you?' Leah asked.

'Disappointing', he admitted nervously.

'Annoying? Unsettling?' she probed a bit more, basing her exploration on visible signs of agitation.

Harry nodded, but tried to trivialise things; he acknowledged Leah hadn't intended to let him down, that circumstances were outside of her control.

Leah nodded. On both counts, factually, he was right.

'But even if that's right, I see it unsettles you. And I wonder if things like this give us an insight into how unsafe things feel – sorry are, or become – when people continue to say one thing and do another?'

This was helpful, allowing Leah to introduce the idea of looking after himself while accepting that some things would remain outside of his control.

'You mean... what the podcast said?'

'Hmm – ish. I suppose. Accepting "what will be will be" doesn't mean "giving up". It might mean we accept limits of what we can do, find a way to manage the degree to which we get unsettled, enough to recover and be ready for the next opportunity'.

Harry pondered what he might do; alone, with his boyfriend or with others. In the next session he reflected on his need to stop 'doomscrolling'.

'Doomscrolling', Leah said, enjoying the clarity of the term.

Harry nodded. 'I need to be more selective in what I subscribe to, the news I follow. For instance, I set new email rules so I check them when I want, rather than all the time'.

This was important, it's not just climate change that impacts people, the tsunami of information is a challenge for many too. While information *can* clarify and facilitate, it stimulates anxiety too.

As sessions progressed, Harry also reflected on his successes, which Leah felt was helpful; successes need celebrating.

ACTION!

An over-focus on 'doing' can lead to burnout, obsessionality and the obfuscation of meaning, but we should avoid the simplistic binary that sometimes bedevils discussions of therapy. It's not 'to do' *vs* 'to be', but rather, we should consider the *meaning* of 'doing' – 'doing' and agency are important aspects of being. This seems especially relevant when clients bring climate-related concerns (Kennedy-Woodard & Kennedy-Williams, 2022).

For many, some degree of action needs to happen around the flow of information. Digital media are programmed to catch us quickly with heightened imagery and meaning, often implicating powerful emotions such as anxiety and aggressivity. When this is coupled with the weight of the crisis and the obligation activists experience to stay informed (Gimalova, in process) it can be overwhelming. Discussing the flow of information can help clients navigate the overwhelm while being informed; taking breaks from constantly fielding *new* information allows for considered thinking to occur.

Action may also help by affording people a chance to move from guilt and a feeling of complicity to feeling they have agency and choice. Action with other people – whether it be joining a litter picking crew, writing to one's MP, or attending campaign meetings, may help break the isolation and overwhelmed feeling reported in relation to the crisis.

Final stage

As therapy progressed Harry was increasingly able to understand that his anxiety was related to the reality of climate change, the *speed* of it and the fact it was happening the world over. There were also the personal experiences of being in nature, and the loss of access to such spaces. A common experience underpinning them was a distrust of those in power to do the right thing. Whether custodians of the Catskill woods, or the UK and US governments, it was hard to feel secure when he could not trust the powerful.

Over the weeks Harry became more mindful about different aspects of his anxiety and the crisis and started to speak of not needing to know everything, that he might become more comfortable with the unknown, the unpredictable and the paradoxical. He started to recognise that disappointment isn't an emotion to run from, it may be warranted. Difficult feelings could be valid as people do let you down, corporations and governments do gaslight the public, and complete withdrawal and mistrust were unhelpful, leaving him feeling alone in the world. Accepting uncertainty seemed to ground him a little, and he thought he might trust people a little more.

As therapy ended, Leah helped Harry consider how he might utilise these insights and the growing confidence in his emotions because, they both realised, the crisis was not going away any time soon.

CONCLUSION

This story is not offered as a watertight suggestion of what clients *will* bring to therapy, nor as an instruction manual of what a therapist *should* always do. Rather it illustrates some common themes as an invitation to think broadly, critically and creatively about possibilities. While it may be most relevant to clinical work with adults and young people, children may be affected by climate change and by the discussion of it too. Therapists may be working with parents as to how they handle difficult news and anxious feelings in very young children.

Much of what is quoted in this account draws on available research and literature – but that is not without its problems. Our economic and ideological structures mean that traditional Western science and therapeutic theory is often privileged, and we need to think as to how and where we broaden our thinking, making space available for research and scholarship from the widest possible perspective, Indigenous psychologies, the realities of the Global South and that which is independent of corporate interests.

REFLECTIVE AND CRITICAL THINKING QUESTIONS

1   How well can I hear beyond my traditional models of understanding?

Draw a line down the centre of a page. On the left-hand side, jot down what you might make of this story using your 'usual' therapeutic model. On the right-hand side consider what else it might have meant – in terms of content and process, in terms of what Harry might have said about it, etc.

2   How well can I conceptualise what is being said in a non-binary fashion?

Make several sets of notes considering what you might take from this story if looked at through a lens considering race; then if considering disability; similarly in terms of gender, power or any other issue of social justice. Don't be fooled by an initial assumption of 'it says nothing about that'. That may be a clue in itself. Consider the relationship between the different insights.

3   How skilled am I at reflecting on the personal and the political, the subjective and the objective?

Spend time reflecting on your thoughts about the personal and the political. What feels self-evident and what do you struggle with? Where do you feel allied to your professional colleagues and where do you feel a bit of an outsider?

RECOMMENDED READING AND RESOURCES

Kennedy-Woodard, M., & Kennedy-Williams, P. (2022). *Turn the tide on climate anxiety: Sustainable action for your mental health and the planet.* Jessica Kingsley Publications.

This book outlines the state of our knowledge about climate change, before exploring different emotions that people may feel in relation to it. Particularly helpful is the focus on moving from anxiety to action and including self-help exercises which could be utilised in practice.

Klein, N. (2014). *This changes everything: Capitalism v the climate.* Penguin. While not addressing psychological therapy, there are few more engaging or knowledgeable writers shedding light on the way that the crisis is intimately interwoven with social justice issues.

Lawrance, D. E., Thompson, R., Fontana, G., & Jennings, D. N. (2021). *The impact of climate change on mental health and emotional wellbeing: Current evidence and implications for policy and practice.* Grantham Institute. www.imperial.ac.uk/ grantham/publications/all-publications/the-impact-of-climate-change-on-mentalhealth-and-emotional-wellbeing-current-evidence-and-implications-for-policy-and-practice.php
A meta-analysis of the evidence on the psychological distress caused by, and in relation to, climate change and the associated health costs incurred.

REFERENCES

Albrecht, G., Sartore, G. M., Connor, L., Higginbotham, N., Freeman, S., Kelly, B., ... & Pollard, G. (2007). Solastalgia: The distress caused by environmental change. *Australasian Psychiatry*, *15*(Suppl 1), 95–98.

American Psychological Association. (2009). *Psychology & global climate change: Addressing a multifaceted phenomenon and set of challenges.* APA.

Blair, L. (2011). Ecopsychology and the person-centred approach: Exploring the relationship. *Counselling Psychology Review*, *26*(1), 43–52.

Cohn, H. W. (1989). The place of the actual in psychotherapy. *Free Associations*, *1*(18), 49–61.

Cox, P. (2020). Extinction Rebellion & Covid-19: The potential impact of civil disobedience upon professional conduct hearings [PowerPoint slides]. National Counsellors' Day 2020 conference. www.onlinevents.co.uk/learn-more/

Doherty, T. J., & Clayton, S. (2011). The psychological impacts of global climate change. *American Psychologist*, *66*(4), 265.

Dose of Nature. (2020). *Dose of Nature prescriptions.* www.doseofnature.org.uk/ doseofnatureprescriptions

Escobar, J. I., Canino, G., Rubio-Stipec, M., & Bravo, M. (1992). Somatic symptoms after a natural disaster: A prospective study. *The American Journal of Psychiatry*, *149*(7), 965–967.

Galea, S., Nandi, A., & Vlahov, D. (2005). The epidemiology of post-traumatic stress disorder after disasters. *Epidemiologic Reviews*, *27*(1), 78–91.

Gimalova, M. (2023). *Being in an emotional storm: Young climate activists and exposure to climate change information.* Psych thesis, Regents University London.

Harkness, C. (2019). *The nature of existence: Health, wellbeing and the natural world.* Red Globe Press.

Intergovernmental Panel on Climate Change. (2014). *Climate change 2014: Synthesis report (AR5).* IPCC.

Johnstone, L., & Boyle, M. (2018). *The power threat meaning framework: Towards the identification of patterns in emotional distress, unusual experiences and troubled or troubling behaviour, as an alternative to functional psychiatric diagnosis.* BPS.

Jones, R. (2020). I took my turn on Friday to be arrested. *The Psychologist.* https://thepsychologist.bps.org.uk/i-took-my-turn-friday-be-arrested

Jordan, M. (2015). *Nature and therapy: Understanding counselling and psychotherapy in outdoor spaces.* Routledge.

Kennedy-Woodard, M., & Kennedy-Williams, P. (2022). *Turn the tide on climate anxiety: Sustainable action for your mental health and the planet.* Jessica Kingsley Publications.

Kesebir, S., & Kesebir, P. (2017). A growing disconnection from nature is evident in cultural products. *Perspectives on Psychological Science, 12*(2), 258–269.

Lawrance, D. E., Thompson, R., Fontana, G., & Jennings, D. N. (2021). *The impact of climate change on mental health and emotional wellbeing: Current evidence and implications for policy and practice.* Grantham Institute. www.imperial.ac.uk/grantham/publications/all-publications/the-impact-of-climate-change-on-mentalhealth-and-emotional-wellbeing-current-evidence-and-implications-for-policy-and-practice.php

Liberty. (2022). *Liberty responds to Commons vote on noise-based protest restrictions.* www.libertyhumanrights.org.uk/issue/liberty-responds-to-commons-vote-on-noise-based-protest-restrictions/

London Councils. (2018). *Demystifying air pollution in London: Full report.* www.londoncouncils.gov.uk/node/33227

Marshall, J. P. (2021). Rolling in the muck, dancing with the law: A story of 'addiction' and the remaking of a self. In M. Milton (Ed.), *Balancing on quicksand: Reflections on power, politics and the relational* (pp. 13–24). Palgrave Macmillan.

Milton, M. (Ed.). (2010). *Therapy and beyond: Counselling psychology contributions to therapeutic and social issues.* Wiley-Blackwell.

Milton, M. (2018). *The political is personal: Stories of difference and psychotherapy.* Palgrave McMillan.

Mooney, C. (2016, June 11). 30 years ago scientists warned Congress on global warming. What they said sounds eerily familiar. *The Washington Post.* www.washingtonpost.com/news/energy-environment/wp/2016/06/11/30-years-ago-scientists-warned-congress-on-global-warming-what-they-said-sounds-eerily-familiar/

Randall, R. (2009). Loss and climate change: The cost of parallel narratives. *Ecopsychology, 1*(3), 118–129.

Rust, M. J. (2004). Ecopsychology: Seeking health in an ailing world. *Resurgence Magazine, 224.*

Samuels, A. (1993). 'I am a place': Depth psychology and environmentalism. *British Journal of Psychotherapy, 10*(2), 211–219.

Searle, K., & Gow, K. (2010). Do concerns about climate change lead to distress? *International Journal of Climate Change Strategies and Management, 2*(4), 362–379.

Searles, H. (1972). Unconscious processes in relation to the environmental crisis. *The Psychoanalytic Review, 59*(3), 361–374.

Taylor, M. (2018, October 26). 'We have a duty to act': Hundreds ready to go to jail over climate crisis. *The Guardian*. www.theguardian.com/environment/2018/oct/26/we-have-a-duty-to-act-hundreds-ready-to-go-to-jail-over-climate-crisis

Uzzell, D. (2021). Integrating the individual and the collective for a transformational response to the climate emergency. *Clinical Psychology Forum: Special Issue: Climate and ecological emergency, 346*, 12–22.

PART 3

BEYOND THE THERAPY ROOM

15
ADVOCACY AND WORKING WITH INDIVIDUAL CLIENTS BEYOND TRADITIONAL THERAPY MODELS

Courtland C. Lee and Marja Humphrey

OVERVIEW

Social justice has become a major construct in counselling and psychological theory and practice. This involves promoting access and equity to ensure full participation in the life of a society, particularly for those who have been systematically excluded based on race/ethnicity, gender, age, physical or mental disability, education, sexuality, socio-economic status, or other background characteristics or group membership. Social justice is a belief that all people have a right to equitable treatment, support for their human rights and a fair allocation of societal resources (Bell, 1997; Lee et al., 2018; Miller, 1999; Rawls, 1971).

For counsellors (or indeed any psychological therapists), social justice implies professional conduct that opposes all forms of discrimination and oppression (Ratts et al., 2015). Therapy practices rooted in social justice seek to challenge inherent inequities in social systems. Significantly, it has been argued that, from a theoretical perspective, social justice is the fifth force in the counselling profession, following the paradigms of the psychodynamic, cognitive/behavioural, humanistic and multiculturalism approaches (Ratts et al., 2004).

To understand fully the construct of social justice and its relationship to the counselling process, the important concept of advocacy must be considered. Advocacy refers to the act or process of advocating or supporting a cause or proposal (Merriam-Webster, n.d.). An advocate, therefore, is an individual who pleads for a cause or argues another individual's cause or proposal (Lee et al., 2018).

Advocacy helps to frame the context of therapy for social justice. As advocates, counsellors or psychological therapists channel energy and skill into helping clients challenge institutional and social barriers impeding their development. In addition to counselling at an individual level, when necessary, counsellors need to act on behalf of marginalised or disenfranchised clients and actively challenge long-standing traditions, preconceived notions or regressive policies that may stifle wellness and human dignity. Acting as advocates, through efforts both with and/or for clients, counsellors can help people become empowered so that they challenge systemic barriers and seize new opportunities (Lee et al., 2018; Ratts et al., 2010).

There are three important aspects of the advocate role for professional counsellors. First, advocates are counsellors who view helping from a systemic perspective. Second, advocates attempt systemic change in partnership with clients who often lack the knowledge or skills to effect such change alone. Third, advocates must understand important systems change principles along with the skill to translate them into action (Lee et al., 2018; Ratts et al., 2010).

The purpose of this chapter is to offer direction on applying advocacy skills to working with clients. These skills move beyond mere counselling with individual clients to intervening as an agent of social justice within problematic systems (Ratts et al., 2015). The chapter begins with an overview of the contemporary context for the role of counsellor or psychological therapist as advocate. Next, a case study will be presented that underscores the need for counsellors to think and act in ways that transcend the traditional one-to-one counselling paradigm. Finally, a discussion of the case study examining the counselling advocacy role will be presented.

CONTEXT FOR PSYCHOLOGIST THERAPIST AS ADVOCATE

The third decade of the 21st century has seen a series of challenges profoundly impact global mental health and wellbeing. This challenging period has resulted in new levels of both individual and collective trauma as communities navigate issues spawned by bigotry, hatred and oppression. The COVID-19 pandemic has changed the nature and quality of life worldwide. Not only have many lives been lost, but for those who survived, the pandemic has exacerbated and exposed long-standing social injustices. Individuals in areas historically marginalised due to environmental concerns, low earning potential, lack of access to medical care or other systemic inequities that impact life have been disproportionately negatively affected.

This period of social and cultural reckoning, underscored by COVID-19 and its impact on human wellbeing, has forced an examination of the current theory and practice of professional counselling and psychological therapy. Traditionally, counsellors have been focused on helping individuals resolve problems and make decisions. Yet, as contemporary world challenges make abundantly clear, the origin of problems and impediments to effective decision-making often lie not within individuals, but in intolerant, restrictive or oppressive environments. The remainder of this chapter will provide a conceptual basis for the advocacy role of counsellor acting as an agent of social justice.

CASE STUDY: THE REDD-SANTIAGO FAMILY

The US-based family in the following case study provides an example of how contemporary social and cultural challenges can impact mental health. It provides a context for understanding the counsellor advocacy role and the importance of thinking and acting outside the boundaries of traditional therapeutic approaches.

Karen Redd, a Black woman, is a teacher at a local urban middle school. In addition to ensuring her students have access to the internet and devices to learn online, she has had to homeschool her own children in between teaching her students. Her partner, Maria Santiago, a Latina, is an essential worker in the cafeteria at the local hospital. She speaks limited English. Due to her work, her exposure to the virus and others who have tested COVID positive has been incessant. Together, these women have two children. Their teenage son, Kevin, is often fearful of what he sees on TV and social media. In the wake of George Floyd's death at the hands of police, Kevin considers himself a target as a young, Black male. Their other child, Raphael, is in elementary school and learning English as it is his second language. He is chronically ill due to asthma and Maria often must miss work to take care of him. She is worried about his health and how many times their health insurance will cover his frequent emergency room visits. The family resides in the state of Florida where they have experienced systemic intolerance due to their LGBTQIA identity. They also feel socially isolated because of recent state legislation about teaching sexual orientation issues in schools that has become known as the 'Don't Say Gay' bill. In their extended family, Karen has an ailing mother who resides in a nursing home. Although Karen would normally visit her mother, Delores, each Sunday afternoon, the shutdowns due to the pandemic have halted her weekly visits. Karen is concerned about Delores as she cannot see her and updates on her health have stopped coming as regularly from the nurses on her floor via telephone and text.

Case Analysis: Beyond Traditional Therapy

Each individual in the Redd-Santiago family could benefit from counselling from a number of theoretical approaches. Karen could deal with her issues of anxiety and stress related to simultaneously having to teach remotely and homeschool her own children. She might also explore her anxiety and guilt related to not being able to see her mother.

Maria could examine her anxiety over her son and his wellbeing and her fear related to being exposed to the virus at work. Both Karen and Maria might benefit from some couples counselling related to the stress of raising children and the isolation they experience as a gay couple in a homophobic environment.

Helping Kevin process his fears as a young Black male living in the aftermath of the George Floyd murder might prove beneficial. Likewise, using an interpreter, Raphael might benefit from exploring his feelings about school and possible illness-related fear or anxiety.

All of the Redd-Santiago family's presenting issues could be addressed with traditional therapeutic approaches including Person-Centred Therapy, Cognitive Behavioural Therapy (CBT), and Play Therapy. However, viewing the family's issues from a social justice advocacy perspective, it is evident that major systemic issues are impacting their mental health. This perspective would suggest that if these environmental challenges are not addressed within counselling interventions, the family will continue to experience problems.

Systemic Forces for Therapeutic Consideration

Many systemic forces are impinging on the mental health of the Redd-Santiago family. First, the global pandemic of COVID-19 must be considered. The pandemic presents a pervasive context for the family's issues and is a systemic threat to each family member's mental health. In particular, Maria's challenges as an essential worker at a hospital require she report for work at a vital health care facility during a major health crisis, despite the fact that she is constantly exposed to the virus. She puts herself at risk daily to help provide for her family as well as offer a support service to the hospital. As a systemic factor, it is important to note that COVID must be factored into contemporary counselling interventions given its widespread impact on mental as well as physical wellbeing.

Second, the educational system and its impact on the family must be examined. Issues related to teaching and learning during the COVID crisis is creating stress for the family. In particular, homeschooling their children is a concern for Karen and Maria. Likewise, Karen is confronted with the difficulties of ensuring technology access for her students. Many families cannot afford internet access or computers which mean their children may be unable to engage in virtual learning experiences. This technological divide is an important equity issue. In addition, the English as a second language programme is obviously challenging for Raphael.

Third, with respect to Raphael's chronic asthma, the impact of the healthcare system on the family must be taken into account. The family is worried about health insurance and whether it will continue to cover Raphael's hospital visits. It goes without saying that if the family were to lose their health insurance, it could spell financial disaster. In addition, due to the COVID pandemic the nursing home where Karen's mother resides has had to change visiting policies and procedures. These changes mean that Karen's access to her mother has been significantly curtailed.

Finally, it is important to consider how the socio-political system is negatively impacting the Redd-Santiago family. For example, Kevin, the oldest son, has had a strong visceral reaction to the death of George Floyd at the hands of the Minneapolis police. He perceives that he lives in an environment where he is at risk simply because he is young, Black, and male. Police policies and procedures that have led to scores of young Black men being killed by police in recent years has established an atmosphere of fear, distrust and anger among many young Black men and their families. Additionally, the family is reacting to a wave of systemic intolerance aimed at members of the LGBTQIA community. This intolerance is symptomatic of a larger systemic force that feeds off fear of the 'other' or someone of a different background or group membership. This fear has spawned a spate of legislation characterised by intolerance and exclusion.

Advocacy and Working with the Redd-Santiago Family beyond Traditional Therapy Models

The systemic challenges inherent in this case study suggest an advocacy orientation that involves not only individual or group counselling, but systems change interventions as well. Individual counselling will help to alleviate much of the stress in each family member's life. However, with the pervasive systemic forces at play in their lives it is safe to assume that if they are not addressed in some manner, the family will continue to face mental health challenges.

Ratts et al. (2010) provide a framework for operationalising a counselling advocacy orientation. The framework begins in a traditional sense with direct counseling that entails helping the client identify systemic barriers, learning approaches to address those barriers and helping them to evaluate those approaches. Going beyond the traditional therapeutic approach, advocacy counselling entails the following components: *client advocacy*, *systems advocacy*, and *social/political advocacy*. Each of these components will be examined in the case of the Redd-Santiago family in the sections that follow.

CLIENT ADVOCACY

Client advocacy refers to actions a counsellor takes to advocate on behalf of an individual client or family. As a client advocate a counsellor identifies barriers to the wellbeing of clients with attention to issues facing vulnerable groups. They then develop an initial plan of action for confronting these barriers in consultation with their client and ensuring the plan is consistent with the client's goals. The counsellor may also negotiate relevant services on behalf of clients. For the Redd-Santiago family, a counsellor may act as a client advocate in several ways.

Karen. 1) Helping her work with school officials and Wi-Fi providers to ensure that all her students have reliable internet access necessary for virtual learning. 2) Aiding her in finding community resources that can provide access to computers for her students. 3) Assisting her in locating resources to enhance her ability to effectively homeschool her own children. 4) Working with her to advocate with nursing home officials to ensure that she gets regular communications regarding her mother's health. 5) Assisting her in exploring with nursing home officials possible ways that she can visit with her mother virtually on a consistent basis.

Maria. 1) Exploring with her ways to improve her English skills through low-cost/free language proficiency programmes. 2) Working with her and hospital officials as well as community resources to ensure that she has access to ongoing COVID testing due to her role as an essential hospital worker. 3) Helping her find the best possible medical care for her son, Raphael. 4) Helping her communicate with her supervisors at the hospital about the nature of her son's medical condition and assisting her in exploring with them possible accommodations that will allow her to care for her son without negative job consequences.

Karen and Maria. Helping the couple work with their insurance provider to examine their health insurance options to ensure they have the maximum benefits and continuous coverage for Raphael's health issues as well as any other family medical needs.

Kevin. Connecting Kevin with a Black male mentoring programme. Such a programme, generally led by adult Black males, would provide Kevin with a supportive atmosphere to explore his Black male identity and develop the competencies for success as well as possible survival in the challenging environment often facing Black male youth in contemporary American society.

Raphael. Engaging the school counsellor to identify a bilingual peer who could help him successfully navigate the academic and social aspect of school, including the improvement of English language mastery. In addition, consulting with school health officials to ensure they can support his asthma management.

SYSTEMS ADVOCACY

Systems advocacy focuses on a counsellor advocating on behalf of groups of clients or within an organisation or community. When a counsellor identifies systemic factors that act as barriers to clients' development, they engage in efforts to change the environment and possibly prevent some of the problems that negatively impact on mental health. This would entail partnering with client groups and community stakeholders to address the specific environmental and systemic issues that impact families such as the Redd-Santiago family. An advocacy-oriented counsellor would be able to participate with and/or facilitate community partners such as schools, religious institutions, businesses and hospitals in identifying the source of problems that families face as they deal with education and health challenges during a global pandemic. Through collaboration with such stakeholders, a counsellor can help set goals and develop action plans to ensure that families receive the community support necessary to thrive and function during challenging times.

One example of this type of advocacy would be having a counsellor supporting Karen and the other teachers from her school in co-ordinating efforts to ensure internet connectivity and access to computers for all students throughout the school system. Another example would be supporting Maria and her co-workers in consulting with hospital administrators about health and safety protocols. If necessary, a counsellor might need to broker the services of an interpreter to ensure that the voices of Maria and her co-workers are clearly understood.

A final example of systems advocacy might involve helping Karen and the relatives of other nursing home residents consult with officials there about greater access to and communication with loved ones during the pandemic shutdown. A counsellor might be able to act as a broker between the families of residents and nursing home officials in revising communication policies and procedures.

SOCIAL/POLITICAL ADVOCACY

A counsellor acting as a change agent in the systems that directly affect the Redd-Santiago family would recognise that some of the concerns challenging the family impact people in a much larger arena. When this happens, a counsellor uses their skills to carry out social/political advocacy on behalf of a client population. The client population in this case might be characterised as working-class families dealing with educational, health, social and economic challenges during a global pandemic. Within this context, counsellors engage in advocacy strategies often independent of specific clients or client groups to address issues they observe.

The case of the oldest son, Kevin, provides a scenario for a counsellor acting as a social/political advocate. As with many young Black males, the killing of George Floyd at the hands of police has shattered Kevin's sense of security as he views himself as a potential target of such violence. Floyd's death has no doubt traumatised him and processing this with Kevin therapeutically is vital. Just as important, however, is addressing the systemic problem of police attitudes and behaviours towards Black males in the country.

A counsellor who is a social/political advocate might engage in activities on behalf of Kevin and scores of other young Black males that challenge policing policies and practices that threaten the lives and wellbeing of Black men. This might involve joining community action groups that are exploring aspects of racism in policing practices and policies. Further, with community allies a counsellor might lobby legislators and other policy makers to enact new culturally sensitive policing policies. Importantly, a counsellor might want to develop and offer workshops to police departments on issues such as cultural sensitivity or communication skills, and/or become active in social justice groups such as Black Lives Matter.

Similarly, a counsellor engaging in social/political advocacy can help the Redd-Santiago family and similar families address the systemic intolerance related to their LGBTQIA identity. Although marriage equality has been established law for a decade in the United States, there have been recent attempts to dismantle the domestic rights that same-sex couples have attained. Concurrently, legislation has been introduced in many parts of the country to stifle attempts to infuse sexuality issues into the educational curriculum.

A counsellor who is a social/political advocate might consider how they could best use their voice to challenge systemic LGBTQIA intolerance. For example, they might want to write advocacy briefings regarding ways to promote LGBTQIA mental health. As appropriate, a counsellor might engage in public awareness campaigns or lobby legislators and educational policy makers about the deleterious effects of homophobia on the mental health of LGBTQIA adolescents and their families. Such efforts might include advocacy for ensuring diversity in educational programmes. Finally, it might be necessary for a counsellor to become politically active in supporting candidates for political office who are supporters of LGBTQIA rights.

ADVOCACY COUNSELLING AND THE REDD-SANTIAGO FAMILY: FINAL THOUGHTS

The ultimate goal of counselling advocacy for this family is to help them become empowered. Acting as an advocate, through efforts both with and on behalf of the family, the counsellor can help each individual develop the competencies to challenge the systemic barriers that impinge on their mental health and quality of life.

The counselling advocacy role with the Redd-Santiago family is based on three fundamental principles. First, viewing counselling from a systemic perspective. Second, engaging in systemic intervention in partnership with clients. Third, understanding systems change principles along with the skill to translate them into action.

CONCLUSION

Professional psychological therapists and counsellors in the third decade of the 21st century must be agents of individual as well as systemic change. This chapter has provided an exploration of how advocacy skills are applied to working with clients. Advocacy moves beyond traditional counselling and psychological models to intervention strategies for challenging problematic systems that impinge upon client mental health and wellbeing. Contemporary counselling must be about not only helping people solve problems and make decisions using traditional therapeutic approaches, but also focusing therapeutic skills on helping to address the profound social, cultural and economic dilemmas challenging society. Through counselling advocacy that transcends traditional therapy models, counsellors can help to empower clients and foster healthy communities as well.

REFLECTIVE AND CRITICAL THINKING QUESTIONS

1   What actual or perceived barriers exist for you as a counsellor stepping into an advocacy role?
2   How readily do you identify systemic challenges in your clients' lives? What impacts your ability to work with clients from an advocacy perspective?
3   How might you encourage self-advocacy for clients from traditionally/historically marginalised populations?

RECOMMENDED READING AND RESOURCES

Al'Uqdah, S. N., Jenkins, K., & Ajaa, N. (2017). Empowering communities through social media. *Counselling Psychology Quarterly*, *32*, 137–149. https://doi.org/10.1080/095150 70.2017.1407747
This article describes how counsellors might leverage social media platforms as a vehicle for social justice advocacy, especially for marginalised communities.

Diemer, M. A., Rapa, L. J., Voight, A. M., & McWhirter, E. H. (2016). Critical consciousness: A developmental approach to addressing marginalization and oppression. *Child Development Perspectives*, *10*(4), 216–221. https://doi.org/10.1111/ cdep.12193
The authors promote critical consciousness as one social justice strategy that professionals acting as advocates can employ and teach to youth from marginalised communities.

Washington, A. R. (2021). Using a critical hip-hop school counseling framework to promote Black consciousness among Black boys. *Professional School Counseling*, *25*, 1–13. https://doi.org/10.1177/2156759X211040039
The author utilises hip-hop music and culture as a backdrop for exploring our societal systems and their impact upon the lives of Black boys specifically.

Williams, J. M., Byrd, J., Smith, C. D., & Dean, A. (2020). Photovoice as an innovative approach to group work with Black youth in school settings. *The Journal for Specialists in Group Work*, *45*(3), 213–225. https://doi.org/10.1080/01933922.2020.1789794
This article offers an example of an intervention designed to uplift students' voices and teach students self-advocacy skills to be utilised within the school system.

REFERENCES

Bell, L. A. (1997). Theoretical foundations for social justice education. In M. Adams, L. A. Bell, & P. Griffin (Eds.), *Teaching for diversity and social justice: A sourcebook* (pp. 3–15). Routledge.

Lee, C. C., Baldwin, R., Micallef Marmarà, S., & Quesenberry, L. (2018). Counsellors as agents of social justice. In C. C. Lee (Ed.), *Counselling for social justice* (3rd ed., pp. 3–20). American Counselling Association.

Merriam-Webster. (n.d.). Advocacy. In *Merriam-Webster's collegiate dictionary*. www.merriam-webster.com/dictionary/advocacy

Miller, D. (1999). *Principles of social justice*. Harvard University Press.

Ratts, M., D'Andrea, M., & Arredondo, P. (2004, September 13). Social justice counselling: 'Fifth force' in field. *Counselling Today*, 28–30.

Ratts, M. J., Lewis, J. A., & Toporek, R. L. (2010). Advocacy and social justice: A helping paradigm for the 21st century. In M. J. Ratts, R. L. Toporek, & J. A. Lewis (Eds.), *ACA advocacy competencies: A social justice framework for counsellors* (pp. 3–10). American Counselling Association.

Ratts, M. J., Singh, A. A., Nassar-McMillan, S., Butler, S. K., & McCullough, J. R. (2015). *Multicultural and social justice counseling competencies*. American Counseling Association. www.counseling.org/docs/default-source/competencies/multicultural-and-social-justice-counseling-competencies.pdf?sfvrsn=20

Rawls, J. A. (1971). *A theory of justice*. Harvard University Press.

16
SOCIAL JUSTICE IN CLINICAL SUPERVISION

Dwight Turner

OVERVIEW

Clinical supervision is one of the core areas of the work that psychological therapists do in the Global North. Clinical supervision, by its very nature, provides a holding and hopefully safe environment for the supervisee to explore the client material that they are holding and working with on a day-to-day or week-to-week basis. One of the main areas of clinical supervision, especially when we consider the topic areas within this book is the weighing up of just how the identity of the client has been impacted by the social constructions of identity which may or may not have hampered their development. Supervisors, whilst there to enable, encourage and facilitate the therapeutic work carried out between the supervisee and the client, also have a duty of care to understand, explore and help the supervisee do the same around issues of social justice and their intersectional socially constructed identities. This, therefore, raises a number of issues for the supervisor which will be covered in this chapter. Specifically, I will consider:

(a) The importance of supervision and supervisors in recognising the socially constructed nature of all our clients, as well as practitioners, and how these formulations are emergent as much out of the political as they are from the cultural and social.

(b) The importance of the supervisor understanding their own social constructions of identity so as to lessen the impact upon the supervisory relationship and therefore the client/therapist relationship beyond them.

(c) How supervisors develop the skills necessary in order to assist their supervisees in exploring the varying layers of intersectional difference which will enter the therapeutic space alongside them.

(d) The supervisor developing their own ability to work with the varying layers of power difference within the supervision relationships they have constructed with their supervisees.

(e) Assisting all parties in developing a comfortable routine around the normalisation of experiences of difference and diversity and intersectionality within counselling and psychotherapy.

CASE STUDY: SPENCER

During the pandemic of Covid-19 which hit Europe in early 2020 much of the psycho-therapeutic work in my practice and in the practice of my supervisees moved online. A particular supervisee of mine, who I shall call Spencer, was working in a clinical setting within a place of higher education in the north of England. During this period of time, his client work had moved online; whilst he found this challenging initially, he realised quite quickly that there were benefits to his working online that he and the practice had not foreseen pre the pandemic.

Spencer is a 40-year-old man of colour who trained on a counselling course in the north of England some 20 years previous. His qualification and his training were some-thing that he was very unhappy with at the time because there was no mention of difference and diversity on his training and he had sought myself out as a supervisor as he wanted to work with a person of colour who would understand difference and diversity.

The pick-up rate for students looking for therapy increased by something in the range of 40%. When we discussed this, what Spencer said to myself was that in discus-sions with his supervisees there was a realisation that because many of them were used to being in online spaces, for them working online within a university setting made more sense than coming in for one-to-one, face-to-face sessions with a therapist. The second argument involved the realisation that this also fitted in with their schedules and the requirements of their own individual courses.

Spencer told me about a couple of particular clients, one of whom, a Muslim woman, had come from a very difficult background whereby she had had to flee her home because her relationship with her siblings and her father had deteriorated to such a level that she was very much afraid for her life. The client was studying for her doctor-ate and by all accounts was doing fairly well in her studies but still found the breaks and holidays difficult because she would often have to return home to a place that she felt unsafe within. Her work with Spencer involved varying explorations of the tension between the desires of the client to live a safe life away from her family unit and the cultural tension brought up by a mother and father who encourage her to return home because that was what she was told would be the normal thing for a woman from her background to do.

CONTEXT

Social justice within the worlds of psychological therapy is nothing new. There have been a number of therapists from the early days of psychotherapy who have advocated for the inclusion or at least the recognition of the impact of the political upon the psychological world of our clients. From Freud (1930), whose experience of the rise of Nazism influenced his writings, to the works of Buber and Levinas, whose existential ideas were very much motivated by the happenings, personal and collective of World War II (Buber, 2002; Levinas, 2006), psychotherapy has always had an aspect within it of the activist, and the fight to acknowledge the rights and wrongs of an era have consistently shaped its environment.

Understanding Intersectionality

Arising out of the Civil Rights fights of the past couple of generations, an intersectional angle to the world of counselling and psychotherapy follows this tradition. Created out of the writings and research of black feminists in the United States of America, an intersectional approach to identity recognised not only that, to reference Lorde (1984b), contrary to the laws here in the Global North, the layers of oppression and otherness are driven not just by one singular identity. She saw quite early on that we hold multiple identities.

   As discussed in several of these chapters thus far, intersectionality and identity is a developing area within counselling and psychotherapy to the extent that we are still very much developing a language to understand its importance and relevance to our profession (Collins, 2019; Crenshaw, 1989; Turner, 2021). This is also echoed very much within the world of supervision. Whereas in the past supervisors on training courses, including the one that I attended some years ago now, were encouraged to be open with issues of difference and equality, the struggle to acknowledge the diverse range of clients and their often-politicised identity constructs has meant that much of this material has, whilst initially being useful, outlived that same usefulness. The work that supervisors are doing now, as they attempt to understand this new intersectional framework, very much builds upon some of the ideas about subject and other intimated by many of the theorists within our profession over the past couple of generations.

Intersectionality and Supervision

Of the theorists who had approached this sort of material in their book around supervision and the helping of professions, Hawkins and McMahon (2020) recognised that supervisors needed to be able to work beyond the egocentric to a more relational and sociocentric experience of the other. The importance of this should not be understated. In the attempt to broaden supervision so that it did incorporate ideas around difference, this understanding, although perhaps basic by today's standards, did recognise that one of the struggles with understanding difference was that often an experience was centred around the therapist or in this case the supervisor, leaving the other, be they the supervisee or the client, invisible.

Any exploration of difference within the world of counselling and psychotherapy though has to do more than to just pay 'lip service' to issues of difference and otherness. As discussed in the writings of those such as Lago (Charura & Lago, 2021; Lago, 2011; Moodley et al., 2004) the importance of taking a more nuanced study of issues of difference and diversity within the helping professions is that it brings a level of safety to the work which clients may not have previously experienced.

Supervision is no different in this respect, and in many ways has been slow to keep up with this need. It is important as practitioners, and therefore as supervisors, that we too are able to cross that inter-relational bridge between supervisor and supervisee. In my practice as a supervisor, for example, dependent upon the stage of development of the supervisee within their career, I will often explore with them the power dynamics in the supervisee/supervisor relationship. What often comes to the surface is of course the sense that I, as a supervisor, hold all the power because I, as a supervisor, am more knowledgeable and more experienced than they are.

Where I sometimes challenge this is in two areas. The first is that on a practical level, as a supervisor, they have hired me to be a clinical representative for their practice. I am a consultant to their business and actually they could sack me at any given moment in time. The second part I always mention is that my relationship with their clients is based very much upon a fantasy; I have never met their client, I will never meet their client and I can only experience their client through the transferential relationship they bring to the space before me. They are, for all intents and purposes, not only the owner of their practice, but the so-called expert in their work with their client, not I, opening the door to a form of relational supervision.

Relational Supervision

This more Buberian understanding of supervision, where it is more about the relationship built up between two people and a third fantasy one in the case of supervising, than it is about subject and object and the power dynamics embedded within that (Buber, 2010). Where this sits alongside ideas of difference and diversity is in re-empowering supervisees so that they can take with them what they need to take into the relationship with their own clients, modelling something in Spencer's case of the re-empowerment that his client needed to go through in order to find her own way forward between the two metaphorical stools of her cultural background and the university background as well.

The second part that supervisors need to remember is that in a paradigm shift away from much of the narrative that we hear within counselling and psychotherapy, they are not politicians. What is meant by this is that counselling and psychotherapy has embedded within itself the idea that none of us should be at all political. Whilst much of these ideas are well-meaning, what is also at play here is a failure to recognise that whilst many parts of our identity are biological or psychological, there are also other socially constructed, and therefore politically influenced, aspects to our intersectional identity. How one's identity then changes is emergent with the realisation that many of our behaviours and socialised qualities are much more influenced and formulated by the political than they are by the cultural and by other forms of difference. The political in this instance, though, is not just the laws and regulations laid down by governments or societies, it is also the ideas and structures about how we are supposed to be as individuals, as men, as women, as those who identify as non-binary, as per our culture, our religion, our family. These varying layers all crowd around and interact together to lay out rules, ways and means that we are then supposed to adhere to and be identified by.

So one of the problematic areas within supervision is that whilst supervisors are often very aware of the cultural context within which a therapeutic dyad occurs, what they struggle to explore is how the shifting sands of the political landscape then impact upon the other. For example, at the time of writing there are widespread Black Lives Matters protests, struggles within the feminist movement post the murder of Sarah Everard, and the battle to have conversion therapy banned by the government of the United Kingdom; the impact of these will have been felt by our clients (ITV, 2021; Morton, 2021; UK Council for Psychotherapy, 2015). In particular, the impact of class for our clients is an often ignored facet of psychotherapy as well as supervision, so attesting to its influence upon the client work is an essential component to understanding our clients more fully (Hey, 2002; Lorde, 1984a).

SUPERVISION EXAMPLE REDUX

For Spencer, for example, one of the things that he needed to explore with myself within our supervision came up predominantly when George Floyd was murdered in May 2020 (BBC News, 2020). In raising his anger and his frustration with his workplace during this period, what he realised for himself was that he had found a way of existing within a landscape where race and difference was not really explored. Yet when George Floyd's murder became a prominent piece of news, he no longer felt that he could remain silent anymore and explored with his workplace issues around difference and diversity and how they might create better and safer spaces for their practitioners and their students, a good number of whom were from minoritised backgrounds of varying types.

The university setting in this instance, according to Spencer, did very little to reassure or to take on board his sense of unsafety and psychological distress to the extent that in the months further on from his exploring this with his managers, he decided that it was time for him to leave the university and find a space whereby he would feel heard and respected as a supervisee, and a counsellor of colour.

The reason I explore this part of the relationship here is that myself and Spencer spent a good deal of time looking at what he might need in order to feel safe in that environment, as well as how his lack of safety in some ways mirrored the lack of safety of his client in her home life.

SUPERVISION AS SOCIAL ACTIVISM

One of the important tasks for supervisors is to help supervisees in exploring their own political identity. This is not to say that a supervisee should not adhere to the power inherent with say systemic whiteness or patriarchy or capitalism. What this means is that the supervisee, with the help of the supervisor, should be able to recognise and hold those parts of their identity accordingly. The reasons for this as such, if we go back to Spencer's example, what I could surmise has played itself out unconsciously, is that the systemic inclusion of racial difference has not only sat within the counselling service, hence Spencer was the only person of colour there, but has also impacted upon the work with the clients.

Supervision is not about suggesting what it right or is wrong; it is about actually owning that which is conscious or unconscious within these difficult spaces, and whilst social justice on an external level is about lending a voice to those who are excluded and developing a moral framework within which people can live, within supervision my suggestion is that social justice within an internal space sits more to the fore. When exploring issues of trauma, one of the things that practitioners fail to recognise in their work with clients is that a core part of the healing is in helping said client to recognise the *internalisation* of that traumatic experience, be it in the form of an abuser, be it in the form of a system which has left one to feel like an outsider, be it in the form of a parent or caregiver who has marginalised and rejected them. That these aspects of our experience will become internalised is a core facet of psychological development within most modalities. This is no different when we bring in a political landscape. We are all formed and moulded by the political decisions made around us and about us by people other than us. Therefore, supervision should be about the recognition of how those structures have come into being in order that the supervisee may attend to them and recognise them within their own therapeutic space.

As previously stated though, it is not about the supervisee having to rid themselves of aspects unless they choose to do so. It is not about them having to feel shame about said aspects either, unless shame is a part of an experience of an internalised, socially constructed identity that they were not aware of. Supervisors, in my view, are not there to shame the supervisee into ridding themselves of some of the power dynamics which they fasten themselves to or have been fastened to. It is about having an open dialogue, an exploration around these structures for the supervisee's sake. This then allows a supervisee to go into a space, hopefully recognising their own internalised system, whatever form that might take, and hopefully holding it well enough and in a contained enough fashion so that it lessens the impact upon their client, especially if they are other to them in some way.

This is one of the flaws often with psychotherapy and with activism, in that there is a sense that there is a position of right or wrong, and actually what supervisors are often challenged with holding is that there is a space in between and it is through modelling this space in between dual narratives, dual ideologies and dual positions that something new and organic, new and spiritual, and new and developmental should emerge for the client and hopefully also the supervisee. In my earlier attempt to re-align the power dynamics in supervision between a supervisor and a supervisee, this openness to experiences alien to oneself is one of the reasons why it feels important to have these dialogues. This also means that the supervisor is helping the supervisee in becoming more comfortable with working with issues of difference, diversity and otherness. That the supervisee becomes more comfortable and less reactive and defensive when working with the other creates for a more exploratory experience of counselling and psychotherapy. So, whilst Spencer was able to offer this for his own client, the difficulty for him was that this safe space was not created in a similar fashion for him within his working environment.

Of course, it goes without saying that for a supervisor to be able to work in such a fashion will mean that they themselves should have done some work, or the work, around their own political positioning and their own socially constructed identities. Prior to this though, what also needs to happen is that the supervisor would need to be able to explore their own sense of otherness. For many of us, we cling to an inclusive aspect of our binary identity, often rejecting even in our psychotherapy trainings, or supervision trainings, the fact that one aspect or more of our intersectional identity has been moulded by the political.

Because all of us are other, this therefore means that we are engaging with aspects of our identity which have not only marked us out as an outsider, but which may have also been pushed into the shadow in order to fit in within the mirrored political landscapes of our trainings and within our practice areas (Turner, 2016). Even Sigmund Freud in some of his earliest works fought long and hard to have his work accepted by the mainstream, yet in doing so marginalised aspects of the work which were seen as outside of the norm by the medical establishment and even those such as Carl Jung who were seen to not be healthy enough from within a Western paradigm to even play a part in this sense of inclusion (Jacobs, 2003). This colonisation of psychotherapy is something which has sat within our profession in a similar fashion to within other modalities in many different ways.

CONCLUSION

Finally, in the future there is another aspect of supervision which I believe will become hugely important. This will involve the decolonising of supervision through an understanding of how this process, the structure of supervision, has itself, like psychotherapy post the days of Freud, become embedded within circles of systemic oppression which exclude or denigrate supervisees and maybe their clients by proxy. This though will involve the supervisor developing more nuanced, unique perhaps and creative or Indigenous ways of working within supervision so as to meet the many different blended learning patterns of the supervisees who they will be working with, be they in placement settings or in private practice. This is where the growth of supervision into a true form of social activism will I feel take place; where the inclusion of more diverse forms and means of conducting supervision have been explored and incorporated, and where supervision then models this inclusive morality.

REFLECTIVE AND CRITICAL THINKING QUESTIONS

1   How has social justice impacted your supervision?
2   Do you feel your awareness of social justice issues has either been incorporated into your supervision, or has been witnessed by your supervisor?
3   Each week think about the wider environment your work with clients is contained within and see if you can construct a narrative around the following:
    a   How have my supervisees presented their problems with the society they exist within in my work with them?
    b   Am I leaving enough space for them to consider social justice issues in the supervisory space?

RECOMMENDED READING AND RESOURCES

Hawkins, P., & McMahon, A. (2020). *Supervision in the helping professions*. Open University Press.
A key textbook on supervision which includes some direction on the importance of understanding diversity and otherness.

Lahad, M. (2000) *Creative supervision: The use of expressive arts methods in supervision and self-supervision (arts therapies)*. Jessica Kingsley Press.
Given the use of creativity in counselling and psychotherapy, this text looks at how to use metaphor and symbolism as a means of accessing the unconscious component of supervision.

Scaife, J. (2019) *Supervision in clinical practice: A practitioner's guide*. Routledge.
A core guide to supervision within the profession offering good easy to access ways of working with peer and group supervision.

REFERENCES

BBC News. (2020). George Floyd death. *BBC News*. www.bbc.co.uk/news/topics/cv7wlylxzg1t/george-floyd-death

Buber, M. (2002). *Between man and man*. Routledge.

Buber, M. (2010). *I and thou*. Martino Publishing.

Charura, D., & Lago, C. (2021). *Black identities + white therapies: Race, respect + diversity*. PCCS Books.

Collins, P. H. (2019). *Intersectionality as critical social theory*. Duke University Press.

Crenshaw, K. (1989). Demarginalizing the intersection of race and sex: A black feminist critique of antidiscrimination doctrine, feminist theory and antiracist politics. *University of Chicago Legal Forum, 1989*, Article 8. https://chicagounbound.uchicago.edu/uclf/vol1989/iss1/8

Freud, S. (1930). *Civilisation and its discontents*. Penguin.

Hawkins, P., & McMahon, A. (2020). *Supervision in the helping professions*. Open University Press.

Hey, V. (2002). Horizontal solidarities and molten capitalism: The subject, intersubjectivity, self and the other in late modernity. *Discourse: Studies in the Cultural Politics of Education, 23*(2), 227–241. https://doi.org/10.1080/0159630022000000796

ITV. (2021). *Trevor McDonald & Charlene White: Has George Floyd Changed Britain?* www.itv.com/presscentre/ep1week19/trevor-mcdonald-charlene-white-has-george-floyd-changed-britain#

Jacobs, M. (2003). *Sigmund Freud – Key figures in counselling and psychotherapy* (2nd ed.). Sage Publications.

Lago, C. (2011). *The handbook of transcultural counselling and psychotherapy*. Open University Press.

Levinas, E. (2006). *Humanism of the other*. University of Illinois Press.

Lorde, A. (1984a). Age, race, class and sex: Women redefining difference. In *Sister outsider* (pp.1–7). Crossing Press.

Lorde, A. (1984b). *Sister outsider*. Crossing Press.

Moodley, R., Lago, C., & Talahite, A. (Eds.). (2004). *Carl Rogers counsels a black client: Race and culture in person-centred counselling* (1st ed.). PCCS Books.

Morton, B. (2021). Sarah Everard: How Wayne Couzens planned her murder. *BBC News Online*. www.bbc.co.uk/news/uk-58746108

Turner, D. (2016). We are all of us other. *Therapy Today, 16*(June), 18–21.

Turner, D. D. L. (2021). *Intersections of privilege and otherness in counselling and psychotherapy* (1st ed.). Routledge.

UK Council for Psychotherapy. (2015). *Memorandum of understanding on conversion therapy in the UK*. www.psychotherapy.org.uk/wp-content/uploads/2016/09/Memorandum-of-understanding-on-conversion-therapy.pdf

17
CRITICAL COMMUNITY PSYCHOLOGY AND PARTICIPATORY ACTION RESEARCH

Eden Lunghy, Sally Zlotowitz and Lita Wallis

OVERVIEW

This chapter describes some of the theories and practices (or praxis – values and theory in action) of critical community psychology (CCP) in the UK and its deep relationship to social justice, both historically and currently. After offering a brief overview of CCP, we go on to describe and delve deeper into a form of research and practice called 'Participatory Action Research' (PAR). We hope to inspire practitioners to consider PAR as an alternative to mainstream 'evidence-based' therapies.

CONTEXT

Overview of Critical Community Psychology

CCP, and the related field of Liberation Psychology, as a whole are vastly neglected within university psychology courses in the UK, with just a handful offering specialism courses in these topics. This isn't surprising given the overall neglect of context within mainstream psychology, with its arguably narrow emphasis. In CCP, the driving idea is 'people-in-context'. In other words, what are the cultural, political, social, community and economic systems and structures that shape people's psychological experiences?

For this reason, it is with some hesitancy that we include CCP within a book about psychological therapies. After all, for most therapies, the emphasis has been on individual change and adaptation, and yet we agree with Watkins and Shulman who state in their brilliant book *Towards Psychologies of Liberation* (2008):

> We do not want to assume that the role of psychology is to help individuals and families adapt to the status quo when this present order contributes so massively to human misery, psychological and otherwise. (p. 13)

The intention of this book is to challenge this assumption about therapy, and no doubt both authors and readers alike wish to change their individual practice to become more socially justice centred. However, it is the context, that is, our culture, political, social and economic systems and structures that keep us pinned down to practising individualistically and from a position as 'experts' rather than truly collaboratively. For example, the UK 'mental health' system, provided by the National Health Service (NHS), is tied to offering only 'evidence-based' therapies. But the research that is conducted to create this evidence base is already a political, economic and social justice issue.

Challenging the 'Evidence Base' of Mental Health Interventions

A report on mental health research spending in the UK between 2007 and 2014 by the independent charity MQ (2015) shows that, firstly, there is significantly less funding for mental health research compared to physical health research. According to the report 'approximately £9 per person affected is currently spent on research. To compare this to cancer, approximately £228 is spent per person affected' (MQ, 2015). Secondly, almost half of the funding for mental health research (46.5%) went on research categorised as 'underpinning research and aetiology', a good proportion of which is on basic psychology and neuroscience. With studies of brain function and dysfunction dominating what we are investigating we can be sure that this will not be considering the impact of wider economic, social or political systems on people's psychological experiences. We can also surmise that such research is oriented towards ameliorative, rather than transformative, interventions (i.e., interventions that relieve symptoms rather than transform the root causes). Bhui (2016) states that '33% of the annual research spend for mental illnesses is on underpinning brain sciences, although the balance is more favourable in the UK (about 33% v. 85% in the US towards neurobiological research)' (p. 510). Finally, this limited research funding is granted predominantly to universities, and astoundingly 'a third of the funding goes to Oxford, University College London and King's College London – each of these receiving more than 10 million on average per year' (MQ, 2015). This means that three academic institutions are significantly shaping the research questions and approach to the 'evidence base' of interventions in mental health in the UK. The report does not mention any funding going directly to community groups or organisations who often serve and represent minoritised communities. The research remains dominated by an individualistic, Eurocentric view of 'mental health' and methods which do research 'on' or 'to' people and brains. It may come as no surprise therefore that there are significant mental health inequalities in terms of experience of distress, access to services and positive outcomes from interventions (e.g., Barr et al., 2015). Injustice and oppression of marginalised groups contribute as root causes to these inequalities and so interventions must avoid replicating these experiences and instead work alongside people to bring about transformative change that challenges these injustices.

CRITICAL COMMUNITY PSYCHOLOGY APPROACHES

CCP has a different underlying set of principles, theories, values, and philosophy compared with mainstream clinical and experimental psychology. It remains underfunded and undervalued, at least partly because it is much less concerned with positivist scientific methods and much more interested in creating meaningful social and psychological research and change that collaborates or is led by those most directly affected. CCP is 'action based on critical theorizing, reflection, and a clear commitment to working for social justice through empowering and transformative practice' (Henderson, 2007, p. 1).

As described above, at the heart of the CCP is a broader analysis of people's experiences which consider the multiple systems of context in which people develop and live, including power dynamics at different scales, such as colonialism, neoliberalism and patriarchy. CCP values and theories include primary prevention, working alongside groups, networks or whole communities rather than doing 'to' them, and centring diverse ways of knowing (Kagan et al., 2011). 'Community' can be understood inclusively whether it is communities of geography (e.g., a neighbourhood), of identity (e.g., Afro-Caribbean community) or of interest. Kagan and Burton (2001) define CCP's core values as justice, stewardship and community.

Psychological 'formulations' of an individual as understood in therapeutic practice (often focused on what is problematic with an individual's thinking) are replaced with community- or group-led analyses of a systemic issue that is affecting the wellbeing of the community, such as violence, institutional racism, poverty or gentrification. These analyses are often co-created through creative, participatory, educatory and dialogical methods that draw on the arts, neighbourhood and/or peer knowledge and resources. They result in multi-level understandings which unpick the different ways in which systems, institutions and resources might be oppressive, supportive or both (Kagan & Burton, 2011).

With these analyses in mind, CCP practice seeks to bring together the community affected, with social justice as a core value and orientation, to find ways of collectively transforming the root causes. This can involve taking collective action, including campaigning and advocacy, non-violent resistance or participating in / organising protests, petitions or other actions to influence local, national or international policy-makers to shift policy, demand community resources or redesign local services. Plus, creative projects such as arts exhibitions, photovoice methodology, theatre performances which may be generated by a group with an aim of raising awareness of issues or for cathartic expression, amongst other purposes.

Other approaches involve peer support, group healing and community-building practices to create the resilience and solidarity needed to resist and overcome the oppressive conditions marginalised people are subjected to. Watkins and Shulman (2008) describe the importance of 'the kinds of free and open social spaces that support such personal and community recovery (Oliver, 2002), where protective enclosures can be created in which individual and community regeneration can occur'. In addition, Sonn and Quayle (2014), emphasise the importance of power in all CCP practice, such that the actions lead to 'actual increases in power (both material and symbolic), thus avoiding the cognitivist and decontextualized focus on an individual's sense of or perceptions of empowerment (Riger, 1993) '(p. 18).

Within these approaches, psychologists bring a set of skills, capital and knowledge that can be useful as part of the wider contribution of skills, capital and knowledges from the community or group (of course psychologists may also be directly part of the community). Psychological ideas are freely shared with the community or group and offered as a perspective but not as having all the authority and expertise. Psychologists often also have good access to resources (such as funding) and social capital (such as policy-makers) and can therefore contribute these where wanted to the wider partnership work.

CASE STUDY: PARTICIPATORY ACTION RESEARCH

PAR is an approach that is often drawn on by community psychologists as it fits with the values and theories described above. The rest of this chapter is dedicated to giving a brief description of PAR and a case study example brought to life through an interview between the two co-authors Eden Lunghy and Lita Wallis. Eden and Lita met in 2018 as part of a PAR project called Take Back the Power (https://thewinch.org/services/take-back-the-power), based at The Winch, a youth and community centre in Camden, North London. At that time, Lita was a youth worker and PAR facilitator, and Eden applied to join the project as a youth researcher. The two have maintained close contact and continue to work together on several projects, including delivering trainings in community psychology and PAR with Sally. We feel that the best way of representing PAR is always through dialogue, to capture something of how such a project might start, experiences of the journey and the huge personal, community and social impacts that PAR can have.

Lita: So What Is Take Back the Power?

Eden: Take Back the Power is a paid, youth led, social action project that was
        birthed in 2017. Each year a cohort of young people are employed to
        undertake research and act against a social injustice that is affecting them.
        In 2017, the cohort explored racism within the education system. They

created workshops, creative outlets such as a zine [https://thewinch.org/services/take-back-the-power/tbtp-2017-ezine/] and ran community hustings to work with other young people in the area. In January 2018 there were six stabbings across the borough in one night which propelled the cohort to select serious youth violence as the next topic. Myself and six other researchers with lived experience of serious youth violence were hired to conduct research and delve into the root of the issue to find positive ways to enact change for our communities.

Eden: What exactly is participatory action research?

Lita: It is a methodology of creating and sharing knowledge that aims to build power, rather than teaching people to consume information. It builds on the foundations of popular education laid by Paulo Freire and his book, *Pedagogy of the Oppressed* (1970).Traditional ways of doing education are from a top-down, hierarchical approach, where the teacher has the knowledge, and the students learn it. In popular education the idea is that everyone has knowledge, and everyone is an expert of their experience. Yes, it is *research*, so it's coming up with questions, something we don't know the answer to, and finding answers through sharing our stories. But it is *participatory*, so it's about making decisions together so that the people in the group are always in charge of the narrative – rather than an external researcher coming in and making their theories and disappearing. It is about *action* so it's more about life than reports – it always has a social justice agenda. It is about building relationships, building knowledge and building power to change the unjust circumstances in which we live... It doesn't belong in an ivory tower; it belongs to all of us.

Eden: So, I wasn't there at the start, how did Take Back the Power get started in the first place?

Lita: There was this group of young people who I would see every week in school outreach. We would have amazing political discussions about race and other social injustices, and so we created a programme together with them to do social justice work at The Winch. And then they never showed up. I managed to get them to come with an offer of a Chinese buffet! When I asked what happened they said 'we don't have the time to be an activist when we need paid work, when we support our families and we are carers of our siblings'. It was obvious we had to create paid jobs for young people to participate.

Eden: I think that process you went through is something that's not yet mainstream when it comes to any type of youth work. There is a growing conversation for young people to not be used tokenistically and a shift to valuing young people as experts in their experience. Being paid was definitely a contributing factor to why I applied. Some employment can infantilise, overwork and underpay you solely because of your age, whilst at Take Back the Power we were paid a London Living Wage. I also felt this helped remove the power dynamic between us, the researchers and you, the facilitators.

Lita: Can you remember anything from those early sessions?

Eden: After the recruitment process, I recall us coming up with our values as a team and that was very much led by the young researchers. We wanted to make it known that we were six Black and Brown young people from North London who had lived experience of serious youth violence. Working out who we were as a collective, our self-identity, skills, talents and heritage were all the richness that made us, and we wanted to showcase that proudly.

Lita: That's an important part of the process – if you set something up, you inherently start with a lot of power, and it takes work to redistribute it. I am glad that you raised that about how to create structures that mean a project can become owned by the collective.

Lita: Are there any other exercises or parts of the process that stick out in your memory?

Eden: Well, there were countless exercises... you always found a way to make us dance! Two exercises spring to mind: Firstly, **Street of Life, inspired by Ncazelo Ncube-Mlilo's Tree of Life** (Ncube, 2006) – the group took components of a house to analyse different aspects of our lives in a symbolic way that we don't think about in our day-to-day lives, e.g., the roots on the ground represent our foundations such as our ethnic background, languages we spoke or religions / belief practices we followed. It was a great way of remembering all the different aspects of your life, so you don't get lost in the hard stuff.

1. **Secondly, we went on holiday!** As the peer researchers, we decided it was vital for us to get out of the city to break away from our usual environments... I'm sure this was a bit scary for you as we were halfway through the process and suddenly decided we needed a residential – we went to the Braich Goch in Wales. I have a vivid memory of us being on the beach and the boys blasting out music and

dancing. Seeing two Black and Brown boys living in their joy had such a profound impact on me especially when this is a side society doesn't always give them space to portray (not that they need permission). The whole trip was a watershed moment for the team. The trip was where we birthed our idea of the Call to Action publication (Lunghy et al., 2019) and our podcast [https://www.mixcloud.com/TakeBackThePower/].

Lita: You guys said, 'we are gonna go on holiday', and for a second I was like 'wait what?' And then I was like, 'You know what, that's an amazing idea!'

Lita: What do you think it was about our holiday that was so essential for our process?

Eden: The trip enabled me to feel like I could be more vulnerable, because of the level of intimacy we built.

Lita: One of my big memories from that trip is of us all wrapped up in blankets with cocoa around the fire, and you telling the story of your family. Profound things happen when we build relationships. We are so cut off from each other most of the time, especially in cities.

Eden: Exactly. It's so important to find time to build familiarity, trust and relationships. We transformed from six strangers to a team who understood each other on a deep level and could see that our experiences were not all that different from each other. The process reminded us that we aren't alone.

Lita: I think at the very least, even if a project doesn't result in any written report or any social action per se, if you can leave a project with a group of people who really trust and respect each other, then the project is a success. PAR can de-individualise our experiences too and take the blame off the individual.

Lita: In an exercise that we called The Wall of Injustice, we mapped it all out, all the incidences of violence that everyone had experienced throughout the course of their life; being moved about between temporary accommodation, racist experiences at school or with the police, everything that people had endured before the actual moment where a knife got drawn, or there was a fight.

Lita: Is it OK to ask how it felt to be in a research process talking so much about issues that were so close to home?

Eden: That's a good question. Throughout the project I was going through a rollercoaster of emotions. For example, in the beginning I felt like an imposter because I had to attend our sessions and then go home and deal with the very real things happening at home. My brother was going through his court case and at the time it wasn't widespread public knowledge, I had a lot of fear attached to that and used to think 'what is X Y Z person going to think?' There was a big juxtaposition of how I presented in the sessions and how I was at home. I don't think this is something people can fully grasp if they aren't in it. I'm very grateful for my friends, fellow researchers and partner, they supported me a lot and kept me going.

Lita: I really remember you saying it felt like you had a 'double life'. I'm glad to hear that having the other researchers around helped to ease some of those feelings.

Eden: The issue is, people expect youth activists to present in a manicured way. Yes, they may be people that deeply care about the topic but a lot of the time they are also young people that are still having to live in the environments they are working to take action on and that's challenging. It's such a part of the culture in which we live, that the things that we do know from our life experiences are so undervalued. The stories of the impact that violence between young men has on young women are often forgotten about, e.g., by the media. Culturally, there is also a lot of stigma around this topic. For my family, the court case resulted in us losing our home, our Congolese community and so much more because of how unsafe it had become.

Lita: And yeah, it's young women like yourself who are holding all this together and living the 'parallel lives' and doing all the emotional work. It's disappointing that you are still experiencing that stigma when you're working so hard.

Eden: Towards the end of the project, concerns were raised by the community about the project being led by two white women. I don't want to centre your emotions, but want to understand how you dealt with those concerns?

Lita: Yeah when those concerns came back to us it was not a surprise, because all along we wondered if we were the right people to facilitate the project. We did stand down the year after yours. We both made the decision for different reasons to step away from the project, and it made sense that the people who took on our roles were both Black women.

Lita: How did it feel for you to hear that feedback?

Eden: I was very taken aback when I first heard it, but I was thankful that Lucy and you shared it with the researchers, it's a testament to both of your ethos on a personal and professional level. The concerns that were raised were from people that didn't have full insight into the project, so it made me question if there were things I wasn't seeing. I believe it's always important to be vigilant of how power dynamics and our intersectionalities play out, so we don't repeat structures we are working to dismantle. However, it was still disheartening to hear – as another member of the community agreed, it felt like all our work as researchers was reduced to the fact the project was facilitated by two white women.

Lita: However you look at it, I think that's a good thing about PAR, the learning that happens is for life. That feedback, I still think about it, I still talk about it in my work now, it's still very relevant. For us as white people, to learn how to be good allies, how to not dominate spaces, how to not centre our experiences, how to use our privilege to raise profiles and power for other people is a lifelong process.

Lita: What do you feel were the achievements of the project?

Eden: So many. That's the thing with PAR it's not solely down to metrics but for the project. My highlights were building community – we came together as a team who wanted to find ways to heal and support each other.

There were also some key outputs; we wrote a tangible Call to Action for anyone and everyone to map out the different ways they can help young people on a communal and systemic scale. We published a podcast describing the real narrative on serious youth violence. I also worked with Sarah Jones, MP and other activists across London to deliver a letter to the PM, demanding that young people be at the forefront of leading the national agenda. When we delivered the letter to 10 Downing Street, I got invited to ITV news, then BBC news and LBC radio! Still waiting for the Prime Minister to respond to my letter... We also set good foundations for others to build on in subsequent projects. Unfortunately, much of the systemic work takes time and our current systems are bureaucratic, so some things end up unfulfilling.

Overall, I am really proud of the community we built and how we got to hold space for each other. On a personal level, Take Back the Power supported me in the midst of my storm, my education and my personal development.

Lita: What would be your top tips for making a successful PAR project?

Eden: Here are my Eden gems for PAR:

- Plan, but use it as a reference point and not as a checklist. It's important to have something to review but don't be afraid if your plans get thrown out.

- Don't feel like you have to stick to traditional forms of data collection, venture out and visit different spaces and learn what others are doing to inspire your work.
- It's easier to bounce back from a break than burn out. Be intentional with your breaks for the team, it's vital that there are moments of respite from the work you're doing. This work can be so emotionally taxing and we are still having to operate in a capitalist system outside of it, let's not replicate the structures we are working to dethrone.
- Celebrate the small and big wins for the project and each other. We were very intentional with celebrating birthdays and milestones that we achieved collectively and individually.

Lita: When you're taking care of your relationships, you're taking care of the project. It's easy to get wrapped up in a capitalist work ethic and be too goal oriented. That's the sure-fire way to kill a project. I think you said 'dethrone' which I love, it's about decolonising our minds...

Eden: ALSO, just find ways to have FUN. Lastly, take time to reflect on the work you're doing whether that's journaling, audio, video diaries etc.

Lita: Nothing is a failure. Everything you do, even if you go to a terrible event or there is tension in the group, or you neglect your journal! Everything in a PAR process is part of the material if you can take space to reflect. Everything is a learning opportunity. I don't think there is ever an end to these projects either. I am still learning now!

CONCLUSION

PAR offers an alternative to mainstream research and practice by democratising knowledge production and orientating processes towards social justice. The process can be deep and have healing and therapeutic qualities at least partly by potentially revealing the systemic root causes of individual distress and co-creating new solutions. This methodology is one of many CCP approaches practitioners can draw on to work alongside marginalised communities to bring about social justice and support healing.

REFLECTIVE AND CRITICAL THINKING QUESTIONS

1   What are the key differences between PAR and traditional psychology research and therapeutic activities?
2   What might be some PAR questions of a community or group you are part of?
3   How could PAR be co-opted or used in a way that it was not developed for and can this be avoided?

RECOMMENDED READING AND RESOURCES

Discovering Community Psychology Podcast. https://podcasts.apple.com/gb/pod cast/discovering-community-psychology/id1552622773. This podcast aims to make community psychology ideas and practice more accessible and gives a good introduction to the topic.

Freire, P. (1970). *Pedagogy of the oppressed*. Penguin. This is a classic text useful to introduce some of the ideas in this chapter.

Lunghy, E., et al. (2019). *Insiders looking out: Solutions to youth violence from people who have lived it*. The Winch. https://thewinch.org/wp-content/uploads/2021/07/TBTP-Call-To-Action-2019-3.pdf

Wakeford, T. and Sánchez Rodríguez, T., (2018). *Participatory action research: Towards a more fruitful knowledge*. University of Bristol and the AHRC Connected Communities Programme.

REFERENCES

Barr, B., Kinderman, P., & Whitehead, M. (2015). Trends in mental health inequalities in England during a period of recession, austerity and welfare reform 2004 to 2013. *Social Science & Medicine, 147*, 324–331.

Bhui, K. (2016). Invited commentary on... Rethinking funding priorities in mental health research. *The British Journal of Psychiatry, 208*(6), 510–511.

Freire, P. (1970). *Pedagogy of the oppressed*. Penguin.

Henderson, P. (2007). Introduction. In H. Butcher, S. Banks., P. Henderson & J. Roberston (Eds.), *Critical community practice* (pp. 1–16). The Policy Press.

Kagan, C., & Burton, M. (2001). *Critical community psychological praxis for the 21st century*. IOD Research Group, Manchester Metropolitan University.

Kagan, C., Burton, M., Duckett, P., Lawthom, R., & Siddiquee, A. (2011). *Critical community psychology*. John Wiley & Sons.

Lunghy, E., et al. (2019). *Insiders looking out: Solutions to youth violence from people who have lived it*. The Winch. https://thewinch.org/wp-content/uploads/2021/07/ TBTPCall-To-Action-2019-3.pdf

MQ Transforming Mental Health. (2015). *Mental health research funding landscape report*. MQ. www.joinmq.org/research/pages/mental-health-research-funding-landscape-report

Ncube, N. (2006). The tree of life project. *International Journal of Narrative Therapy & Community Work, 1*, 3–16.

Oliver, K. (2002). Psychic space and social melancholy. In K. Oliver & S. Edwin (Eds.), *Between the psyche and the social: Psychoanalytic social theory* (pp. 49–65). Rowman and Littlefield.

Riger, S. (1993). What's wrong with empowerment? *American Journal of Community Psychology, 21*(3), 279–292.

Sonn, C. C., & Quayle, A. F. (2014). Community cultural development for social change: Developing critical praxis. *Journal for Social Action in Counseling & Psychology, 6*(1), 16–35.

Watkins, M., & Shulman, H. (2008). *Toward psychologies of liberation.* Palgrave Macmillan.

18
INFLUENCING POLICY AND SOCIO-POLITICAL CHANGE

Dan O'Hare and Melernie Meheux

OVERVIEW

Our aim in this chapter is to demonstrate that influencing social policy, as psychologists, is both possible and worthwhile. We will do this by providing insight into how we, as two educational psychologists, have used research and practice to influence policy and social change to promote social justice. We will briefly describe what we mean by 'social justice' and then provide an overview of the educational psychology role. We will present a case study exploring how we worked to influence socio-political changes in light of a narrative of children needing to 'catch-up' as they returned to schools after COVID-19 restrictions eased. We structure this section using the '5 T's principles to influence policy'.

CONTEXT

The COVID-19 pandemic sparked an interest in social justice issues within education, and society more broadly. The nation saw children without access to laptops, internet data, spaces to work or play – and were reliant on the generosity of charities, broadcasters and local companies to access home schooling, despite the reported provision of this by the government. Families worried about feeding their children and the nation campaigned alongside the professional footballer Marcus Rashford for children to have free school meals at home. This passion for social justice was spread across social media and became something that people spoke about and engaged in (whether they knew it was social justice or not!).

How We Understand Social Justice

Our view is that social justice is increasingly at the forefront of people's minds. This is particularly so in recent years as inequalities between people have been exacerbated by worldwide events, such as the COVID-19 pandemic, the Black Lives Matter campaign, the increasing influence of climate breakdown, wars around the world leading to displacement and refugees seeking safety, and the cost-of-living crisis in the UK.

When we think of definitions of social justice, we recognise our assumptions:

1   All groups in society do not currently enjoy full and equal participation.
2   Some people are not afforded equal participation due to a lack of consideration about how policies might exclude them, while others are actively excluded.
3   The distribution of resources in society is not equitable.
4   There are some members of our society who are not physically or psychologically safe and this is about structures and systems.
5   The unequal or inequitable distribution of power or resources that some groups of people experience is sometimes justified simply because of membership to a particular group.

Schulze (2017) explored how UK educational psychologists (EPs) define social justice and found that EPs placed great importance on taking action to tackle discrimination and marginalisation, to promote inclusion, fairness and diversity. These discussions were linked to uncovering and then working to equalise or re-distribute power and privilege. There are two quotes that are particularly relevant here, about how psychologists might influence policy and socio-political change. The first speaks to uncertainty about how to do social justice:

> to begin being more socially just, EPs need to know what that would look like. (p. 67)

The second quote speaks to an aspect of practice that risks being overlooked in discussions that focus on working towards a more socially just society, namely, influence:

> Educational psychology was judged to be able to influence governmental policy but it was acknowledged that this required people being in positions of influence. (p. 66)

Educational Psychology

EPs facilitate life outcomes for children and their families. They support the training and development of educational practitioners, ensuring high-quality provision for children and young people. They have a significant role in the identification of special educational needs and contribute to statutory plans that aim to detail the needs of young people, and the educational arrangements or 'provision' that might be put in place to support learning and wellbeing. EPs work directly with children, but also the key adults in their lives, to effect change indirectly. Educational psychology work happens across different levels including the child or family; whole school; and whole local authority levels.

The Currie Report (Scottish Executive, 2002) discussed five core functions of the role:

1   Consultation
2   Assessment
3   Intervention
4   Training
5   Research

Importantly, each of these functions can be realised at each of the levels that EPs work (see Soni & Shotter, 2019, for a fuller, accessible discussion).

Most EPs work in local authorities, but work across a variety of sectors is becoming more prevalent (Department for Education, 2019). EPs often have a holistic understanding of the child or young person they are working with, and also a clear, but often under-recognised, holistic view of the systems influencing a child's life (K. Rowland, personal communication, 2022).

Doctoral training programmes are distinctly oriented towards social justice. In the 'Statement of Intent' in the BPS Accreditation standards there is a recognition that:

> Interventions are developed that aim to promote autonomy, educational and social inclusion and wellbeing, and to empower and enable those in educational settings, thus minimising exclusion and inequality. (BPS, 2019, p. 8)

The BPS Practice Guidelines (2017) recognise that psychologists will work with a range of people who may not experience 'full and equal participation' and address the need to work towards social inclusion, an aim we see as specifically relevant to notions of social justice given the wording of the guidelines:

> Promoting social inclusion is a broader task than promoting equality and tackling discrimination and stigma. It requires psychology professionals to address wider structural issues in society which maintain excluding processes and power differentials. (p. 36)

CASE STUDIES: TIME TO PLAY AND 'CATCH-UP NARRATIVES'

Background

In 2019 the BPS Division of Educational and Child Psychology published a position paper that advocated for children's right to play (Hobbs et al., 2019) and brought together EPs, academics, play experts and campaigners to highlight that opportunities for play in children's lives are diminishing, and that high-quality child-centred play is essential for development.

In Spring 2020 national restrictions were in place in response to the COVID-19 pandemic. For many children, this meant not going to school and a breakdown of daily routines and ordinary social contact. At the time there was a shift towards 'home learning' but many schools and families found this exceptionally difficult.

In this context both of us were involved in work that aimed to highlight the importance of play for children's development. Underpinning this was a recognition of the different 'starting points' for many children and families. We were acutely aware of families who had children attending perhaps three different schools, all trying to share one mobile phone. In June 2020, with the support of the BPS, several films were produced to refocus attention on the myriad benefits of play, particularly child-centred play and a message centred on creativity, imagination and time.

As vaccination rates and the focus on education increased, a strong narrative around 'catch-up' and 'lost learning' began to emerge. This sets the scene for this case study where we discuss the process and actions we took, alongside others, to influence policy and try to effect socio-political change.

Being Part of a Broad and Skilled Team

This 'step' is probably one of the most important regarding any attempt to influence policy. This step recognises that psychologists are best-placed to influence policy when they belong to a multi-disciplinary team, with colleagues from outside the psychological disciplines. Work to counter, add depth and nuance to the headline 'Catch-Up' was undertaken within a context of support provided by a larger organisation (in this case, the British Psychological Society).

This meant that even the earliest tentative discussions were supported by a strong team with expertise in areas that psychologists might not share, including:

- **Policy advisors** – with knowledge about the process of influencing policy. Insight into the structure of government with a focus on 'horizon scanning' to identify new opportunities.
- **Communications staff** – with skills in translating psychological knowledge into accessible and easy-to-read information.
- **Media professionals** – with extensive experience working with the media (e.g., TV, radio and print), and relationships with key journalists and media outlets.
- **Social media team** – with knowledge about the different social media channels that might be most effective, when and for what audience.
- **Website managers** – who have skills in making sure psychologists' work is in the right format and written appropriately for the web – a way of writing that is different from professional or academic writing.

What we go on to discuss in the next section would, in our view, be difficult for psychologists to do alone. When we talk about the actions we took and the decisions made, these were part of a collective team effort, although we try to highlight what we as psychologists did.

Using The 5 T's to Influence Policy

The 5 T's for policy engagement is a common and useful set of principles to structure any policy work (Pike, 2019). In using our previous 'Right to Play' and 'Time to Play' work in the context of 'catch-up' narratives, these principles helped to increase the potential to influence policy.

The 5 T's are:

- Targeting
- Translating
- Timing
- Tools
- Talk

Targeting – Identifying the Right People to Talk To

This first step is about identifying who is going to be best to talk to even before you begin to decide what you are going to say, through what channel or how. Reed (2016) suggests adopting a 'pincer' strategy to identify the right targets for your policy work, i.e., top-down and bottom-up. A top-down strategy might be about identifying other powerful groups or organisations already working on this area and are credible and reliable sources of policy information, e.g., charities or campaign groups. A bottom-up approach might be identifying relevant policy advisors within government and working to build connections with them with the aim of accessing decision makers such as private secretaries or ministers of state.

The most common tool used to identify various stakeholders is the Interest/Influence matrix (Mendelow, 1991). This is often plotted on a four-quadrant graph (see Table 18.1).

The Interest/Influence matrix is not a perfect science and isn't meant to be limiting. It can provide a snapshot in time regarding who is best to target. It may allow you to spot gaps, such as too much energy being directed towards stakeholders who have high interest, but little influence in changing the policy landscape.

Such an exercise might provide you with the opportunity to spot connections between groups or organisations that might make them useful allies if they work together. It is often this act of many groups coming together, with a shared aim, that can move them from being 'subjects' to 'key players'.

Table 18.1   Interest/Influence matrix

High influence, low interest	**High influence, high interest**
Context setter	Key players
Must keep satisfied / meet needs	*Must engage closely*
Low influence, low interest	**Low influence, high interest**
The crowd	Subjects
Low effort required – monitor	*Keep informed, collaborate – potential to become highly influential*

Some of the key stakeholders we were able to identify to target included:

- The Education Committee
- The Children's Commissioner's office
- Department for Education 'Mental Health Tsar'
- Playing Out
- Play England
- The PSHE Association

Translating - Getting the Message Across

Psychological research, theory and practice is often complex and messy. Academic papers are too long for policy advisors or members of parliament to spend time on. We were concerned that the emerging narrative focusing on 'academic catch-up' was too deficit focused and did not recognise the complexity of experience that children had over the course of the pandemic school closures. We were also concerned to ensure that schooling and education were understood to be about more than academic learning.

This meant working with communications and policy experts to consider a wide range of psychological theory and research about: learning, school readiness, emotional wellbeing, grief, recovery, resilience, play, child development, strengths-based practice, community and family experiences, poverty, relationships, child voice, the education system, digital inequality. Essentially, far too many topic areas to address entirely.

These discussions with policy and communications team members led to translating all this psychology into several **key messages**:

1 Children's wellbeing is just as important as their academic achievement.
2 Many children learnt new things and developed new skills throughout the pandemic; these should be recognised and celebrated.
3 Play is essential to children's development and learning, not just an add-on.

Timing - Getting the Time Right

Given that there were 'rumblings' for some time about children needing to 'catch-up' at school due to 'lost learning' we were able to prepare our key messages so we could respond rapidly when policy announcements were made. Examples include:

- *Policy announcements to extend the school day* – communicating the importance of wellbeing, social development and play.
- *The appointment of a 'catch up tsar'* – advocating for extracurricular activities, sports, music, drama, play and social time for children and young people.
- *Individual tutoring to get children to catch up* – focusing on the importance of teacher expertise, teacher–pupil relationships, recognising where children had developed skills and the importance of high-quality instruction and high-quality feedback in children's learning.

Engaging with policy allows psychologists to draw on previously completed work to support and reinforce key messages. This is something we were able to do regarding the importance of play at school.

Some of our previous work had included films where children and young people talked about the negative and positive aspects of school closures, particularly if they were shielding (BPS, 2020). Similarly, we had been involved in supporting policy colleagues to create a YouGov Survey to explore parent's views of play (BPS, 2021). This meant that we were able to draw directly on the views of children, young people and parents to advocate for the importance of play at school.

Tools - Using the Most Effective Channels

Brownson et al. (2018) highlight that while public health professionals or professional advisors might draw on 'science' or evidence reviews to inform policy decision making, elected officials (like MPs) often have the shortest amount of time to dedicate to an issue and strongly rely on 'real-world' stories and the media. This has implications for what tools are chosen to reach the people that you need to reach.

Research demonstrates that politicians from different parties rely on different news media outlets (Phillips, 2014). When looking at daily newspaper readership, *The Times* is the most common newspaper for Conservative MPs while *The Guardian* is most common for Labour MPs. Phillips' work also shows that a high proportion of MPs from both main political parties rely on news broadcasting from Sky News or BBC News, whereas very few (if any) report watching ITV News or Channel 5 News. This sort of information is key to determining the most effective channels through which to communicate key messages.

Our approach was to use a variety of channels to ensure we were able to target a range of relevant people. Examples include:

- Press and media work – newspapers with wide readership, local radio stations, national radio, local TV.
- Social media – targeting our existing community and other interested organisations through informal communication means.
- Individual meetings with MPs and policy influencers – working with the wider team here was essential (i.e., policy advisors) who could connect our messages about play with areas of interest that specific MPs had.

Policy Briefings

A key way to support successful meetings with politicians and policy influencers was to work with policy advisors to create an effective policy briefing. Briefings should make it clear what is being asked for and what the policy recommendations are. A strong policy briefing should contain the following (adapted from Reed, 2016):

- **Title**

Short and catchy that grabs attention and has a clear focus.

- **Overview/introduction**

Describe what the problem is and how your work is relevant to current policy gaps.

- **Research and practice findings**

Discuss the findings from your research or practice that can answer some of the problems or gaps in policy you have identified. Be clear and direct. Use short sentences and make good use of subheadings and bullet points.

- **Policy recommendations**

  Clear recommendations that relate to specific policy issues. Examples from our work include:
  - Ten minutes extra play a day
  - A focus on a varied and enriching curriculum
  - Prioritise unstructured play
  - Make play a ministerial priority within the Department for Education

- **Key references and contact details**

A maximum of two key references if someone wants to read further, and a clear way for policy maker to contact you

Talk - Building Relationships and Networks

The 'talking to people' part of this process is where all the planning you have done comes to fruition. It is not any more or less important than say, targeting or translating, because without that preparation work it is more difficult to build effective relationships and networks of people who can trust you as a source of information and influence in their own views on policy. Reed (2016) advises:

> although policy-makers find out about research from many sources, it is
> information from face-to-face contact with people they trust that most
> commonly influences decisions... Creating a policy briefing is not enough: it is
> what you do with your policy brief that counts. (pp. 205–206)

At this stage we spoke to civil servants, MPs, government advisors and importantly representatives from other organisations that would support our overall asks (see the key messages described in 'Translating' above). Building a network is a key step as this can help to add credibility to your message and policy asks – these are the supportive stakeholders that you will have identified in step one, targeting.

It is easy to lose track of what your focus is. We know that MPs or civil servants have many demands on their time, and it can feel like a 'now or never' situation where you need to communicate all your views about everything because you might never get the opportunity to speak to this politician again. This means key stakeholders may leave a meeting not really being clear about the aims, purpose or outcomes. Be focused, clear and confident that they are meeting you for a reason and want to hear what you have to say.

It is also important to remember the types of evidence that an elected official might draw on to make decisions – real life stories. These stories can make your work come to life and can demonstrate the change that you are advocating for. For example, our policy asks were around increasing play time at school and as EPs we were able to draw on many examples where increasing the amount of play has benefitted children's well-being and learning.

Relationships and networks can also be created in less defined, informal spaces, such as social media. Platforms like Twitter mean you can instantly respond to policy conversations directly with MPs or key influencers. It is not uncommon to have one-to-one conversations with key names in a field, politicians or other big policy influencers. This has implications for how you have your information readily available. While a PDF policy briefing might be useful to email to a civil servant, it is not as helpful for a social media exchange. This means that you need well written, accessible online materials that you can direct someone to (you can see an example here: www.bps.org.uk/time-to-play).

Putting It All Together and Thinking about Impact

With any work to influence policy, the obvious hope is to have an impact. Having said that, it is uncommon for policy change to happen immediately following your excellent work. Policy change is often a slow burn, happening over time, involving many stakeholders and, sometimes, piecemeal. This makes impact and evaluation even more important, so that you can track over time the effect of the actions you have taken to influence socio-political change.

Weyrauch (2012) highlights the importance of distinguishing between product and activity indicators (more short term) and impact indicators (medium to long term). Product and activity indicators might be things like:

* Number of meetings with civil servants, policy advisors or MPs
* Number of media interviews
* Number of times that social media activity has been viewed
* Citations of your work (papers, presentations, blog posts, media interviews)

Longer term impact indicators include (Jones & Villar, 2008):

* Getting issues on the political agenda
* Encouraging discursive commitments from policy decision makers
* Securing change in policy and decision-making processes
* Affecting policy
* Influencing behaviour change in key people

Activity indicators are usually easier to measure and track. You will know how many meetings you have been invited to about your policy area, and you can often get views of social media posts or web page views easily from your organisation team.

Understanding the broader policy impact of your work will likely take time and it can be important to have reflections and feedback from some of the key stakeholders involved in your work. Some of the longer-term impacts of the work we have been involved in include:

- A shift in tone of media coverage about post-COVID recovery, and how this is conceptualised and spoken about (getting it on the agenda)
- Influencing how MPs speak about 'recovery' e.g., more time for play and extracurricular activities at school (discursive commitments and influencing behaviour change)
- Schools changing their policies to increase play times or bring back afternoon play (affecting policy)

It is important to reflect that some of these longer-term changes have happened within a wider context of many people and organisations advocating for policy change in broadly similar areas. This is common and as Weyrauch (2012) comments:

> it is difficult to attribute them to the daily work of only one organisation, since they are often multi-causal and the fruit of the actions of several actors. Nevertheless, it is possible to select certain indicators to identify how [your] organisation contributed to the medium and long term changes in public policy. (p. 3)

CONCLUSION

We conclude by advocating for psychologists to hold on to their passion for social justice issues and be more organised in its activism. There are ways that this can be achieved. Knowledge and methods about how to influence policy needs to be considered explicitly on all practitioner psychologist training courses. More research needs to be undertaken in relation to social justice and policy influence within the psychological professions – what it looks like, what it means and how it can be achieved. Trainee psychologists in the UK need to be taught about the structure of the legislature and how policy influence can be achieved.

We have outlined here examples of things that psychologists are doing already and also what can be done to start a journey towards influencing policy and socio-political change. Whilst it is important to recognise the work that needs to be done within individual and systemic practices, we also wonder whether psychologists need to get better at recognising the work that they already do, that could be regarded as influencing socially just policy. This needs to happen alongside increasing the visibility and awareness of such work within the public. Paying more attention and being more mindful of social justice in our actions will lead to more of the same.

REFLECTIVE AND CRITICAL THINKING QUESTIONS

1   Who in your organisation or professional body will you work with to support you on your journey to influencing policy? (e.g., policy team, media, public engagement)
2   Can you articulate, simply, why you want policy to change? (this is about identifying policy gaps)
3   Can you explain why your work is important and its implications in under two minutes, using plain English? (think of this as the elevator pitch)
4   What distinct and specific policy asks do you have and what government department briefs do these policy asks fall under?
5   Do you have real-life stories to support your claims and policy asks?

RECOMMENDED READING AND RESOURCES

Read, M. S. (2016). *The research impact handbook*. Fast Track Impact.
An accessible and comprehensive guide for anyone wishing to ensure their research has impact, complete with a range of templates and guides to plan your work.

UK Research and Innovation. (2022, January 27). *How to influence policymakers*. UKRI. www.ukri.org/councils/esrc/impact-toolkit-for-economic-and-social-sciences/how-to-influence-policymakers/
An introduction to the process through which you can influence policymakers highlighting the vital role research has in public policy making.

The National Coordinating Centre for Public Engagement: www.publicengagement.ac.uk
A treasure trove of advice, support and resources.

Oliver, K., & Cariney, P. (2019). The dos and don'ts of influencing policy: A systematic review of advice to academics. *Palgrave Communications*, *5*, 21.
A systematic review that presents eight recommendations for how to influence policy – relevant to researchers and practitioners.

REFERENCES

British Psychological Society. (2017). *Practice guidelines* (3rd ed.). BPS.
British Psychological Society. (2019). *Standards for the accreditation of Doctoral programmes in educational psychology in England, Northern Ireland and Wales*. BPS.

British Psychological Society. (2020, September 3). *Children and young people's experiences of shielding and isolating due to Covid-19 (full version)* [Video]. YouTube. www.youtube.com/watch?v=Rof1YYWEW-U

British Psychological Society. (2021, September 22). *BPS launches Time to Play campaign as survey reveals high level of parents' fears about effect of pandemic on primary school playtime.* BPS. www.bps.org.uk/news-and-policy/bps-launches-time-play-campaign-survey-reveals-high-level-parents'-fears-about

Brownson, R. C., Eyler, A. A., Harris, J. K., Moore, J. B., & Tabak, R. G. (2018). Getting the word out: New approaches for disseminating public health science. *Journal of Public Health Management and Practice, 24*(2), 102–111.

Department for Education. (2019). *Research on the Educational Psychologist Workforce.* Department for Education.

Hobbs, C., Atkinson, C., Barclay, M., Bristow, S., Casey, T., Finney, R., Goodhall, N., Mannello, M., & Woods, F. (2019). *DECP position paper on children's right to play.* Leicester: British Psychological Society.

Jones, N., & Villar, E. (2008). Situating children in international development policy: Challenges involved in successful evidence-informed policy influencing. *Evidence and Policy, 4*(1), 31–51.

Mendelow, A. L. (1991). Environmental scanning: The impact of the stakeholder concept. In *Proceedings from the Second International Conference on Information Systems* (pp. 407–418).

Phillips, C. (2014, April 9). *Communicating with MPs: The power of the media.* Ipsos. www.ipsos.com/en-uk/communicating-mps-power-media

Pike, L. (2019, May 2). *The '5 Ts' of policy engagement: PolicyBristol's approach to supporting academics.* PolicyBristol Hub. https://policybristol.blogs.bris.ac.uk/2019/05/02/the-5-ts-of-policy-engagement-policybristols-approach-to-supporting-academics/

Reed, M. S. (2016). *The research impact handbook.* Fast Track Impact.

Schulze, J. E. (2017). *Exploring educational psychologists' views of social justice.* [Unpublished doctoral dissertation, University of Manchester].

Scottish Executive (2002). *Review of the provision of educational psychology services in Scotland (The Currie Report).* Edinburgh: Scottish Executive.

Soni, A., & Shotter, A. (2019, December 2). *'Interweaving MATs' – EP work across schools in a multi-academy trust.* edpsy. https://edpsy.org.uk/blog/2019/interweaving-mats-ep-work-across-schools-in-a-multi-academy-trust/

Weyrauch, V. (2012). Toolkit N°3: Design/establishing the pillars of M&E strategy. In *How to monitor and evaluate policy influence?* (pp. 3–4). CIPPEC.

POSTSCRIPT

Social Justice in Psychological Therapies: So, What Now?

Laura Anne Winter, Divine Charura and all contributors

Consistent with the overall ethos of this text, we aim in this final chapter to reflect on the 'so, what now?' of social justice in psychological therapies. When we as editors came together to work on this text, we firmly agreed that the book needed to demystify social justice: it needed to make it something tangible, applied and importantly something possible for psychological therapists to truly engage with and bring into their work. To close, we have brought together all the authors' voices to provide the reader with a summary of what psychological therapists can tangibly and straightforwardly *do* to work towards the goals of social justice.

SO, WHAT NOW?

- Mental health professionals need to critically examine and dismantle the very 'sentence' of psychological therapy to create a novel healing space 'inside the sentence' where effective and responsible engagement with minoritised and racialised individuals can occur. Clinicians must reflect on power and privilege in their own lives, and on how their particular social locations have shaped their values and worldview, and how these in turn affect their clinical work (Chapter 2 authors).

- Acting on social justice issues requires courage, commitment and resilience. Moving from the relative 'bystander' position inherent in being a therapist to shifting to the explicit expression of views related to matters of social justice in the outside world is quite a shift. There are many instances and issues in our current world that are polarising opinion. Beyond expressing views connected to social justice, psychological therapists, by virtue of their training and professional experience, are somewhat equipped to engage with, seek to understand and explore opposing points of view. I believe that we need to move beyond the comfort of our interviewing rooms and seek to engage in the exploration of socially contested issues with others (Chapter 3).

- Rather than 'sitting on' knowledge in the guise of adhering to traditional frameworks of psychological therapy, integrated approaches to working with principles and action of social justice can be of assistance to clients. As therapists, we can facilitate direct interaction with, and challenging of, wider systems in collaboration with clients. It would seem this can be achieved by continuously working in the best interests of our clients and formulating the *individual in context*, whilst aligning with professional competencies and ethical guidelines (Chapter 4).
- Develop, train in and practise theoretical models that have a social justice dimension at their core. If your model doesn't explicitly account for social, political, economic and/or environmental sources of distress, it needs changing (Chapter 5).
- Familiarise yourself with the three core principles of social justice informed therapeutic work, which provide important scaffolding for any enactment of social justice informed therapeutic practice: (1) relational, socially just ethical practice, (2) transformative practice, and (3) politically informed practice. Engage with collaboration and broaching (deliberately engaging in conversations in therapy as well as supervision which explicitly name and challenge injustice that clients may have experienced and acknowledge the importance of social justice). Be curious, be reflexive and open to learning with and from others (Chapter 6).
- Address and name oppression in therapy; contextualise stressors people suffer from within social context; utilise strengths-based approaches; facilitate empowerment; acknowledge and manage privilege; engage in effective advocacy. Congruence is key for effective therapeutic and psychological contact. Start by learning to be congruent with yourself by recognising and understanding your implicit bias, when this comes into your awareness it will help you understand and connect to your client authentically to foster a non-judgemental and safe therapeutic space to explore identity and difference (Chapter 7).
- Be proactive and research signposting options for clients who might benefit from tailored support outside of the therapy room. For example, your local citizens advice or welfare bureau, food bank information, free debt advice charities, community groups. Keep helpful lists updated and invite your colleagues to collaborate and share (Chapter 8).
- Every day, everywhere, see, reflect, listen, reflect, ask and learn. See again, ask again, listen again, learn again, reflect again. Keep seeing and listening. Keep learning. Never stop reflecting. This in itself is action and will always lead to knowing why, how and when to act (Chapter 9).
- Get to know what is 'normal' for your clients. Clients may come to therapy with previous invalidating experiences about themselves, so taking the time

to understand their perspective and create a shared narrative of understanding is important. Hear narratives of exclusion and marginalisation. Begin with an assumption of diversity and not an expectation for your client to adapt to a/your neurotypical default (Chapter 10).

- Therapists provide a medium through which marginalised people and communities can explore and express their voices, perceptions and experiences. There are 'roots and shoots' to inspire therapist action. For example, the Therapists Connect social media group now has over 12,000 members and is growing. Professional bodies advance equality, diversity and inclusivity challenges and actions. Through individuals, groups and organisations, we can challenge, change and contribute; however, we need organising forces to transform actions and influencing into impactful, sustainable and politically meaningful change. Step forward colleagues! For some clients, their experience of being in therapy can inspire them to action and into work within therapeutic contexts. Finding one's voice also can elicit people's desire to challenge injustices and extend social justice agendas. Psychological therapist demographics are slowly changing to better reflect wider social and cultural heritages. That said, professional bodies and training organisations could generate impetus and support diversification and inclusivity through targeted training bursaries. Strength exists in numbers – mustering therapists to group and form not-for-profit or community interest companies can provide one medium through which therapists can collaborate to create inclusive, compassionate, affordable and accessible mental health and wellbeing services (Chapter 11).
- Be aware of the impact of oppression on clients and help them locate the source of their distress in the oppression they endure rather than a sense of brokenness in their self (Chapter 12).
- At a time of increased forced migration and public debate about refugees, therapists will encounter the consequences of this negative discourse upon the mental health of those who seek asylum. Living with the fear of detention or forced return and navigating complex systems within a hostile or ambivalent environment will exacerbate or trigger significant mental health difficulties, thus social justice informed practitioners will attempt to challenge the narratives and practices that perpetuate negativity towards asylum seekers and refugees. Standing in solidarity with refugees, speaking to colleagues, writing to politicians and supporting campaigns that safeguard the rights of refugees are just a few steps psychotherapists can take to promote social justice for refugees (Chapter 13).
- Get to know the natural world nearby. Experience it fully and regularly. See, smell and experience the way it shifts across the seasons and watch the ways in which people respond to it. Be curious about the deep-seated relationship we have with the natural world and bring that heartfelt care to your work as a psychologist (Chapter 14).
- Counselling practices rooted in social justice seek to *challenge* inherent inequities in social systems (Chapter 15).

- Remember that none of us can do this work without our support networks. Family, friends, relationships, can all serve as fortresses of solitude providing us solace and peace as we take stock and rest up from the latest paper we have written, presentation we have given, or workshop we have run on these important but draining issues. Knowing that we have this grounding can be the difference though between the descent into madness of a Nietzsche and the career longevity of an Obama (Chapter 16).
- Consider how you can bring community or liberation psychology principles and models into your everyday practice. Outside of professional employment get involved in social justice campaigning and activism with grassroots groups – it will provide the insights you need to improve your practice (Chapter 17).
- Don't bury the lead. Psychologists can find it difficult to be upfront with the policy implications following from their work. Often the approach mirrors what you'd find in an academic piece of writing, i.e. slowly building a good academic argument that leads, eventually, to a well-reasoned and academically sound conclusion. Policy makers don't have time for this. You should lead with how your work (research or practice) is relevant to a particular policy area, and the key change or ask that you want. Be clear about how your change relates to the policy interests of the MP or civil servant you're talking to and be ready to confidently state your ideas for change (Chapter 18).

A NOTE TO END ON: TAKING CARE OF ONE ANOTHER

Social justice action can, and often does, come with risks for the individual(s) or community groups who engage in action and activism. This is particularly the case where the individual is minoritised or marginalised themselves and advocating or engaging in social justice work connected to their marginalised identities. Historically, we know there are many examples in which activists were murdered or suffered political violence and silencing. There are costs to engaging in this work, and these should not be ignored. We need to acknowledge these costs, and take care – of ourselves, and of one another as we progress in trying to change things for the better. We hope that the ideas contained within this book help our professions to do just that.

INDEX

Note: Page numbers followed by "*f*" indicate figure and "*t*" indicate table in the text.